PELICAN BOOKS

A HISTORY OF THE UNITED STATES

VOLUME ONE

Russel B. Nye was born in Wisconsin in 1913 and educated
at Oberlin College, Ohio, and at the University of Wisconsin. He began teaching English and American Literature at the University of Wisconsin and is now Director of
Languages and Literature at Michigan State University.
His interest in American history led to a biography of the
historian George Bancroft, which won a Pulitzer Prize, and
to studies of the Anti-Slavery Movement and of Mid-
western politics. His latest book is a study of the American
Constitutional and Early Republican period.

J. E. Morpurgo is Professor of American Literature at
the University of Geneva, Visiting Lecturer at Leeds and
Deputy Chairman of the National Book League. Born in
London in 1918 and educated at Christ's Hospital and
the College of William and Mary in Virginia, his first
academic career began in 1939 and lasted for only six
months before the War turned him into an artillery officer.
In the next three decades before returning to an academic
life he was a publisher, General Editor of the Pelican
Histories from their inception until 1960, Assistant
Director of the Nuffield Foundation, adviser on book
matters to various Asian governments and for fifteen years
Director General of the National Book League. He also
built up a considerable reputation on radio and television,
wrote several books on American topics and on English
literature as well as two travel books. He holds three
honorary doctorates from American universities.

A HISTORY OF
THE UNITED STATES

BY

R. B. NYE AND J. E. MORPURGO

VOLUME ONE

THE BIRTH OF
THE U.S.A.

PENGUIN BOOKS

Penguin Books Ltd, Harmondsworth, Middlesex, England
Penguin Books Inc., 7110 Ambassador Road, Baltimore, Maryland 21207, U.S.A.
Penguin Books Australia Ltd, Ringwood, Victoria, Australia

—

First published 1955
Reprinted 1961
Second Edition 1964
Reprinted 1967
Third Edition 1970

—

Copyright © R. B. Nye and J. E. Morpurgo, 1955, 1964, 1970

—

Made and printed in Great Britain
by Hazell Watson & Viney Ltd, Aylesbury, Bucks
Set in Monotype Baskerville

CONTENTS OF VOLUME I

LIST OF MAPS

CONTENTS OF VOLUME II

LIST OF MAPS

INTRODUCTION

SEEN from the American side of the Atlantic, through the eyes of proud heirs, American colonial history is a record of growing wisdom, of developing unity, and of increasing devotion to the ideals of personal and communal freedom. Looked at thus, the years between the landfall of the *Sarah Constant* and the American Revolution ring with possibilities and with promises; successful rebellion against European tyranny is the payment on these promises, and the subsequent history of the colonies united into a new nation fulfils the possibilities: the United States of America, greatest and best of the nations in the twentieth century, appears as the glorious flower which has sprung from the wonderful seed of the Thirteen Colonies. But looked at from Britain, through eyes that even after the disillusionment of the last thirty years still find imperial success more familiar than failure, the history of British colonial enterprise in the territory which is now the United States is bitter and tragic. The English historian looks at what there was in the beginning, sighs over the lost opportunities and the disintegration of an empire, and regrets what might have been: the American historian, who has all around him the happy consequences of English mistakes, and who has been brought up to be aware and proud of the abundant initiative which has gone into the creation of a new power, can only rejoice in the fact that the mistakes were made.

This *History* is the result of a collaboration between an Englishman and an American (in that, so far as the authors know, it is still, as it was when it was first written, unique among histories of the United States) and regarded as it were from Mid-Atlantic, certain of the fundamental problems in America's early story seem to stand out more clearly than they might have done had this book been written either by an American, with all his natural prejudices, or by an Englishman, whose prejudices are no less obvious and no less natural. How much was Colonial America the child of sixteenth-, seventeenth-, and eighteenth-century Britain? How much was its thought, its social habit, its economic and political progress conditioned by Cisatlantic events and the predominantly Anglo-Saxon ancestry of the early settlers? How much was the eventual break with Britain a rebellion against British control, or how much was the very Britishness of the ideas and culture of the Americans responsible for their rebellion against tyranny which they regarded as incompatible with their Anglo-Saxon heritage?

From first to last, from the days of Raleigh to the days of Washington, it is impossible to treat American colonial history without frequent investigation of the history of what was still the homeland. American history was not made merely out of the colonies, it had its influence on and it was influenced by what was going on up in Canada and down in the West Indies; above all it was touched, twisted, and designed by events in Britain itself. From first to last, from the settlement of Virginia to the signing of the Declaration of Independence, the Americans were, some to greater extent and some to less, but all in some degree, British abroad. Despite the fairy-tale efforts of many historians, and particularly of American historians, the European colonizer was not miraculously Americanized in the moment he set foot on American soil, nor, at least until the middle of the eighteenth century, were colonial leaders remarkably equipped with prescience and primarily inspired by the need to sharpen the ideals, the ideas – and the swords – of the colonies for the coming struggle with Great Britain. It is a disease common to historians: this desire to show on the screen of the present the clear image of a distant future. Yet, and the resolving of this paradox must be one of the main concerns of any book on Colonial America, the common exaggerations have in them some elements of truth. From the first, though they were certainly not Americans in the modern sense, the colonials were not as other Englishmen. In the second century of colonial history many of them were not

Englishmen at all, even by ancestry, though for the most part they were inclined to take to themselves the English language, English customs, and habits of mind, which, if not English, were certainly more English than Continental. From the first, relations, often strained relations, with Government in London were a major factor in hastening the process of Americanization.

CHAPTER I

WEST TO THE EAST

IN the investigation of significant historical developments it is often impossible to follow, with any conviction, the old logic of cause and effect. Events crowd upon circumstances, seemingly unrelated details coincide, individuals, unknown to each other and inspired, it would seem, by motives that are utterly disparate, set to work in the same direction, but in various parts of the world; accident plays its part, and then, suddenly and almost fortuitously, the pieces fall into place and mankind has changed direction. It was thus with the early exploration and exploitation of the New World. Economics, scientific progress, religion and the persecution which often goes with religion, personalities, and what is loosely called 'the spirit of the age' all conspired together to bring about events that made possible the voyages of discovery and settlement; these things, geography, national characteristics, and again accident (it is impossible for the historian to ignore the force of accident) gave the dominion over what was eventually to prove the greatest empire of them all, to the countries of the North-West Atlantic Seaboard: to France, Holland, and England.

The scientific improvements of the late fifteenth and the sixteenth century made navigation from an act of faith into a science. The development of printing techniques and their application to map-making furthered the work of Cartographers like Mercator, Ortelius and the hydrographer Wagenaer and helped to relieve seamanship of the fantastic legends of the middle ages.

Shipbuilders played their part. To their designs the stern-castle almost disappeared, the outline of the ship was revised to reduce resistance, and these improvements much reduced the hideous take-in of bilge water, one of the principal horrors of early voyaging. There was devised, too, a new scheme of sails in the median plane of the ship, rudimentary fore and aft rigging. All these refinements made long sea voyages feasible. (Later, early in the eighteenth century, the introduction of the use for ships' furniture of mahogany, a very close-grained hard wood which allowed fine cutting, was to make possible a great increase in the comfort and regularity of ships' runs across the Atlantic.)

Curiosity and greed preceded, ran parallel, and succeeded upon the scientific developments, and there were always available, as there always are, individuals who were ready to attempt just a little more than convenience or progress would justify. Before the astronomical work of Copernicus convinced scholar and adventurer alike that the world was a revolving globe, Columbus had already acted upon an assumption that had not yet been proved.

Already, early in the sixteenth century, the centre of European mercantile power had moved from the Mediterranean to the Atlantic. Portuguese seamen, trained by Henry the Navigator, using the newly developed caravel (narrow at the poop and wide at the bow), by the not-so-simple expedient of visiting and claiming for themselves new lands, had extended their country's domains to include the Azores, Guinea, parts of India, Brazil, and the Spice Islands. Exploitation, missionary endeavour, exploration, and empire-building were with them, as with most of the early imperial powers, indistinguishable, but their efforts did much to break the virtual monopoly which Venice had long held over the spice routes to Europe. Spain, which had been fortunate enough, or wise enough, to accept patronage of the explorations of Columbus, followed up his discovery of the West Indies with immense vigour, considerable courage, and little foresight.

From the beginning of the fifteenth century, Portugal had been groping for a route to the riches of the East by way of Africa; Spain too had had dreams of easy wealth, and the stumbling discoveries of Columbus, a hireling to the Spaniards, seemed to give to that country an unfair advantage in the quest. So, in 1493, Portuguese jealousy and Portuguese disappointment took the rivals before the only man on earth who could arbitrate effectively between two giants. Pope Alexander VI had read his Old Testament; his position as God's temporal representative he took seriously, the words of the ninety-fifth Psalm he took literally: 'In His Hand are all the corners of the earth', and, a most exclusive Solomon, he cut the world in halves, gave one half to Portugal and the other to Spain. The eastern end of Asia, so men were coming to accept, was on the other side of the Atlantic; the Portuguese were prepared to get to it by going eastwards, the Spaniards by going westwards, and at the other end of their journey there was obviously enough for both. The Pope's line from pole to pole through the ocean which Columbus had crossed could separate their discoveries and, by keeping off each other's territory, still both nations could become rich. It is hardly surprising that both countries accepted the decision for, without wasting their energies fighting each other, they still gathered in all that they wanted and used the Pope's blessing to keep all other trespassers away from the harvest.

The journeys of Vasco da Gama in 1497 seemed to give the lion's share of the division to Portugal. Albuquerque and Almeida built for Portugal an empire in the East yielding immediate and tangible profits, an empire which shone mightily beside the miserable promises and the few natives' feathers that were all that Columbus could offer. But this very success diverted Portuguese energies from the New World, and for the next fifty years Spain had virtually no rival in western waters.

Columbus had set his course due west. His followers went north and south from the point where the land mass of Central America had stopped the greatest explorer of them all; south towards Darien, Maracaibo and the Orinoco, north towards Honduras and the Gulf of Mexico. Ojeda, Bastidias, and Pizarro went after the other Spanish explorers and conquistadores began to open up South, Central, and North America. A wild adventurer named Balboa (not despite Keats, 'Stout Cortés') climbed the peak in Darien and first looked upon the Pacific. Cortés himself landed, in

1519, on the shores of Mexico, and with less than six hundred Europeans, two hundred and fifty Indians, fifteen horses, and ten brass cannon, conquered that country for Spain.

In the inventory of that expedition, those ten brass cannon are of the greatest significance. For close on four hundred years the white man had to fight for the control of the American continent against those who had owned it before he came. Often he suffered disaster at their hands, sometimes, particularly in the early days of settlement, his hold on the newly won lands seemed about to be broken, but always he had behind him the inventive and industrial genius of Europe and of Europeans transplanted, always he had at his disposal weapons of destruction which the Indian could not equal. At least his peer in the skills of pitched battle, and, to the very end, his master in fieldcraft, the American Indian soon learnt to use the white man's weapons – and soon learnt to steal them – but the manufacture of firearms, their invention, and their improvement, he never learnt. By the time the Indian had the muzzle-loader, the white man was already at work on a breech-loader, by the time the Indian had the breech-loader, the white man was rifling his weapon, when the Indian had caught up with this development, his enemies were preparing repeaters and machine-guns. The organization, both industrial and military, which is necessary for the use of artillery, the Indian was never to master.

At the time when their use was becoming general, Blaise de Monluc, Marshal of France, described firearms as 'the Devil's Invention', and Don Quixote, as if quoting and elaborating his contemporary, spoke violently against artillery in his 'Curious Discourse on Arms and Letters':

Whose inventor I firmly believe is now receiving the reward for his devilish invention in Hell; an invention which allows a base and cowardly hand to take the life of a brave knight, in such a way that, without his knowledge how or why, when his valiant heart is fullest of furious courage, there comes some random shot – discharged perhaps by a man who fired in terror from the flash the accursed machine made in firing – and puts an end in a moment to the consciousness of one who deserved to enjoy life for many an age.

But without this 'Devil's Invention' Don Quixote's coun-trymen of that 'hideous and unchivalric Age' of which he complained could not have prospered so rapidly in their journeys for wealth, nor could their successors have held untamed lands and driven back untamed enemies.

At about the same time that Cortés was in Mexico, Magellan clarified the vague outlines of the southern part of the American continent by beating his way round the cape which now bears his name and sailing on out into the South Pacific. It is one of the strange quirks of history that Magellan himself was a Portuguese who had learnt his navigation under Albuquerque in the East Indies, but that his greatest voyage was made under the inspiration of Charles the Fifth of Spain. Spanish explorers were now familiar with the Gulf of California and the mouth of the Mississippi River.

On 14 April 1528 the first considerable expedition landed in territory which is now the United States. Three hundred men and forty-two horses commanded by Panfilo de Nar-vaez came ashore close to the site of the present city of Tampa, Florida. This first expedition ended in tragedy and wonderful heroism. Massacre, storm, and slavery in the hands of the Indians accounted for most of the party. Only three Spaniards and one Negro slave managed to escape the Indians, and this party of four found its way eventually to the Spanish settlements in Mexico.

The leader of this miserable band of survivors, one Cabeza de Vaca, was in part responsible for the impulse which added great strength to Spanish efforts in North America in the middle years of the sixteenth century and, indirectly, for the impermanence and disasters which followed upon tem-porary success. On returning to Spain he seems to have for-gotten the horrors he had endured, and the hardships of the continent. His traveller's tales, fortified by evidence of great wealth which Pizarro was sending back from Peru, aroused the curiosity and the greed of Spaniards in Mexico and Spaniards in Spain. Two great expeditions, one under de

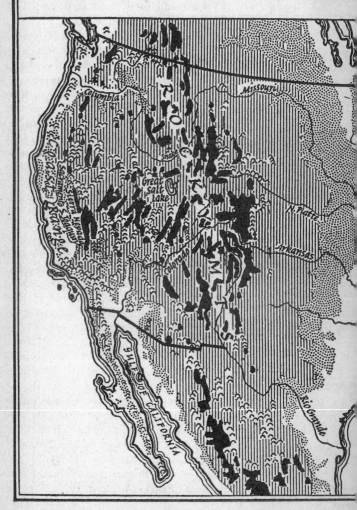

RELIEF: 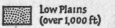 Low Plains (over 1,000 ft)

Lake Superior

Lake Michigan

Lake Huron

Ottawa   St. Lawrence

L. Ontario

Lake Erie

APPALACHIAN MOUNTAINS

Cape Cod

Long Island

Ohio

Cape Hatteras

Mississippi

Tennessee

Alabama

GULF OF MEXICO

Bahama Islands

Straits of Florida

CUBA

Soto and the other under Coronado, set forth after gold and silver. Florida, Arkansas, Louisiana, and Texas were all explored, Coronado's party reached the Rio Grande and even looked down into the Grand Canyon, the story of gold not far away led them on and on into the wilderness. The gold was never discovered. Some settlement was achieved particularly around the coasts of Florida, but while gold and silver still poured in from Peru and Mexico Spaniards could never devote much attention to the more unfruitful lands to the north.

In Europe, the sudden flow of riches from Central and South America, riches that were increased in magnificence as the Spaniards exploited the Peruvian silver mines, had results quite different from those that their exploiters wished. Slowly at first, and after the middle years of the century more rapidly, the influx of silver forced up the general price level in Europe. The sensitive mechanism of international credit was ruined and the silver, which might have fostered industrial development, was squandered in Spain on luxury, speculation, and war. By the end of the century, Spain was in effect ruined by wealth, and it brought down in its economic collapse the city of Antwerp, the one northern centre which had seemed likely to share its prosperity.

Opportunities were now open to other countries, who could take their eyes off the blinding glitter of precious metals and look instead to the land and to the seas around the land.

Meanwhile in Northern Europe, France, Holland, and England were being prepared by circumstances to take the opportunities that were thus presented to them. If any one detail can be said to explain the sudden emergence of northern countries as colonial powers, it is, strangely enough, a change in the habits of fish. In the Middle Ages, the herring had made his home principally in the Baltic. From about the end of the fifteenth century shoals of herrings began to appear in the North Sea. In the pursuit of these fish men of the northern countries learnt to be sailors; even when all three nations had developed a mercantile marine and some kind of navy it was still the search for fish that lured them out into the North Atlantic and sent them (particularly the English and the French) as far afield as the waters around Newfoundland.

On the North American continent the French were the first to dispute the overriding claims of Spain. In 1534, and again in 1541, Jacques Cartier had explored the St Lawrence, and had given to France some rights (unrecognized of course by those were were faithful to Papal decisions), some authority over the land, which, at all events, the Spaniards did not want. Spain was prepared to realize the need for permanent bases. (As early as 1526 an attempt had been made to set up a settlement somewhere between the Savannah and the Chesapeake Bay.) But the French had more reason to establish themselves in continental America and greater opportunity to make their settlement successful. French sailors were, many of them, Huguenots suffering persecution at home. With a base on the American side of the Atlantic, they could live as Frenchmen and as Protestants. At the same time, there is little doubt that they realized that the good French habit and the good Protestant habit of preying on Spanish treasure convoys could be more effectively pursued from the coasts of South Carolina than from Dieppe or La Rochelle.

On 27 May, 1562, two French ships, under the command of Jean Ribault of Dieppe, sailed in between the headlands of St Helena and Hilton's Head into the waters of Port Royal, South Carolina, and there established a French settlement.

Ribault was the precursor of many French leaders, though before very long French interests began to centre themselves around the Gulf of St Lawrence and the Gulf of the Mississippi, and before very long Catholic Frenchmen joined their Protestant compatriots in the tasks of exploration.

CHAPTER 2

THE AUGMENTATION OF THE INDIES

AND what of the English? It is now difficult to realize the smallness and the unimportance of England when the first of the Tudors came to the throne. The English were island-dwellers, cut off from the mainsprings of European endeavour and exhausted by cross-Channel struggles and by civil war; an island with nothing to do but look after itself. But the English *were* island-dwellers, and that very fact gave them inspiration and ability which eventually enabled them to make up for much lost time. Henry the Seventh let slip his chance to sponsor Columbus, though he made some amends by granting a Royal Patent to Giovanni Cabota, known to Bristol and to English history as John Cabot, and to this Genoese by birth, Venetian by naturalization, and man of Bristol by temporary residence, Henry paid a reward of ten pounds for the discovery of Cape Breton Island.

But Henry the Seventh's principal contribution to the future of an island race was indirect. In the words of Francis Bacon, 'he could not endure to see trade sick'. At the time of the battle of Bosworth, England was essentially an agricultural country, such wealth as it had drawn not from industry or merchandising but from the growing of wool. The one considerable advantage which the English held in international trade was that the city states of the Low Countries were dependent upon England for this essential raw material. Yet such was the insignificance of English power that the authorities in the Low Countries put a heavy import duty on wool. The English had it, the Netherlanders wanted it, but the English had nowhere else to sell it, and so were forced to pay for the privilege of selling to others what the others wanted. Henry the Seventh acted quickly against this state of affairs. He placed an embargo on the export of raw wool and then set up at Calais – the last remnant of England as a Continental power – a monopolistic market to which all must come for the purchase of English wool. The Netherlands were glad to make a commercial treaty with this high-handed merchant king.

Similarly, Henry passed through his first Parliament a Navigation Act which reserved to English ships the right to import wines and dyes from France. By dint of commercial sharp practice he managed to persuade the Spaniards to sign a trade treaty.

As yet England had no navy and no mercantile marine worth the name and this Henry, ever capable and energetic in the pursuit of profits, set about to correct. He began to construct ships (and to design them) and he built the first dry dock at Portsmouth. He was even prepared – unusual practice for a monarch – to charter out his ships to private commercial undertakings.

Henry's ships were not what we could now call naval vessels; they were armed, and effectively armed, against possible depredations by rivals, but they were designed to bring money and not victories to their royal ship-owner.

Henry the Seventh's son suffered in his mercantile and nautical endeavours from the years when he was under the thumb of Cardinal Wolsey, for Wolsey was essentially a European statesman, his intention plain: to make England once more a force on the Continent. He had no conception of the fact, which was already becoming obvious to other men, that England's destiny lay elsewhere. But once Wolsey's services to his God and to his King had been thrust aside, Henry the Eighth continued his father's policies, and in the history of English overseas expansion (as in the history of the English arts and of English religion) Henry the Eighth deserves creditable mention, if no more.

England's slow start in exploration served to tighten the springs of national effort. Pride, greed, and the growing diplomatic importance of England in the affairs of Europe, demanded that England should not remain for ever outside the exciting treasure hunt.

Henry the Eighth, though his life was much taken up with international and amorous intrigue, still had time and the ability left to choose the right men to lead the English enterprises. By showing particular favour to William Hawkins, who between 1530 and 1532 made three voyages to Brazil, Henry's royal smiles launched into adventure and profit the family that, more than any other family, was to fly its flag over British seafaring success throughout the century.

For the most part, however, English adventurousness was still limited and ill-informed, following but tamely in the steps of the Continentals. In the Mediterranean, and on the nearer coasts of Africa, on fishing voyages around British shores, the coasts of Iceland and Newfoundland, the English seamen trained, while at home the English merchants grew rich in peace.

Merchants and seamen alike inspired each other to covetous dreams of Cathay and the Indies.

The imitation of other powers was obviously fruitless. Though England shared with all nations the belief that wealth would come from the East, the English soon realized that it was only by slipping competition and going out by different routes that they could tap the great wealth which was in the East available. While Edward the Sixth, a sickly youth, was at his pious task of mending the educational mischief wrought by the dissolution of the monasteries, Sir Hugh Willoughby, with Richard Chancellor as his pilot-general, set out to find riches for the Court and for the City of London. It was their intention to find a way to India through the Arctic – the North-East Passage. Willoughby died in Russian Lapland, his courageous and rather pathetic log book the first in a long series of English classics of exploration. Chancellor sailed on into the White Sea and made his way, by land, to Moscow. He returned safely to England and there helped to initiate the first of the great trading companies – the Muscovy Company. His second voyage to Russia, again by the northern route, ended in disaster. He himself was lost at sea, but his convoy brought back to London a very real proof that progress had been made: the first Russian Ambassador.

Anthony Jenkinson succeeded Chancellor, and thrusting out from his predecessor's fruitless exploration, reached the Caspian and went on to Persia; ever nearer and nearer to the fabulous East, but not yet by a route that could be considered practicable for permanent commerce.

English effort in discovery had hardly got under way when Mary came to the throne. The advent of a Catholic monarch married to a Continental king, inevitably forced England back into European affairs and took away some of the impetus to more distant voyages. But Mary was a Tudor and, therefore, something of a merchant, and Mary was English and, therefore, not eager to force inactivity upon England's sailors. Philip the Second, however, whose madness was not altogether unwise, cared little for the interests of the kingdom which would not recognize him and was scrupulously careful of the interests of the kingdom which was his own. He did all that he could to prevent the English from muddling their way into competition with Spain.

Yet even the Marian interlude acted as a spur to English ambitions. Calais was lost, and with it went the last European vent for England's excess energy. Hatred of part-Spanish rule hastened the choice of the Spaniard as the Englishman's natural enemy; there was little chance of interfering with Spanish power where it was strongest – on the Continent of Europe – and patriotic Englishmen began to look eagerly at Spain's sensitive extremities in distant seas. Mary's Catholic zeal turned martyrology into a national habit, made the horrors of the Inquisition more comprehensible, drove Protestantism firmly into England's national character, and increased the sympathy which Englishmen were already feeling for the other seafarers of Northern Europe: the Dutch and the French Huguenots.

Mary's reign saw a considerable setback in the health of the national economy, but the country had experienced prosperity and was no longer content to do without it. So, when Mary's Protestant sister came to the throne and lifted once more the national hem from the dusty path to Rome, the energies of England were released, and amongst a hundred other activities, privateering upon Spanish trade routes and upon Spain's Imperial preserves (vastly increased in 1580 when Spain conquered her only maritime rival, Portugal) became at once a patriotic pastime, a religious duty, and a gainful employment.

While England's policies had been directed from Spain it was inevitable that such exploration as had been attempted was designed to discover a North-East Passage to the Orient, a passage that might be used without giving offence to Spain. Under Queen Elizabeth, who knew no foreign control, the Crown transferred its patronage from the North-East Passage to the North-West. In 1576 Sir Humphrey Gilbert, in his 'Discourse on a North-West Passage to India', set out the geographical arguments which could support the new political inclinations and not all the doubts that were caused by reports of the voyages which Martin Frobisher made in 1576, 1577, and 1578 to the terrifying coasts of Labrador, nor all the failures of other explorers, could quite destroy English hopes or stultify English efforts.

The search for a North-West Passage was, of course, fruitless, but in this search there took growth the most significant development of sixteenth-century mercantile policy. Others, among them the greatest of Elizabeth's sea captains, Sir Francis Drake, used the Straits of Magellan as a golden gateway to plunder, but Sir Humphrey Gilbert, his half-brother Sir Walter Raleigh, and their neighbour and cousin Sir Richard Grenville, began to cast their eyes upon the east coast of America. Their intentions were at first hardly different from the intentions of most of their contemporaries. They still looked to the East for riches and merely hoped that if they could establish trading posts in North America, these posts would pay for themselves by engaging in bartering with the American Indians and would act as revictualling stations for English ships on their way to more lucrative trade with the Indians of Asia. Nor were strategical considerations outside their reckoning: a base capable of being used against the Spaniard was always a goal to Drake's contemporaries.

But gradually the eyes of England focused on America itself, and prospects of colonization took the place of ideas of temporary settlement.

In 1583 Gilbert landed at St John's, Newfoundland, a place which fishermen from the Grand Banks had been using for drying their catch for almost one hundred years. Gilbert had with him a royal patent, authorizing him to make grants of land, to bring settlers from England, and to set up a system of local government under the laws of England. As many, perhaps even most, of the fishermen who used this place were French, Gilbert's laws appear as somewhat arrogant. One of them, for example, stated that:

If any person should utter words sounding to the dishonour of Her Majestie, he should lose his ears and have his ship and goods confiscate.

But such arrogance is the stuff of empire.

Gilbert's attempt to settle Newfoundland ended in disaster. He himself was lost at sea on his way back to England, and his patent lapsed, but America was now firm in English consciousness.

At home the geographers, advertising agents of adventure, settled to the work of popularizing new projects, and the writings of one of them, Richard Hakluyt, at once records of the past and incentives for the future, rivalled Foxe's *Book of Martyrs* as a best seller of the day.

Humility and backwardness in empire-building now disappeared altogether from English habit. 'The English Nation,' wrote Edward Hayes, historian of Gilbert's expedition,

onely hath right unto these countreys of America from the Cape of Florida northward, by the privilege of first discovery, unto which Cabot was authorized by Regall authority; and set forth by the expense of our late King, Henry VII.

Thus England set aside the Pope, Spain, and Portugal and used convenient, if almost imaginary, history to give authority to the fulfilment of national desires. England, said

Cecil, had no intention of recognizing Spanish monopoly in the Americas,

either because of donations from the Pope or from their having touched here and there upon these coasts, built cottages and given names to a few places.

Only when history supported English claims would the English accept its authority. If the Spaniards actually inhabited the place, then, for the time being at least, the English nation would respect their suzerainty, but Spanish claims could

not hinder other Princes from freely navigating those seas and transporting colonies to those parts where the Spanish did not actually inhabit;

a very convenient formula, as the English were now, of all peoples, the most actively contemplating 'inhabiting' the shores of America.

Sound economic considerations were uppermost in the minds of those who planned and dreamed at home. The need to relieve England of surplus population – in the twentieth century the main argument of enthusiasts for emigration – was not yet a factor, and the younger Hakluyt actually argued that the country could maintain five times its contemporary population. But the vision was fading of immediate and tangible wealth in the form of gold and silver, the vision that had well-nigh ruined Spain, and though some still imagined

that the discovery of a good Mine, by the goodness of God, or a passage to the South-sea, or some way to it, and nothing els can bring this Countrey in request to be inhabited by our nation,

others had taken note of Spanish successes that the Spaniards themselves had hardly noticed, the agricultural developments in the Caribbean colonies, and contemplated similar American projects under English dominion.

England, faced always with the threat that Continental war would isolate her from her trading markets, needed other and safer sources of profit and produce; sources, as the elder Hakluyt wrote, that would free her from dependence on 'infidels or our doubtful friends'.

On 25 March 1584, the direction of Elizabethan colonial thought came to a head and was set on the way to eventual fulfilment, by the issue of a patent to Sir Walter Raleigh,

to discover, search for, finde out, and view, such remote, heathen and barbarous landes, countreys and territories not actually possessed by any Christian Princes, nor inhabited by Christian people.

Acting on this authority Raleigh immediately sent out two ships to find a suitable site for a colony. The area allotted to this reconnaissance, the coasts of America north of the Spanish settlements in Florida, seems to suggest the usual two-edged motives in Elizabethan colonial policy – economic gain and strategic advantage. Most of the products which English economy demanded, and in time of war could get from elsewhere only at great risk, required a Mediterranean climate (these were, many of them, the same products which the Spanish West Indies were already producing) and, at the same time, a colony firmly established close to Spanish Florida would be a threat indeed to the power of Spain in North America.

Raleigh's scouting vessels, under Amadas and Barlow, sailed impudently close to the shores of Florida, worked up the coast to Roanoke Island, there took possession in the name of Queen Elizabeth, and having taken on board two friendly Indians – as exhibits to delight the stay-at-homes and as subjects for leisurely interrogation by those who would venture forth once more – returned to England to report.

Raleigh himself seems to have been well satisfied with their findings and the Queen accepted eagerly the honour of having this new England called Virginia, in proud celebration of the state in which she, rare among women, found it convenient and happy to remain. In December 1584 a bill was presented to the Commons for the confirmation of Raleigh's Patent – the first item of American legislation to appear in the records of Parliament.

As ever, piety came first. God could not be left out of the

reckoning. The Queen was 'desirous that the knowledge of God and trewe religion might by her heighnes Labors be propagatyd Amongeste foreign Nacions'. Prosperity, in the statecraft of Elizabethan England never considered as far behind godliness among the virtues, was appropriately discussed next – the Bill rehearsed the 'Infynite Commodities' of Virginia and suggested that by their exploitation much benefit might come to England. A thumb to the nose at Spain was never so much as hinted.

But when in 1585 Raleigh's second expedition set out, in seven ships under the command of Sir Richard Grenville, its composition was entirely male and almost entirely military, and it may well be that the original conception had been changed considerably; that even the strategic notion had been adapted to tactical ends: to establish a base in 'Virginia' which might protect the route of Francis Drake's West Indian expedition of 1585 and 1586 at the same time as Bernard Drake created a diversion by attacking the Spanish Newfoundland fisheries – all in preparation for a projected occupation of the Spanish West Indies by a force under the command of Sir Philip Sidney.

If this was the plan there must have been some last-minute modification. The party which was settled on the shores of what is now North Carolina was hardly big enough to establish a firm military base – only just over a hundred men were left at Roanoke Island under the command of Ralph Lane. But whatever the reasons for the organization of this party, its activities do not contain much of promise for the future of American colonization. Lane seems to have contrived to turn the Indians from friendly and curious neighbours into violent and treacherous enemies. Reliefs and stores from England never arrived when they were expected, and:

The hand of God came upon them for the cruelty and outrages commited by some of them against the native inhabitants of the countrey.

Lane's party was fortunate indeed to be taken off by Sir

Francis Drake on his way home from his own private wars against the Spaniards in the Caribbean.

But failure did not dishearten the merchants of London, though, for a time at least, it did dissuade Raleigh from further endeavour.

In 1587 a new company was formed, known as the City of Raleigh in Virginia, which leased the rights from Sir Walter Raleigh himself. Following the pattern which throughout the sixteenth century and well into the seventeenth was customary in voyages of exploration, this new company was composed of adventurers of two sorts: the one, nineteen of the original thirty-two members, London merchants who risked nothing but their money; the other, the voyagers themselves, who put their experience, their energies, and their very lives into the exploit.

Three ships took out to America the members of the second colony. Again there were something over one hundred in the party, but among that hundred there was a significant addition: seventeen of them were women and nine children. Elizabethan England had realized that colonization implied more than mere exploitation.

On 18 August 1587, the first English child was born in Virginia, the grand-daughter of the Governor, John White. In honour of her Queen and her new homeland, she was named Virginia. White came back to England to arrange for reinforcements and supplies; the excitements of the year of the Spanish Armada prevented him from getting a ship back to his 'Discomfortable Company' until 1589, and by the time that he returned the City of Raleigh in Virginia and its famous child, Virginia Dare (who had been known to history for only nine days) had disappeared into the mists of tragedy and speculation. What happened to them no one knows. Starvation, disease, or massacre may have been their fate. There is some slight evidence that they had followed the advice of friendly Indians and moved up towards Chesapeake Bay, where a few of them survived until their final destruction by Powhatan not long before the first successful settlement established itself at Jamestown in 1607. There is even more evidence, though still inconclusive, that some of them found their way across the Carolinas and into Georgia. But Virginia Dare and her elders were lost, not only to Elizabethan England, but still, after almost four hundred years, to the investigations of historians.

As yet, nothing had been established; even that 'Vegetable of singular strength and power', tobacco, which Raleigh's colonists had sent back to England, was of no economic importance until the next generation, when John Rolfe, generally known for his romantic essay in miscegenation, his marriage to Pocahontas, invented a method of curing that made the plant palatable to European taste.

There was, as yet, no empire. Such energies as were directed to the establishment of Englishmen overseas were concentrated, for the most part, not on America, but much closer to home: on Ireland. A wise after-the-event playwright (Shakespeare or Fletcher?) put into the mouth of Cranmer a prophecy on the omnipresence of the English monarchy:

> Wherever the bright sun of heaven shall shine
> His honour to the greatness of his name
> Shall be, and make new nations.

But the glory of empire was with James the First and not with Elizabeth.

Nevertheless, long before the death of Elizabeth, England had lost her parochial mentality; the far corners of the earth were no longer so very far away. The hunt was up, and the quarry no longer the sole purpose of the chase: the excitement, the desire to travel and to explore had been planted alongside the desire to make profit in the English character, and the gossip and the idiom of voyaging had taken root in the English intellect. When Shakespeare, who was never given to writing above the heads of his audience, described Malvolio as 'smiling his face into more lines than are in the new map with the augmentation of the Indies', the groundlings knew very well what he had in mind.

So far as America was concerned, English achievement in

the sixteenth century was slight indeed; the solid work of settlement still lay ahead, but not so very far ahead. Without the bold, if unsuccessful, efforts of the merchant-buccaneers, the pirate-patriots and the fighter-dreamers of the sixteenth century, there would have been no successes in the century that followed.

CHAPTER 3

SETTLEMENT AT JAMESTOWN

As the reign of Queen Elizabeth drew to its close, England became conscious of its flexed muscles; conscious too, almost to the point of desperation, that, though much had been attempted nothing had been achieved in American colonization. Under Elizabeth, a pattern had been set, which, for almost two centuries, was to be followed in many English overseas enterprises; the pattern of granting to a chartered company the monopoly of trade in a particular area. Frequently with trade rights went permission to negotiate treaties with foreign powers, and the authority to maintain armed forces. (In the case of the East India Company, the control of a private army was maintained for over two centuries). Thus it was that chartered companies had been set up with royal permission and solid commercial backing to undertake all trade with Russia, the Muscovy Company; with the Baltic, the Eastland Company; with the Levant, with Spain, and with Venice. Of these companies, most were concerned with old-established trades, and it had become almost an axiom of Elizabethan economic policy, an axiom much resented by the 'interlopers', that as soon as a trade became important enough to warrant control, royal favour gave exclusive rights to some chartered company, usually consisting of already prosperous merchants in the City of London. If, however, the effect of the foundation of companies in old-established trade was to divert profits into the pockets of a few privileged persons, and they mostly Londoners, there was more excuse for the formation of a chartered company to undertake the exploitation of new trades and new areas, and it is doubtful whether the colonization of Virginia could ever have been successfully carried through had it not been for the formation, in 1606, of the London and the Plymouth Virginia Companies. Individual adventuring had proved itself incapable of continuing to success such a complicated venture; it remained for corporate enterprise to establish what had hitherto been a dream which always turned into a nightmare.

By the Charters of 1606 the two groups, the Virginia Company of London and the Virginia Company of Plymouth, were authorized to choose territories between the Cape Fear River in North Carolina and the forty-fifth parallel up in what is now Maine. The London Company kept its eyes firmly fixed on the portion which had been specially allotted to it, the southern section, and thought from the first of a colony on the shores of the Chesapeake Bay. The Plymouth Company looked to the north, to the sterner coasts of Maine.

In the year 1606 money and men came readily to the Virginia Company of London. James the First was on the throne, but the babblings of Stuart incompetence had not yet dimmed the light that shone from Tudor vigour. By December of 1606 the Company had three ships ready for the voyage to America, and on the last day of the year the expedition, under the command of Captain Christopher Newport, up-anchored and sailed for the open sea. Like the second great founding expedition, the Pilgrim Fathers, Newport's fleet found it more difficult to leave England than to cross the Atlantic. It was almost two months before the ships finally cleared the South Coast ports; only two months later, they were between Cape Henry and Cape Charles (named by them after the Prince of Wales and his brother Charles, Duke of York). Having left ten men at Cape Henry as 'Centinels' against the Spaniards (and having become the first Englishman to indulge in the debate that still continues, upon the comparative merits of Whitstable and Chesapeake Bay oysters) Newport hastened on up the nearest great river – which, lest the King think that he had been slighted in favour of his sons, he called the James River. For two weeks he searched for a suitable landing place, and finally decided to settle on a peninsula to the northern bank, a peninsula so nearly surrounded by water that it is still called Jamestown Island. History was to prove that this was an unfortunate choice. Even today mosquitos breed in the nearby swamps. If it is raining anywhere in Virginia it is raining in Jamestown and if the sun is unbearably hot elsewhere in Virginia it is hotter still in Jamestown. But knowledge of mosquito-borne dangers was still two hundred years away; it was May when the first settlers landed, and in May Virginia, even Jamestown Island, has that delicious freshness and warmth which has always made Englishmen envy Mediterranean climates. In addition the one consideration which was to Newport truly important was the defensibility of his site. For that, at least, his selection was ideal.

So here, on a muddy peninsula, a hundred adventurers, many of them still fooling themselves with Elizabethan dreams of quick riches, and hardly any of them properly equipped by experience or inclination to the tasks before them, began the true history of the British Empire and Commonwealth.

In looking back at the early history of the Virginia colony, there is a natural tendency to contrast its origins with the origins of other American colonies. Massachusetts Bay and Maryland took their inspiration from religious impulses; Pennsylvania from that borderland between religion, philosophy and politics where all Utopias are created; Georgia was the direct creation of the sentimentality and instinct for philanthropy which are among the virtues and vices of the English-speaking peoples. Beside all this, Virginia may seem an exceedingly worldly, even a sordid creation: the creature of a joint stock company. Yet while stockholders in London never took their eyes off percentages, nor did they ever cease to protest their devotion to a higher cause, and their protests were not entirely without substance and honesty. As proudly as the Spaniards before them, those interested in Virginia announced that it was among their interests to convert the Indians. King James himself, in granting the Charter of 1606, insisted that his purpose in granting a patent was 'in propagating all Christian religion to such people as yet live in darkness and miserable ignorance of the true knowledge and worship of God'. When the first fruits of commercial enterprise were brought back to England in 1608, there came with them an early example of the advertising pamphlets which were to pour out of America for fifty years, John Smith's *A True Relation*, to which was prefaced another note, comforting those at home with the thought that the most arduous and most practical step had now been taken, Virginia was settled, and that there but remained the less exhausting part of the work,

the end, to the high glory of God, to the erecting of true religion among infidels, to the overthrow of superstition and idolatrie, to the winning of many thousands of wandering sheepe unto Christ's fold, who now, and till now, have strayed in the unknowne paths of Paganisme, Idolatrie and superstition.

Smith, himself, in the usual manner of front-line soldiers cursing the behaviour of 'scarlet majors at the base', would not accept the honesty of the Company's intentions:

For, I am not so simple to think that ever any other motive than wealth will ever erect there a Commonweale.

And in his denunciation of the policies of London, which certainly painted a sweetly untrue picture of conditions in Virginia in order to lure out colonists, Smith further disagreed with his anonymous introducer:

We did admire how it was possible that such wise men could so torment themselves, and so, with such strange absurdities and impossibilities; making religion their colour when all their aime was nothing but present profit.

Yet these first colonials were Elizabethan born; they saw the hand of God in all things, and were eager and ready to assist His work. Most of them essentially middle-class, and most of them touched with the notions that Calvinism had foisted upon the English Church, their attitude towards the purpose and structure of the colony hardly differed from the attitude of the first settlers in New England, save perhaps in one aspect which still tinges the attitude of the South towards the Old World: that the Virginians did not come to seek refuge from religious persecution.

Time was to come when the writing of American history was to be almost entirely the prerogative of Northerners, and then it was that the myth was created which still persists in the public imagination on both sides of the Atlantic, the myth that somehow the antecedents of Virginians are less solid and less worthy than the antecedents of New Englanders. Yet one only has to look at the pious truth behind the story, which, as fable, is so well-loved by Americans – the story of John Rolfe and Pocahontas – to realize the essential similarities of spirit in the colonists of the Virginia Company and the Pilgrim Fathers.

To Rolfe, an enterprising, hard-working, intelligent, and undoubtedly self-seeking colonist, redemption was still the 'ultimate issue'. He found himself 'inthralled in so intricate a laborinth' by his thoughts of the Indian Princess 'that I was even awearied to wind myselfe thereout', and spent much time at his devotions in an effort to overcome these 'diabolical assaults'. The charms of Pocahontas were so great that even prayer could not overcome them, and then it was that Rolfe saw the way out of his dilemma: God, he insisted, demanded of him the sacrifice of marriage to this heathen girl. Even after he had been separated from her for some time, 'which in common reason (were it not an undoubted work of God) might breede forgetfulnesse of a farre more worthie creature', he could not forget her. But by marrying her he would convert her, 'and I will never cease (God assisting me) untill I have accomplished, & brought to perfection, so holy a work in which I will daily pray God to blesse me, to mine and her enternall happines'. That the marriage would also serve to set the seal of alliance upon friendship between the colonists and Pocahontas' powerful father, the crafty Indian ruler, Powhatan, but added to the holiness of the project.

Rolfe's services to the stability and success of the Virginia colony were not confined to his convenient marriage, nor is his piety the entire measure of his typicality. In many senses, he can be regarded as the first in a long line of Virginia planters, and the planter was for two hundred and fifty years the corner-stone of Virginian life, economic, political, and social.

The earliest tobacco sent to England from Virginia had been much affected by the long sea voyage, and the first settlers on Jamestown Island had no thoughts of making tobacco their staple product until Rolfe's successful experiment in the cultivation and curing of the tobacco plant proved his contention that the Virginia leaf would 'compare with the best in the world'. Once this was achieved the colony's economic future was established.

With this development came an increased demand for labour of a different sort than had hitherto been available to Virginia. To meet this demand, in England 'barbarous offenders were winked at and innocent souls, either out of private spleene or for greedy gaine, sent awaie to Virginia'. Philanthropic persons – with an eye on profits from philanthropy – swept the slums of London and the provincial cities for the poverty-stricken who were prepared to go anywhere rather than stay at home, and the Virginia Company took over and transported to Virginia the old English system of apprenticeship and indenture.

The Company was constituted no differently from any other company of the time, and to such companies apprentices were integral. A note on the eight hundred and seventy-one men and women 'sent to Virginia by the Treasurer and Company in the year 1619', lists one hundred as being 'boyes to make apprentices for these tenants'. Soon after this it became the practice of the Company to publish advertisements stating the number of apprentices needed for Virginia, and when the full numbers were not forthcoming, the Company was of necessity forced to find some other method of enticement to obtain apprentices for the Colony. In England it had long been the custom to put pauper and orphan children to apprenticeship, and this custom seemed to provide an ideal solution to the problems of the Virginia Company. The City of London was only too glad to acquiesce in the scheme; the children were not always quite so ready to accept transportation as an honour and a privilege.

The Citie of London have, by act of their common counsell, appointed One Hundred Children out of their superfluous multitude to be transported to Virginia; there to be bound apprentices for certaine yeares, and afterward with verie beneficiall condicions for the Children; and have granted moreover a levie of Five Hundred pound among themselfs for the aparelling of those Children, and toward their charges of transportacion. Now it falleth out that among those Children, sundry being ill-disposed and fitter for any remote place than for this Citie, declared their unwillingness to goe to Virginia; of whom the Citie is especially desirous to be disburdened; and in Virginia under severe Masters they may be brought to goodnes.

So wrote Sir Edwin Sandys, Treasurer to the Company; the children were sent, with their consent or without it.

Along with them came the indentured servants, who were to receive no wages until they had served their seven years. Lured by the announcement that eventually they would have 'a share of all the products and the profits that may result from their labour, and . . . a share in the division of the land for those, and their heirs, for evermore', attracted by the broadsheets which insisted that once in Virginia they would have 'houses to live in, vegetable gardens and orchards and also food and clothing at the expense of the Company', they sold themselves into service. Great numbers died of fever, either on the way out or after landing; those who survived found swamps instead of orchards and vegetable gardens. They were marched in gangs to their work in the tobacco fields. The products of their labour went back to the Company, such riches as remained in the colony seemed to remain in the pockets of a very few. Tales of the miseries of the indentured servants leaked back to England and increased the difficulty of obtaining labour.

And, in August 1619, John Rolfe reported that 'there came in a dutch man of warre that sold us twenty Negars'. The significance of this cargo cannot be lost upon the twentieth-century observer, yet at the time only the colour of their skins was cause for comment, for these were not slaves, except in the sense that all indentured servants were slaves for their seven years' service; they were, in fact, immigrants coming out under the same conditions of willingness, or unwillingness, that had been shown by many of their English contemporaries. (Incidentally, the 'Dutchman' was an English privateer, still indulging in the old habit of preying on the Spaniards, but hiding her nationality under a convenient pseudonym lest her activities bring down Spanish military might against the Jamestown Colony.)

Craftsmen, skilled and unskilled labourers were not the only citizens required, if the colony was to achieve permanence. The country needed women. So, starting in 1619, groups of young women were packed off to make wives for the planters. The Company in London instructed its officials in Virginia to guard these girls carefully and see that they were not married against their wishes (their choice, however, was somewhat limited) and to make sure that every colonist who selected a wife from these consignments should return to the Company the price of her passage out to Virginia in the form of one hundred and twenty pounds of best tobacco.

The impulse to permanence came early to the Virginia colonists. Even in the first generation, Virginians realized that they had crossed the Atlantic not merely to bolster the tottering economy of King James' England, nor merely to increase the wealth of the already wealthy members of the Virginia Company. They were not in Virginia, as the French in Canada, suffering temporary discomfort so that they might return home more prosperous and more popular in that their prosperity had added to the prosperity of the Court. Like the French, it was their intention to subdue the Indian by the Bible or by the sword. Their dream of 'The Virginias' had no geographical limits, but in imagination stretched on into a fairyland beyond the mountains, fabulously rich, fabulously extensive, and fabulously dangerous.

Virginia
Earth's only Paradise.

Michael Drayton had called it in 1606 – with a touching optimism and a blatant hypocrisy prophetic of modern travel advertisements, for, in 1606, few Englishmen had seen Virginia and Michael Drayton was not of the few. But, imagination, greed, and ambition were, to the early Virginians, all ephemeral; their immediate purpose was to make stable what they knew, to build homes for themselves and to fashion, in Virginia, a home for their descendants. They realized immediately that if their aspirations were to mature, if they were to create something more permanent than a business enterprise on American soil, they must ensure a supply of labour, and the future education of the young of the colony.

Apprenticeship, a method by which young men could be brought to Virginia and inspired to make their homes there with a livelihood ensured and prosperity at least promised, was 'to be a great support of bothe Plantations', and so fairly easily organized. Education was not so simply arranged, and the early efforts of the Virginia Colony to overcome their difficulties were hampered by many and grave disadvantages. The lack of town centres in which to build schools, the pioneer existence forced upon the first generation, and the ever-threatening menace of Indian raids, all these factors served to delay the inauguration of any system of education.

Nevertheless, not ten years after the settlement of Jamestown, the colonists, encouraged by the Company in England, were already looking beyond elementary education and seeking the means for the erection of a college in Virginia.

The first proposal was for an institution in which to educate Indian youths, and it was for this cause that, in 1617, King James authorized his bishops to make collections. It is conceivable that it was not so much missionary zeal that encouraged this fantastic notion of preferring the Indian to the white children, but rather a cynical appreciation of the Englishman's nature that always doubts that charity begins at home, and that the colonists, while quite willing to include some Indians in educational benefits, from the first intended that such money as was collected should be diverted to the advantage of their own children. At all events, by 1618, a scheme had been drawn up for a university at Henricopolis in which the Indian college was to be but a small division.

By 1620 the college had no mean endowment: ten thousand acres of land from the Virginia Company of London, fifteen hundred pounds from English congregations, a library and a Communion set were all the property of what would have been the first English-speaking university outside the British Isles. 'Workmen of all sorts for the erection of the university and college', farmers to cultivate some of the ten thousand acres, a manager for the college lands, all were appointed, and on 17 April 1622, the Reverend Patrick Copland, a clergyman who had been serving in Surat, India, but who had taken a great interest in the ambitions of the young Virginia Company, preached in London a sermon offering thanks to God for the great success of the college in Virginia. His gratitude, personal and theological, was premature. On 3 July he was appointed a member of the council in Virginia and Rector of the college, but a few days later Captain Daniel Godkin arrived in London with the dramatic and tragic news of an Indian massacre; news that not only destroyed hopes for a college and for other educational institutions, but also threatened the very existence of the colony.

The colonists had been lured into a state of unpreparedness by the apparent amiability of the Indians, but on Good Friday the Indians had abandoned pretence and with a devilishness emphasized by its careful organization had attacked the almost defenceless colony. George Thorpe, manager of the college lands and an eminent member of the London Company, was dead, and with him more than three hundred and fifty colonists.

Revenge was now the prime business of the Jamestown settlers. An aspiring journalist among their number (there were many such) hurried back to England his description in verse of the preparations for settling accounts with the Indians: *Good Newes from Virginia*, 'Sent from *James* his Towne the present Moneth of March 1623, by a Gentleman in that Country. To the Tune of *All those that be good fellowes*':

> No English heart, but heard with griefe,
> the massacre here done;
> And how by savage trecheries,
> full many a mothers sonne:
> But God that gave them power and leave,
> their cruelties to use,
> Hath given them up into our hands,
> who English did abuse.
>
> For many reasons long we lay,
> and no revenge did take,
> Till Noble *Wiat* Governour,
> caus'd all the Counsell make
> A firme decree, that worthy men
> should venture to oppose,
> In just revenge to try their force,
> against their heathen foes.

(Three hundred and twenty-five years later, a copy of this piece of doggerel, 'the earliest known piece of printed American verse', originally sold on the London streets for one penny, was priced at four thousand pounds.)

In the face of such preoccupations, the college could not be. With this dream went the aristocratic dream of a public free school for the particular benefit of the planters, to save them 'from the great costs to send their children from thence to be taught'. (A scheme, for which the same patriotic Copland on his way back from India had collected the superlative sum of seventy pounds from the crew and passengers on the ship in which he travelled.) And with it went another plan for the education of the Indians, originated by a mysterious letter signed D. and A. (Dust and Ashes) which gave five hundred and fifty pounds 'to see the erecting of some school or other whereby some of the children of the Virginians (Indians) might have bin taught and brought up in Christian religion and good manners', either by being brought over and educated in England, or else by the erection of a free school in Virginia 'wherein both Indians and Virginians may be taught together'. Apparently the followers of the chief, Opechancanough, had other plans for their sons than sending them to England or permitting them to sit beside white children in the Virginian school, and their love of children did not extend to the children of the white men who had not been spared in the Good Friday massacre. But, even in this dark hour, there was some comfort for those who believed in education and the Christianizing of the Indians, for it was a young Indian, Chanco, who had been educated by the English, who saved Jamestown and the colony from total destruction by warning his master of the imminent horror. Nevertheless, after the massacre, the thoughts of the colony turned rather to retaliation and to military strength than to the peaceful pursuit of education.

Not until 1633 was another school set up in Virginia, and sixty more years were to pass before Virginia had its first institution of higher learning, but one scheme, which failed through the dishonesty or inefficiency of those who had control of money set aside for its furtherance, deserves at least casual mention, both because it comes so soon after the massacre, and because it demonstrates, thus early in Virginia history, the great influence that Oxford University was to have on higher education in Virginia throughout the Colonial Period. In 1624 Edward Palmer set aside his lands in Virginia and New England, for the establishment of a university and schools, on an island site in Susquehanna, to be called *Academia Virginiensis et Oxoniensis*. If there is any truth in the great differences between Virginians and New Englanders, it may well be drawn from the fact that, in the early days, Cambridge inspired New England and Oxford Virginia.

For the moment the Virginia Colony had to be content with persuading parents and the masters of apprentices to educate their children, nor did such enforced education demand very much effort from the adult:

Anne Chandler, orphan of Daniel Chandler, bound apprentice to Phylleman Miller, till eighteen or day of marriage, to be taught to read a Chapter in the Bible, ye Lord's Prayer, and Ten Commandments, and sempstress work.

reads a note of one early indenture.

The poetic Gentleman of Virginia voiced the views of his compatriots – still to the tune *All those that be good fellowes* – that when the business of revenge was complete the attentions of Virginians, and all those Englishmen who cared for the future of Virginia, should be turned to the prosperity of the colony:

> The Iron Workes and silke workes both,
>   and vines shall be replanted:
> Great store will be of euery thing,
>   that we so long haue wanted.
> Indico seed, and Sugar Canes,
>   and Figtrees prosper well:
> With euery thing particular,
>   that beares true tast or smell.
>
> Ship Carpenters are come great store,
>   to do our Country good:
> For which no Country can compare,
>   to equall us for wood.

to its strength:

> A blokhouse on the rieuer side,
>   is making very strong:
> That we shall neuer neede to feare,
>   our foraine foes ere long.

and its future population:

> Thus wishing God will turne our mindes,
>   of many for to come:
> And not to liue like dormise still,
>   continually keeping home.
> Who euer sees *Virginia*,
>   this shall he surely find:
> Whats fit for men, and more and than
>   a country man most kind.

But the real problems of Virginia were in the next few years centred upon constitutional affairs. Already, just before the massacre, the Virginia Company had sent out Sir George Yeardley as Governor, and he it was who on 30 July 1619 had gathered in Jamestown the first Virginia House of Burgesses. The comfortable sentiment of nineteenth-century American historians has made of this convention a tiny seed which was to grow the great plant of 1776, and of Yeardley and his London patron Sir Edwin Sandys, the statesmen who had had a pre-vision of the philosophy which was to inspire Franklin, Jefferson, Washington, and Adams. But the connexion between democracy, the American way of life, and this first House of Burgesses is remote indeed. The new influence of Sandys in the affairs of the Virginia Company sprang not from any conviction that freedom was not having its due way in the American wilderness, but from impatience for profits on the part of one group of shareholders, and the efforts of Yeardley to gather the colonists into council was merely the result of the Englishmen's age-old inclination to set up a committee when something needs organizing; in this case, the providing of the profits to those who had invested in their adventure.

Yeardley was the successor to an inefficient system. In 1607 the very first colonists had appointed for themselves a Council. Even, the Council had appointed itself, justifying the appointments, if justification were needed, only by the obvious worth, prosperity, and social status of the Councillors. From this Council the members had themselves elected a president. John Smith was violent about the misgovernment that resulted, but blamed the misgovernment not on the aristocratic nature of the political structure but on the remoteness of Virginia and the natural inclination of mankind towards depravity. 'In Virginia,' he wrote, far from decent authority and the restraints of established civilization, men's minds became so undisciplined that they 'neither do well themselves nor suffer others'. By 1610 the Company had had to admit that 'licence, sedition and furie are the fruits of a headie, daring and unruly multitude'. Under the second charter, of 1609, the Company resolved to mend its ways, appointed Lord De La Warr to rule over Virginia, with an absolute commission to implant severe discipline in the Colony, and the *Lawes Divine, Morall, and Martiall* which were to be his weapon were authoritarian beyond the imagination of twentieth- or even eighteenth-century Americans. The carcass of such a distinguished Peer as Thomas West, Lord De La Warr, like the carcass of John Pory, a less eminent applicant for the post of Colonial Secretary, could not be adventured 'in so dangerous a business for nothing', and De La Warr appointed a succession of Deputy Governors in his place. But all accepted the autocratic view of the *Lawes*, the predominantly military view of the Committee, and the authority of a Governor which were therein contained.

De La Warr himself did not venture forth until 1618 and, as if his previous fears were justified, died on the way. Yeardley was his successor.

It is true that Yeardley repealed the *Lawes*, but his repeal was tactical rather than philosophical. He had no concern for the rights of citizens, but rather the desire to encourage citizens to make Virginia their home. 'No man will go from hence,' wrote Smith, 'to have less freedome there than here.' Liberty, according to the accepted usage of the time, meant little more than the right to profit in a station preordained by God. If Yeardley, Sandys, and the Virginia Company were prepared to adopt some of the trappings of parliamentary organization, it was only in the hope of giving new, and much needed, stimulus to Virginian dividends.

Yeardley's efforts were hardly successful, and to their failure the massacre of 1622 contributed its considerable share. To all the doubts, the disasters, and the failures of Virginian colonization, seventeenth-century England knew only one answer: direct monarchical government. King James prepared to take over the control of Virginian affairs, and his intervention in 1624, far from being a check to the progress of democracy, was in the minds of contemporary Englishmen, in whose number Virginians undoubtedly counted themselves, a return to the decent system under which all Englishmen should live, and a happy escape from the mercenary inspiration of government by joint stock company. When Francis Wyatt succeeded Sir George Yeardley as Governor of Virginia, the Virginia Company of London was no more, and Virginia had become in every sense a royal Colony.

CHAPTER 4

THE FOUNDATIONS OF NEW ENGLAND

THE establishment of the Jamestown Colony, despite disappointment, feud, bloodshed, and massacre, settled the future of America as an English-speaking and primarily Protestant nation. Much lay ahead; rivals, white and Indian, had to be overcome, a continent still undreamed of by Smith, Rolfe, Yeardley, or Wyatt had to be explored and settled; in perplexity and often in pain a sense of nationhood had to be acquired before it could be said that America was a spiritual reality. But already, before ever the second of the major groups of Englishmen had settled themselves farther north on the shores of New England, the long process had begun which turned Europeans into Americans.

Yet, though these first Virginians and their heirs were to contribute much to the ultimate history of their nation, though they were to give it life and light and leadership for almost two centuries, and though still today the Virginian background contributes something irreplaceable in reason and charm to the American character, it is nevertheless true that to the ultimate triumph of Americanism the landfall of the *Mayflower* was more important than the landfall of the *Susan Constant*.

The occasional semantic inadequacy of the English language trips even those who speak it. It has been thus with the word *puritan*. Coined to describe a form of churchmanship, it came to be associated with a moral and, above all, a social code. And the confusion which has resulted has been heightened by the fact that even in origins the inspiration of the Puritan creed was not far removed from the inspiration of puritanism; a closeness which was to prove in later years convenient to those who wished to foist the narrowness and bigotry of their own mean spirits upon the American people, and could appeal for their precedents to the proud and beloved history of the Plymouth colony; this without much fear of contradiction, though to associate the *mores* of the passengers on the *Mayflower* with the *mores* of Volstead or the Boston Watch and Ward Society is historical error and also flagrant libel against William Brewster and his companions, both Saints and Strangers.

For the Pilgrim Fathers were not dummies set up in an edifying Victorian waxworks. Hardly less than their Virginian contemporaries they danced to the tunes that Elizabethan England had struck up in the hearts of Elizabethan Englishmen. They were restless, enthusiastic, bold, and, by no means least, full-blooded. To them the humility of Uriah Heep and the humility of Saint Francis of Assisi were alike foreign. They loved argument among themselves and, where necessary, battle with their enemies. No man, but only God, they recognized as their superior; tribulation they accepted, yet not in any spirit of complacency but in the certainty that the need for tribulation had to be overcome. Slapped on the cheek, they turned the other cheek – only to hide the fact that they were feeling for a cudgel. The world was theirs to enjoy, and if they had to settle in bleak New England it was because they wished to ensure that their enjoyment could not be interfered with by edict of King or Archbishop. The pleasures of ultimate salvation took precedence in their minds over all else, but not to the complete extinction of all else.

New Englanders and Virginians alike had Elizabethan excitements in their hearts; a zest for adventure and the faraway possessed them as it had possessed Drake or Raleigh. To them the land that they occupied was *tabula rasa* on which they could write what they willed, without hindrance from the forms and traditions of an older society. Against them stood the enemy: disease, impiety, the Indian, and the wilderness, but on their side was the strength of a dream which has encouraged their descendants to the present day. Here, in the early seventeenth century, with the forces of persecution, of economic convenience and expedience, must be reckoned this dream of 'America, land of opportunity'.

Geography, not religion nor character, was to determine

the eventual distinctions between the society of New England and the society of Chesapeake Bay. Though ultimately in both regions people began to believe that their genius had made the characteristics of their regions, the priorities were in fact reversed: New England was poor agricultural land, Virginia (like Maryland) was rich, and rich above all in the elements which encouraged the particularly agricultural economy which Rolfe and European demands had established. The New England coastal plain was cramped, held in by a line of rocky hills which hindered navigation and exploration to the west and prevented the easy acquisition of such large tracts of land as those which made possible the establishment of planter aristocracy in the South. Inevitably, New England turned to commerce and manufacture. If the rivers were less navigable than the York or the James, they were, on the other hand, eminently suitable for turning the wheels of mills. If the New Englanders were held to the coast, it was at least a coast well furnished with harbours. And as commerce, shipbuilding, and seafaring forced the New Englander close to his neighbour and made him into an urban dweller, so the wider spaces of the South encouraged the Virginian to be a countryman.

Ultimately New England was to have an aristocracy of commerce, as proud in its own way as the Virginian aristocracy of agriculture, but even in origins the existence of an aristocracy was in both regions recognized, and to the North as to the South, the acquisition of wealth was a sign, not of man's wickedness or cunning, but of especial efforts on his own part and of God on his behalf.

From the very beginning, the Puritans showed some of the traits which they have passed on into the American character. Theirs was God's own country because they were God's chosen people. In that they were practical they could be cooperative – the early history of Plymouth and Massachusetts Bay is a more shining example of the virtues of cooperation than the somewhat turbulent history of Jamestown – but even their spirit of cooperation was but an extension of their fierce individualism. To them success, and what is more important, salvation, depended upon the efforts of the individual, and if their reasonable minds understood that the individual could not succeed unless he worked with his neighbours – then they would work well with their neighbours. Simple, because simplicity was necessary to overcome the enormous practical difficulties that they faced, hard-headed, because it was necessary to be hard-headed to survive, they achieved much from the combination of their simplicity and their hard-headedness.

The naming of places is often a form of historical record, and nowhere was this to be more true than in America. When John Smith christened New England, he settled, by that very act, something of the future of the region and its people. And, as reputation so often is the yardstick by which men live, so, from the very first and until today, have New Englanders held to a remnant of old Englishness.

Smith came to New England after fish and fur; no new effort for a European, as Englishmen, Frenchmen, and Spaniards had known the wealth that could be drawn from New England for well over a hundred years; and far up in the North Sir Ferdinando Gorges and the Plymouth Company had recently made an unsuccessful attempt to settle a colony at Sagadahoc, but new rivals had appeared on the scene and the English were learning a sense of urgency from the intrusions of the Dutch. Hitherto the region had been 'Northern Virginia' to the English, and 'Canada' to the French. The Dutch, having defeated their Spanish masters and refused the invitation of the Virginia Company to share in the task (and the expense) of establishing a Virginia colony, were now energetically at work seeking profits from the fur trade. They had established a post on Manhattan Island and a fort near the head of navigation on the Hudson River (near the site of Albany) and they had set up in Holland the United New Netherland Company to explore and exploit all the lands 'between New France and Virginia, now officially known as New Netherlands'.

Such facile conquest by edict and words could not please the English. The Dutch threat not only persuaded John

Smith to renewed efforts, but also gave new enthusiasm to the almost defunct Plymouth Company, so that in 1616, again making its effort too far north for comfort, that Company employed Richard Vines to spend the winter on the coast of Maine.

But not until 1620 could it be said that England had found a home in the North-East of America; not until the Pilgrim Fathers landed, perhaps, but only perhaps, at Plymouth Rock, could it be claimed that the boasts of France and Holland to suzerainty over the land between the forty-first and the forty-fifth parallel were merely boasts.

The Pilgrims came to America out of persecution, and persecution that had religion as its origin. Their journey was long, their difficulties not all physical, they argued as much amongst themselves as against the rigidity of governmentally controlled worship. They were at times utterly incompetent in the face of the climate and the conditions of a pioneer life. But their endurance and their eventual success made them, more even than their Virginian predecessors, the fathers of the American way of life. They came out of persecution and thus set a pattern which has only recently been broken. But to them democracy was an unknown word and a word which, if they had known it, would have meant but little. Government they had to have; they set it up by the common will, but by the common will they remained still Englishmen under the Crown. And the Crown, which had in one sense driven them out, was nevertheless eager to accept the benefits of their pioneering, so that on 1 June 1621 the settlement already established at Plymouth was legalized by a patent from the New England Council.

To the religious causes of New England migration must be added causes that were primarily economic, and it is not enough to think that all of the early Puritans came to New England because they were Puritans. The years which saw the first great migration were, in England, years of depression; New England, with its promise of land, held out greater hopes to the impoverished than did the Virginia colony with its system of land tenure based upon quit-rents.

The New England Council, but recently set up, was not, like the Virginia Company, a mercantile organization. Rather did it approximate to a government department and gather its profits not from actual trading ventures but from fees, rents, and licences. The Plymouth colony paid it dues; the Bushrode Associates of Dorchester, who followed the Pilgrims out to New England, paid their dues and settled their plantation at Cape Anne. Another group landed, and made its headquarters at Wessagusset. The Council appointed Robert Gorges, the son of Sir Ferdinando, as Governor for all New England.

But there was no such thing as 'all New England'. Each colony was an independent unit and each mistrusted the other to the point of war. The Pilgrims, those gentle and upright creatures, employed their own mercenaries and actually went so far as to attack the colony at Wessagusset, where the colonists were so much less God-fearing than the Pilgrims that they actually lived on amiable terms with the Indians. It was the Pilgrims' chief cut-throat (*pace* Longfellow), none other than Captain Miles Standish who drove the Wessagusset colonists out of Massachusetts Bay and 'took leave and returned to Plymouth; whither he came in safety, blessed be God! And brought the head of Wituwamat with him.' Wituwamat was one of four Indian leaders who seem to have had no quarrel with Standish's countrymen, but who had, nevertheless, been lured into a room by Standish and there hacked to pieces.

There was force of character in the Pilgrim colony and more in Massachusetts Bay colony, that gave those settlements pre-eminence in New England, but there was force of arms as well. Rivals, even English and Protestant rivals, could not be tolerated. One of them, who lived under the severe shadow of Pilgrim bigotry for many years and who was, no less than they, a refugee from intolerance at home, finally gave up the harsh struggle and moved to Rhode Island with the bitter explanation: 'I came from England because I did not like the Lord Bishops, but I cannot join with you because I would not be under the Lord Brethren.'

Yet within a year of the incorporation of the Massachusetts Bay Company on 4 March 1629 the Puritan element had gained control of Massachusetts Bay.

The advantages of leadership in New England, which were to remain with Massachusetts for one hundred and fifty years, were already obvious in the very early days of the Company. Alone among the colonization stock companies, the Massachusetts Bay Company vested control not in the hands of a board of governors in England, but in the hands of those stockholders who themselves emigrated to America. It regarded itself as subject only to the control of the English Crown. And the particular success within the Company of the Puritan element is not hard to explain. Though there was a considerable difference – in social origins, religious ideas, and economic status – between Plymouth and the Massachusetts Bay colony, the foundation of success was at Plymouth; on to those beginnings could be built future strength. But the materials which made the colony endure and gave to its building such extraordinary impetus between 1629 and 1640 were provided by two who would not have wished any good thing upon Puritanism: by King Charles the First and Archbishop Laud.

Only two days before the charter was handed to the Massachusetts Bay Company, Charles, in his magnificent Stuart conceit, had denied to his subjects in England their right to the voice of Parliament. For eleven years that voice was silenced. In 1632 Laud became Archbishop of Canterbury and, in the full vigour of his office, set about the task of turning back the clock, of denying the logic of Protestantism, of substituting Canterbury for Rome, and a Canterbury (with its acolyte bishoprics and its supporting monarchy) as the only authority for a man's conscience. The heritage of Elizabethan adventure, as earnest and as energetic in theology as in geography and the arts, was against Arminianism. Within the Church of England, and within the body politic of England, Englishmen had learnt to look for authority to their conscience and the scriptures; the word of an Archbishop could never be enough. And if they could not practise their beliefs in England, then New England beckoned.

The leaders of these new expeditions were educated men, even, many of them, men of position. Cambridge, as if resenting the fires that Oxford had lit under Cambridge martyrs, was the centre of their thought. In Cambridge, above all at Emmanuel College, not only poor divinity students but also the sons of courtiers and country squires had learnt the harshest discipline of all, the discipline of personal decision. (Early in the history of the Colony of Connecticut there was one Cambridge graduate for every two hundred and fifty of the population, and it has been said that between 1630 and 1690 there were as many university graduates in New England *per capita* as there were in Old England.)

In the first wave of emigration, which followed upon the grant of a charter, came John Winthrop, squire of Groton in Suffolk and a prominent if not financially successful lawyer. Around him, when he became Governor in the autumn of 1629, was formed a group of distinction and political acumen. (Incidentally, among them were some whose names still echo into Anglo-American history: Winthrop's brother-in-law was Emmanuel Downing whose son, a graduate of the first class at Harvard College, gave his name to Downing Street; another of the group was a Saltonstall; in fact, it is not so much descent from the *Mayflower* complement which should be honoured in New England, as descent from this first great mass emigration.)

Like Francis Drake or John Smith before them, these Puritans were tempted by the romance of far-off places; to their adventure the effort of conquering a new land added zest. They considered themselves chosen of God to build the New Jerusalem in this land—against the opposition of man, the Indian, who was so much less than man, and the Devil that they knew to be in themselves. Such comfort and such beauty as was in the world they considered theirs by birthright and sweat. Democracy meant democracy among believers; freedom meant freedom within God's boundaries, a freedom, as Winthrop said, which is just, good, and honest. For the nicer principles of democracy, as it was to be interpreted by their twentieth-century descendants, they had no more patience than their Virginian contemporaries. The elect must rule, the unbeliever be trampled into belief or extinction, and the only equality they recognized was the equality before God of all true believers – a concept most difficult to translate into Common or Constitutional Law.

To their Elizabethan curiosity and Elizabethan courage they added the dutiful intellectualism of their faith. God had made the world: physical, spiritual, and political. In order to understand the nature of the Creator it was incumbent upon His people to understand His creation; hence their great faith in learning, intelligence, and education. Satan planned 'to keep men from the knowledge of the Scriptures': the Puritans pursued with energy a policy designed to confound his effort, a policy which would ensure that 'learning may not be buried in the grave of our fathers'.

William Brewster, the bailiff, innkeeper, and postmaster of Scrooby who founded the Pilgrim church, owned in his old age more than four hundred books, most of them theological works, but also Machiavelli's *The Prince*, Bacon's *Advancement of Learning*, Hornsby's *Scyrge of Drunkards*, books on medicine and the cultivation of silkworms, and a copy of the *Tragedy of Messalina, the Roman Emperesse*, 'as it hath been acted with general applause, divers times, by the Companie of his Majestie's Revells'. Even Miles Standish, soldier-in-chief to the Pilgrims, and no scholar, died possessed of an excellent little library of more than sixty books, among them, appropriate to his faith, 'three old Bibles', and, appropriate to his profession, Caesar's *Commentaries*, and Bariffe's *Artillery*. He had a translation of the *Iliad*, a history of the world, a history of the reign of Queen Elizabeth and, outlandish to his chosen habitation, a history of Turkey.

In the year following upon the grant of a charter to Massachusetts Bay, Massachusetts became the refuge of two thousand new colonists. Before Parliament raised its voice once more and its physical strength to halt the excesses of

King and Archbishop, more than twenty thousand had left England for Massachusetts. Not all of them stayed; some were disillusioned, finding New Jerusalem both physically and spiritually less comfortable than Old England. Some returned home when the Protectorate gave them hope of freedom to follow their own particular style of bigotry. Many died. And of those who remained, not all were Puritans. It is impossible to give accurate statistics of Church membership in New England, but it has been said that only one-fifth of the population of the New England colonies before 1750 was composed of Church members, and if this figure is an underestimate it does at least give some indication of the uncertain strength of the Church. Nor must it be forgotten that, from the very beginning, Puritanism faced dissension from within as well as disagreement from without. Its history in New England is one long story of compromise and retreat.

But the manner, the circumstances, and the material of this mass emigration ensured to the Puritan sect, and above all to its clergy (sixty-five ministers arrived in the colony between 1630 and 1641), a position of leadership in Massachusetts Bay, and encouraged in the colony the devotion to bookishness and learning which was already settled in the Puritan faith.

Bookishness brought with it book-writing. Perhaps, for modern taste, pleasure in early New England literature demands attention first to rebels: to Thomas Morton of Merrymount, most un-Puritan of Massachusetts pioneers, to Roger Williams, a Puritan perhaps, but one so unorthodox that he achieved for himself banishment from Massachusetts, and to such untypical poets as Ann Bradstreet whose work, at all events, has been somewhat over-estimated through natural surprise that a Puritan woman, the mother of eight children, should be able to write poetry at all on this harsh frontier. But, despite the unchallenged supremacy of these 'artists', the strength and weight of New England writing and New England reading was theological.

Morton's *The New English Canaan*, published in Amsterdam

in 1637, might satirize the worthy but solemn qualities of the Puritan leaders, and therefore win smiles of approval from Englishmen who were beginning to feel the heavy hand of Calvinism upon their national, and natural, pleasures; Morton's proclaimed Anglicanism could bring to his support that strong minority in England which was not certain that the way of temporal and eternal happiness lay in the footsteps of John Calvin: but so far as Massachusetts itself was concerned, Morton's book was as vicious and its author better known. One can imagine a few angry Fathers dipping into *The New English Canaan* in the secret corners of their beds, and seeing each his neighbour in Morton's description of a Pilgrim 'prophecying' one man rising and talking like a grocer, 'weighing everything'; another 'of a more cutting disposition' tailoring from his text a comely holy garment and urging his congregation to put it on as it was in 'such a fashion as doth best become a Christian man'; another talking like tapsters 'filling up the cup of repentance'; and yet another running off so fast with his given text that no one in the congregation could follow him – 'and doubtless his father was some Irish footman'. One can imagine that, as the Puritans were very human, and only a generation removed from their lusty Elizabethan fathers, some of these secret readers were greatly tempted by Morton's open delight in 'carnalle pleasures', and almost all of them by his enthusiasm for moneymaking. But, though its subject is Massachusetts, *The New English Canaan* had no general currency in New England, for Morton himself was the central figure in the first great muckraking in American history. His book, an earlier *Hudibras*, belongs rather more with the history of the Civil War in England than with the history of an established theocracy in Massachusetts. For Civil War postulates lack of conformity even to the point of violence; theocracy demands orthodoxy.

The Puritan concept of art was that it was functional, rational, and divinely centred. 'Art is from God and should glory God.' Generally, the Puritan leaders were opposed not merely to carnal pleasures but even to sensual delights.

Such opposition was apparent in their worship and in their literature; the two came together in the plainness and directness of the Puritan sermon. Here logic was the driving force, and such passion as there was came from the determination to convert and control and not from the emotions. When the Puritan preacher used imagery at all, he shunned the suggestive images of the poets and went instead to the fireside or the shop, to the events of everyday life instead of to the wilder, more wonderful circumstances that come with love, hate, or physical beauty.

Thomas Shepherd of Emmanual College (who also wrote the first law code for Massachusetts), and John Davenport, the first minister in New Haven – and, rarely for that place at that time, an Oxford man – were, with many of their contemporary preachers, men of considerable learning and certain literary equipment. Nor were they without wit of a kind. Nathaniel Ward, for example, whose stay in Massachusetts lasted for only twelve years, and those between the fifty-seventh and sixty-ninth of his life, had been brought up in the England of the Euphuists, and his own vigorous word-coinage suited well his intolerance and cynicism, but was, nevertheless, witty after the fashion of his earlier days:

When I heare a nugiperous Gentledame inquiring of the dresse the Queen is in this week: what the nudiustertian fashion of the Court; I meane the very newest: with egge to be in it in all haste, what ever it be; I look at her as the very gizzard of a trifle, and product of a quarter of a cypher, the epitome of nothing, fitter to be kickt, if shee were of a kickable substance, than either honour'd or humour'd.

As New England prospered and as the seventeenth century moved forward towards scepticism, the intellectual grip of Puritan leaders was weakened. To this process certain ministers set up sturdy opposition and some of the greatest Puritan theocrats appeared when the theocracy was already dying, standing Canutelike against the tides of tolerance and worthiness. The greatest of these was Cotton Mather, third in a distinguished dynasty, himself a philanthropist and something of a scientist, but so devoted to the memories of Massachusetts' great days that he would have called the world flat to reclaim the colony for strict Puritanism.

In popular knowledge, his name is most associated with the Salem Witch Trials, but in the elderly life of Mather, the Salem Witch Trials served merely as the spur to the writing of his greatest book, the *Magnalia Christi Americana*.

It is worth pausing for a moment to consider the events, the access of reproach, delusion, misery, and hate which suddenly engulfed Essex County, Massachusetts, in 1692, for in them was evidence of the great mental changes which growth and increasing social certitude had wrought in Massachusetts. The story is well known: how the eleven-year-old niece and nine-year-old daughter of the Reverend Samuel Parris had been taken ill with ailments for which no physician could prescribe; how they had named, as their tormentor, the minister's Negro servant, Tituba; how other and older girls had developed, or imagined for themselves, the same symptoms, and blamed them on anyone who seemed a suitable person for the title of warlock, and upon anyone who threatened to overthrow their exciting status as informers against the devil; and how, as the magistrates and the Court of the Commonwealth took up the chase, the Witch Hunt and the Witch Trials became the vent for superstitions, for local hate and local revenges. There is, in the story, enough material for a dozen casebooks in psychiatric investigation. Mass hypnosis, sexual aberration, power lust, and fear complex; these and many other explanations from the jargon of the psychologist are all implied; but eventually the Witch Trials must be considered as a battle between the old and the new in Massachusetts. Everywhere the century had been a century of struggle; everywhere battle had been joined, science armed against religion, scepticism against superstition, reason against authority. New England had come late into the conflict and had fought it out over many subjects, among them witchcraft. When men of the intellectual ability of Chief Justice Stoughton, Judge Samuel Sewell, and Cotton Mather championed – some more and some less certainly – a belief in witchcraft, it was because, consciously or unconsciously, such beliefs were in their minds identified with the old faith, because they were concerned with resisting implications, to them all evil, in the new scientific septicism. Witch Trials were the practical symbol of their contemporary success. The intellectual struggle is typified by the difference between Cotton Mather's *Memorable Providences, Relating to Witchcrafts and Possessions* ('God tells Mankind that there are Devils and Witches') and his father, Increase Mather's much more humane *Cases of Conscience*. The eventual victory of the 'Enlightenment' is demonstrated by the short duration of the hysteria and in the fact that by the beginning of 1693 justice and sanity had returned to Massachusetts.

To the history of the time the Salem Witch Trials were by no means peculiar. Most of the executions in New England were confined to one year; in the whole of the seventeenth century there is evidence of only thirty-four executions for witchcraft in the New England colonies. In the same period, Scotland executed almost one hundred times as many. The New England Courts, however close to panic, never attempted spectral evidence as did British Courts for almost one hundred years after the Salem Trials. Salem and New England generally came to its senses rather quicker than did Old England.

In Salem twenty witches and two dogs had been executed. The public revulsion against these cruelties helped to break the declining power of the clergy. But Cotton Mather, who, though he had always been certain of witchcraft, had never been so sure that witches should be executed, was nevertheless completely certain that the future of Massachusetts depended upon a return to the past great power of the Massachusetts ministry.

The beginning of the en**d** of the theocracy had its origins, of course, long before the Witch Trials. Roger Williams, in himself and in his writings one of the finest of the New England theologians, was as much a rebel against theocracy as had been Thomas Morton before him or the sceptics after him. Politically, he is the most interesting of all New England's early thinkers, for his thought founded a colony in Rhode Island, and established for the American people a precedent, a political-cum-religious toleration which was to have its eventual result in the first amendment to the American Constitution:

Congress shall make no law respecting an establishment of religion or prohibiting the free exercise thereof.

Williams, more spiritual than the most spiritual of his Massachusetts enemies, was one of those Cambridge divines who came to Plymouth in the Great Migration of 1629. As restless within the bounds of the Puritan Church as he had been within the bounds of the Established Church in England, from his pulpits in New Plymouth and Salem he preached political and ecclesiastical heresy: separation from the English Church (the fiction of connexion was stoutly maintained by Massachusetts ministers long after the reality had disappeared), the invalidity of New England land-titles (because the settlers made no compensation to the original land-owners, the Indians), and, above all, religious toleration, a dangerous doctrine which he held far more drastically than his most advanced contemporaries. God, he insisted, commands that

a permission of the most Paganish, Jewish, Turkish or Antichristian consciences and worships, bee granted to all men in all Nations and Countries; and they are onely to bee fought against with that Sword which is onely (in Soule matters) able to conquer, to wit, the Sword of God's Spirit, the Word of God.

Such radical opinions could not be permitted either in the Massachusetts Bay area or in Plymouth. Williams was banished. After a difficult winter in the Narragansett country, early in 1636 Williams, true to his principles, bought some land from the Indians and called the place Providence. Others followed Williams to Providence Plantation, and although the colony never became, in any sense, a rival to the commercial prosperity of Massachusetts, the hard-working farmers of Providence managed to keep alive by raising cattle and growing corn. The example of their leader brought other liberal thinkers to build up settlements in the region: William Coddington in Portsmouth and eventually in Newport, Samuel Corton in Warwick. By 1644 there were these four settled communities in Rhode Island. They had little in common except devotion to the idea that religion was a matter for the conscience of the individual and that the organization of Church and State should be separate. But Roger Williams, who had gone back to England to attempt to secure a charter for the whole colony, partly because of his personal friendship with State officials at home (including Milton), and partly because he was able to do a little pamphleteering on behalf of the English Independents in their struggle with the Presbyterians, succeeded in persuading Parliament to grant the charter, and succeeded, on his return to Rhode Island, in holding the four separate communities to a loose federation.

If priorities are valuable, then Rhode Island can claim that it was the first colony to achieve anything like democracy after the eighteenth- or twentieth-century style. There, all had a vote; except the insane and women, except children and bachelors. In 1647, almost a half-century before the Salem Trials, Rhode Island abolished trials for witchcraft; in the same year, almost two centuries before Charles Dickens, Rhode Island abolished imprisonment for debt.

The settlement of Connecticut was based on considerations far less laudable than the settlement of Rhode Island. It was, in a sense, nothing but a suburb of Massachusetts, whither went Puritans to be more pure, the avaricious to grow more rich, the power-seekers to gain more power; all away from the competition of Massachusetts. The rich river lands along the Connecticut were attractive to farmers tired of the sterner soil of Massachusetts, stories of fur trade brought in pilgrims and Dutchmen from New Amsterdam, rumours of general prosperity aroused the interest of English merchants and English noblemen. Massachusetts Bay could claim the area as an extension of Massachusetts, but the claim was denied by the number of those leaving Massachusetts on the assumption that Connecticut was separate. Eventually, in 1635, a King's Bench decision placed ownership elsewhere, with a group of English noblemen, among them Lord Saye and Sele, and Lord Brook. Ultimately, even this proprietary grant finished, though its terms did give to Connecticut the most active of its earlier settlers, the Winthrop family, and when, in 1662, a new charter was granted to the colony by Charles the Second confirming the colony's rights, it was at the insistence of the son of the proprietor's first governor that Charles the Second acquiesced.

Although there were among the Connecticut settlers many who echoed, in part at least, the democratic notions of Roger Williams, and although there was in the settlement at New Haven (it was not merged into the Connecticut colony until 1662) some element of self-determination, succeeding settlements followed, often horribly and sometimes with even more violence, the theocratic notions of Massachusetts Bay.

> Let men of God in Courts and Churches watch
> O'er such as do a toleration hatch,
> Lest that ill egg bring forth a cockatrice
> To poison all with heresy and vice.

The system of government in Connecticut was not in any outstanding respect different from that in Massachusetts. There was, it is true, some extension of the franchise, but to nothing like the same extent as in Rhode Island, and, therefore, the relations with Massachusetts were on the whole more favourable than the relations between Massachusetts and Rhode Island.

Religious persecution at home had been the origin of Massachusetts. Religious persecution in Massachusetts established not only Rhode Island but also New Hampshire, where John Wheelwright, the Antinomian, settled Exeter. Not far away, at Dover, Lord Saye and Sele had his agent, Thomas Wiggin, who brought in settlers from anywhere, even from Massachusetts, and at Strawberry Bank, the oldest settlement in the province, Captain John Mason held title based on a patent from the New England Council.

At Hampton was a trading post occupied by agents from the Bay, themselves orthodox Puritans. There was, in New Hampshire, no obvious unifying theological or political concept to bring these tiny colonies into a combination. Massachusetts claimed jurisdiction over all the settlements, and while the Protectorate prospered in England the claims of fellow Puritans were upheld. Not until 1679 could New Hampshire obtain a charter as a royal province.

So too in Maine. East of the Penobscot, what is now the State of Maine was dominated by the French. At Pemaquid there was a fur-trading post owned by English merchants. From the Kennebec to the Piscataqua was Sir Ferdinando Gorges's province of New Somerset, a group of small settlements under the governorship of Sir Ferdinando's nephew, William, and in the whole of Maine there was a good deal of quarrelling; here, not over doctrine – most of the settlers in Maine accepted the Church of England liturgy – but over land-titles.

Still, in the middle of the century, though Massachusetts Bay had its difficulties, it was in power, prosperity, and population the most forward of the New England colonies. Fifteen thousand settlers were under its undisputed jurisdiction. A further two thousand five hundred in the Connecticut Valley had their own ideas but accepted the leadership of the Bay; New Plymouth, in like case, had only a thousand. There were another thousand in Maine, five hundred in New Hampshire, and rather fewer than five hundred in Rhode Island.

This preponderance of settlement gave to Massachusetts a preponderance of political influence, and when, in 1643, fear of the French to the North, the Dutch to the South, and the Indians everywhere, forced upon the New England colonies some degree of cooperation as 'The United Colonies of New England', it was Massachusetts Bay that called the tune, Massachusetts Bay that refused to admit to the Confederation the rebels in Rhode Island.

While other smaller colonies were still pioneering, Massachusetts was able to turn its attention to trade, and to trade not merely internal or with England, but also with the West Indies, with the Dutch at New Amsterdam, and with the French in Acadia.

Inland there was timber, and the forests were full of acorn-fed hogs, a valuable item of commerce when salt pork was the substance of seafarers' food. In the forest too was the source of furs, and the source of oaks and pines for ship-building. The seas were full of fish, and the coasts were full of harbours.

On 4 July 1631 John Winthrop launched the first sea-going vessel to be built in Massachusetts, a thirty-ton ship, *The Blessing of the Bay*, and from that day shipbuilding became one of the major industries of New England; from the middle of the century New England seafarers and New England fishermen went about their business in New England-built ships.

It was not until late in the century that the prosperity of the New England sea-coast began to settle on the triangular traffic between New England, the African coast, and the West Indies: the traffic in rum and slaves. It was not until early in the eighteenth century that the New Englanders began to take over, and to improve upon, the West Indies' prerogative of distilling fermented molasses into rum. But already in the seventeenth century, Boston had become the major seaport of the American colonies.

Across the Charles River at Cambridge, Massachusetts Bay had established, in 1636, a college, soon to be called Harvard College, which was to take over from Emmanuel in the other Cambridge the task of training Puritan preachers. In every township of fifty householders, the general court of Massachusetts Bay insisted that there should be provided a schoolmaster to teach reading and writing, and every township of one hundred households had to provide a Latin grammar school based upon the model of the English schools.

The Bay colony was determined that, in all things, it would be equipped to lead the way. Grace, refinement, was never part of the New England artistic nature; Boston never did achieve the fine beauty of Williamsburg or Annapolis, a beauty European in origin, yet touched by the sun of the South. But by Puritan hard-headedness and the endeavours of preacher, politician, farmer, and merchant, Boston had become the metropolis of England in America.

CHAPTER 5

MARYLAND, THE LAND OF INCREASE

ON 13 May 1625, only a few weeks after he had come to the throne, Charles the First laid down his colonial policy, declaring, as his full resolution:

> to the end there may be one uniforme course of Government in and through Our whole Monarchie, That the Government of the Colonie of Virginia shall immediately depend upon Our Selfe, and not be committed to any Company or Corporation, to whom it may be proper to trust matters of Trade and Commerce, but cannot bee fit or safe to communicate the ordering of State-Affairs, be they of never so mean consequence.

That King Charles denied his own policy by approving the Massachusetts Grant of 1629 is not easily explained, but 1629 also saw a compensatory extension of the policy when, against all the hopes of the still grasping shareholders in the defunct Virginia Company, Charles gave to his Attorney-General, Sir Robert Heath, a province to be known as Carolina. Nearly five hundred miles along the coast, the boundaries of this Carolina grant took in not only the southern portion of what had been regarded as Virginia Colony, but also much land which had long been conceded to Spain. That the southern boundary was only a couple of days' march from the Spanish fortress of St Augustine was proof of the sad decline of Spain as a power on the North American Continent, and the fact that Heath intended to settle Carolina with French refugees from Catholic oppression added insult to the injury of the proof.

Heath's plan fell through, and it was not until the middle of the century that Carolina was settled. (It then included not only what is now Carolina, but also the present State of Georgia.) But, meanwhile, to the north of Virginia another colony was established, again by refugees of a kind: by Catholics under the patronage of George Calvert, Lord Baltimore.

Looking back on a reign when the King himself was a fellow-traveller with Catholicism and the Queen an unrepentant Roman, it is difficult to accept notions of victimized Catholics, but the traditions died hard, and in England Catholics still lived as they were long to live, on the edge of their nerves. Persecution is a many-headed monster. Behind the glories of Tudor England had lurked discontent and cruelty. England was changing and change always has its victims. Catholic Mary had tried to resist change by torturing and burning its supporters; her Protestant successor had attempted to foster it by exactly the same methods; Mary's persecution of Protestants was followed by Elizabeth's counter-persecution. And, in the reign of Charles's father, the discovery of the Gunpowder Plot, a Catholic plot, had done much to revive, in the minds of Englishmen, their hatred of Catholicism. English memories were long; the three hundred men and women who had died for their faith in the five years of Mary's reign were not yet forgotten, and the existence of the Inquisition on the Continent kept bitterness alive. In addition, a statesman of the calibre of George Calvert could read the signs; the power of the King to defend his Catholic subjects was shaking and their need for defence might increase as the more virulent forms of Protestantism increased their hold not only over the sentiments of the public but also over political power.

Calvert was himself an old pioneer and hungered for land, as many a gentleman was hungering whose dignity was beyond his exchequer. From 1627 to 1629 he had tried, with his family, the hardships of life in Newfoundland. From there he had gone to the more equable climate of Virginia, and, in 1629, he had asked King Charles for a grant of land south of the James River to the northern boundary of Heath's grant in Carolina. But on this occasion both the colonists along the James River and the shareholders of the Virginia Company had cried out against the Catholic, and Charles, uncertain of his own strength, had urged Calvert to look elsewhere.

Calvert looked to the area immediately north of the

Potomac and persuaded Charles to give him a patent on all the land between the Potomac and the area 'where New England ends', roughly the line of the present city of Philadelphia. This grant, not to a company of merchants or a group of colonizers but to one man who was, in an almost feudal sense, the vassal of the King, was the first successful fulfilment of Charles's colonial policy. By the time the patent was sealed, the winters in Newfoundland had worked their worst upon George Calvert, who was dead at the age of fifty-two, and absolute authority over the new colony had passed to his son, Cecilius.

In the charter which he had drafted, the elder Calvert had left blank the name of his colony. His son diplomatically informed the King that he would have wished to call it Carolina had not that name already been pre-empted, and that now he wished to call it *Crescentia*, the Land of Increase, but Charles had other ideas. Courtesy to the royal family demanded that it be called after his Queen, *Terra Mariae*, in simple English, Maryland.

Laudable charity to his co-religionists was no surety of financial success, and financial success was the main purpose in the mind of the Proprietor of Maryland, so when in the late summer of 1633 Cecilius Calvert gathered together some two hundred settlers on the *Ark* and the *Dove* in the Thames, there were among their number both Protestants and Catholics. But, though these settlers were asked to take the Oath of Allegiance, the Oath of Supremacy, obviously and intentionally anti-Papal, was not demanded of them. Off Southampton three Jesuit priests were taken aboard, and on 25 March 1634, on a small island in the Potomac, one of these, Father Andrew White, celebrated the first Mass and conducted the Catholic settlers in a procession to erect 'a trophy to Christ our Saviour'; a not-too-violent breach of the instructions given by his brother to the Governor:

To preserve unity and peace among all the passengers upon Shipp-board, and that they suffer no scandalls nor offence to be given to any of the Protestants, whereby any just complaint may heereafter be made by them, in Virginea or in England, and for that end, they caused all Acts of Romane Catholique Religion to be done as privately as may be, and that they instruct all the Romane Catholiques to be silent upon all occasions of difficulties concerning matters of Religion; and that the said Governor and Commissioners treat the Protestants with as much mildness and favour as Justice will permitt. And this to be observed at Land as well as at Sea.

Protestant neighbours were not inclined to be so careful of Catholic susceptibilities. In Calvert's colony there were none of the troubles with Indians, with disease, and with famine that marked the early story of Plymouth and Jamestown, but there were troubles enough with the Virginians and particularly with one, William Claibourne, a member of the Governor's Council of Virginia, who, before the arrival of the Calverts, had established himself on Kent Island in the Chesapeake, and who for almost four years was in open rebellion against the Proprietor.

The feudal nature of the Maryland grant made all dwellers in Maryland tenants of the House of Baltimore. Estates in Maryland could be awarded by the Calverts to whom they chose, and remained with the tenants of their choice so long as the holders paid their quit-rents to the Proprietor. It was not likely that William Claibourne would submit to this arrangement, and his dispute with the Proprietor over his right to trade in furs with the Indians dragged on in England and in Maryland for many years.

The Lords Baltimore, as Catholics, were in a difficult position as Puritan power grew in England. The reservoir of potential Catholic or High Church landowners dried up. The King could not afford to honour or help with grants of land in Maryland those whose services at home were essential to his military success. In 1648 the Proprietor appointed a Protestant Governor, and in 1649, when an axe stroke in Whitehall removed his royal patron, Calvert opportunely urged his assembly to pass through a Toleration Act offering protection to all who professed to 'believe in Jesus Christ'. Puritans from Virginia settled on the eastern bank of the Severn River opposite the site of Annapolis, and as soon as they arrived began to flout the authority of the Proprietor by refusing to take the Oath of Fidelity which the proprietorial system demanded. Claibourne sided with them, and in 1655 the dispute again came to the point of battle. Baltimore's governor of the time, William Stone, himself a Protestant, and his little army were defeated and taken prisoner, and the leader of the Puritans, anxious to

> Prove their doctrine orthodox
> By Apostolic blows and knocks

was inclined to shoot all his prisoners, but, having executed four, was dissuaded from making the slaughter wholesale.

The salvation of proprietorial government came from a strange quarter, from Virginia, where the settlers, predominantly Royalist by inclination, could not bear to see Puritanism triumphant, and were content to sink their old jealousy in the effort to hold Maryland for the King. The return of Charles the Second buttressed proprietorial government in Maryland. In 1661 Cecilius, Lord Baltimore, appointed his son Charles as Governor and also appointed the Governor's 'private, secret and continual council', the Chancellor, Chief Justice, Secretary and all the justices of the provincial court. This was feudalism such as England itself had not seen for two hundred years or more. The whole administrative and financial control of the colony was vested ultimately in one man. The Charter demanded a popular assembly and some such body had existed from the very beginning, but in 1670 Cecilius Calvert forced a law limiting the suffrage and summoned but half the members of the Assembly in order, as he said, to save the counties half the costs of their travel and upkeep. Throughout his proprietorship he instructed his son to reserve to himself the power of initiating legislation. He struck his own coins and even planned his own honours and awards (though the proposal was never implemented).

Nevertheless, although proprietorial government lingered on until the American Revolution, it had from the beginning suffered many checks to its feudal inclinations even from the friends and co-religionists of the Baltimores, who had come to Maryland to get rich and were not inclined to accept the dictatorial authority of the Calverts. More and more they insisted upon their own right to make laws for themselves, and when Protestant William and Mary chased Catholic James from the throne, Maryland seized the opportunity and, with the approval of the King, dispossessed the Baltimores. The change was emphasized by moving the capital of Maryland from the Catholic St Mary's City to the Protestant Annapolis. In 1715 proprietorial government was restored, but now much limited by powers granted to the Maryland Assembly.

CHAPTER 6

NORTH AND SOUTH

THE history of the first century of Colonial America is like
an amateur pageant for which the actors in one scene
rehearse separately from the actors in others, and neither
know, nor seem to care, what happens in any but the scene
of their immediate responsibility. There is the history of
Virginia and the history of Maryland; the Pennsylvanians
show some Quakerly concern for their neighbour Quakers
in Jersey; the leaders of Massachusetts are at least covetous
of Maine and New Hampshire, but these are the interests
of contiguity and not the interests of community. For the
most part, only in quarrels did the seventeenth-century
colonies show any obvious sign of relationship.

If there was a tendency towards standardization or unification, it came rather from Government in England than
from the colonials themselves. The New England Federation, the threat of *Quo Warranto* employed against some
colonies and held over them all, the gradual extension (hastening towards the end of the century and culminating in
the Trade Act of 1696) of the power of the Lords of Trade,
and the existence of an embryo Colonial Civil Service,
whose members, such excellent administrators as Sir Edmund Andros and Francis Nicholson among them, were
transferable from one colony to another and who were therefore far more knowledgeable about America than most
native-born Americans – and far more inclined to see it
whole – these things were the beginnings, the very vague
beginnings, of unity. Both as such and in themselves were
much resented by the colonials.

That it may be for his Majesty's Service, [suggests John Usher
in 1698] to have Pensilvania, the two Jerseys and New Yorke,
Annexed into one Govermtt, which will better secure the Acts of
Trade, and the Plantations from the Intrusions of French and
Indians, by Sea and Land, and Make the Charge of the Govermtt

bore with more ease – being all one mans Children. And the Secureity of New Yorke and Albany is the Secureity of the Jerseys and Pensilvania. All reason in the world they should doe their parts. For New Yorke begins to Grunble: Shall we pay dutys of Impostt and Excise when our Neighbours Pensilvania and Jerseys doe not – noe, we will lay it downe.

There is the governmental argument for unity concisely put – and something of the colonial objection.

Yet similarity of experience was already forcing upon the colonies some degree of emotional congruity, some union in distaste and disrespect towards the unifying power of Britain. In considering the history of the second century of America it is well to remember two facts about the first century: that in that time, the whole period of American consciousness, the British monarchy had been twice degraded by Englishmen, and, that, in almost all the colonies, the colonial political experience had consisted of struggles with power imposed from without. Among Englishmen respect for the Crown came as much from consciousness of ancient grandeur as from knowledge of present power. The Crown, less than in the days of Elizabeth the First (and certainly less than today under Elizabeth the Second) but still to a very real extent, was part of the national *mythos*. Crécy, Agincourt, the defeat of the Armada, the King's touch, and the quasi-spiritual position of the monarch; all these things overshadowed even the memory of Charles the First's trial and execution, of James the Second's flight and defeat on the Boyne. But for the colonials the mystery was too distant to hold much allure, the current disgrace far more persuasive.

The Crown was distant, but the Crown's servants only too close. In some colonies the royal Governor was principal whipping-boy to the colonials.

Of these Virginia, the oldest royal colony, was outstanding, and Sir William Berkeley the Governor who aroused most fury. And in Virginia, Berkeley's vigour placed the Virginians time and time again on the horns of a dilemma.

For example, though the Virginians felt little love for the Cromwellian Commonwealth, only the blustering of their ardently Royalist Governor could have led them to such dangerously extravagant defiance of Cromwell as they practised between 1649 and 1652. And if it so happened that in this case the interests of the Governor and of the leading citizens of Virginia came together ultimately so that together they could, though near-rebels, force from Cromwell's commissioners a remarkably comfortable series of concessions, the same cannot be said for the activities of the last and tyrannical years of Berkeley's long governorship. It was these activities which led to the tragedies of 1675–6, to the ill-designed but so nearly successful rebellion led by Nathaniel Bacon, and the eventual dismissal, not too soon for any Virginian, of 'William Berkeley, governor of Virginia until his most Sacred Majesty shall please to determine otherwise'. In these moments of crisis few prominent Virginians wished to choose one or the other of the protagonists. They were for authority, but not necessarily for Governor Berkeley's; for the rights of Virginians ('except the Common People') but not necessarily to the extent of supporting the 'General by Consent of the People', Nathaniel Bacon.

In Virginia under Berkeley, as in other colonies under their royal Governors or Proprietors, a pattern of obstruction to authority was forming, but, even at the end of the seventeenth century, neither the issues nor the methods of obstruction were yet clear to colonial Americans.

As there was at the end of the century still comparatively little in the political life of the colonies to justify the general term 'American', so was there as yet but little social, economic, cultural unification.

It is estimated that, by the end of the seventeenth century there were approximately a quarter of a million Europeans in America. Among them were men of many national origins, many trades, and many religions. They, or their immediate ancestors, had come to America for many different reasons, and had been brought out by many different methods. Religious groups, indentured servants, transported criminals, voluntary migration, all had helped to people America; these, and the remarkable fecundity of pioneering people, forced up the population and slowly but inevitably forced back the frontiers of settlement.

And if among these diverse elements there was any common factor, anything approaching a 'typical American', it was the small farmer, industrious, independent, a natural isolationist and, by the very manner of his lonely life, something of an anarchist. Even at the time of the American Revolution all but one-tenth of colonials (by 1775 there were almost two and a half millions) owed their livelihood to the land.

Of their relations with the larger entity, the 'Empire' ruled from London, most of these colonials knew little and cared less. There was in them, as yet, no sentiment of Americanism. So far as they had learnt patriotism it was to the colony, so far as they had grouses – and this far was often very far – they were against the government of the colony.

But economic policies wrought in London were already forcing upon thoughtful American colonials some consciousness of their peculiar and thwarted status. Independent they might be in their own economic ambition but the current British conception of mercantilism stood between them and independent economic development.

The English had bettered the Spanish notion of quick profits from empire. Long-term prosperity was the national goal: it was regarded as the first function of the colonies to produce the raw materials which Britain manufactured, to aggrandize and make rich the British shipping trade. Such policies were not primarily directed *against* the colonials but were part of an inevitable plan to make England economically independent of her great mercantile rivals and eventually more powerful than any of them, economically, politically and in military strength. But, translated from theory into statute by a series of mid-seventeenth-century Navigation Acts, culminating in the Staple Act of 1663, the effect upon the individual colonial was cramping indeed. He could sell only at home or to Britain, he could buy manufactured goods only from Britain, or, their price much increased by duties and handling charges, by way of Britain.

In exchange, it is true, he gained certain advantages: a virtual monopoly in the English market for some of his goods – notably tobacco; tariff protection for other goods, such as cotton, sugar, and indigo, even against the economic interests of the British consumer, and subsidy for still others: wine, silk and naval stores among them.

But, particularly in New England, which grew few of the products that were favourably regarded except timber for naval ships, the mercantilist ideal was never regarded with favour by the colonials.

The New Englanders quickly found an alternative to the notion of a neat, interdependent empire (in which the colonies were to be permanently in a position of economic inferiority). The sea was theirs and they used it. They built ships for world trade and fishing. With the aid of some equally businesslike Englishmen, they virtually invented the slave-trade against which their descendants were to rave for a century and a half and from which the South, which provided the profits, has never quite recovered. They took to manufacturing rum and industrial goods for themselves and for sale in the Middle and Southern colonies. They became merchants, commission-men, and middle-men. And, as the Mercantile Acts were often but laxly enforced and the British Empire still the greatest and the richest trading area in the world, New England grumblings against mercantilism were often more explosions of New England bad temper than justified grievances.

In the Middle colonies too, where the balance between commerce and agriculture was comfortably set, British economic policies caused little hardship. The sugar-growing colonies in their turn, supported in pressure brought at Westminster by the powerful group of West Indian absentee owners, soon won concessions and eventually, in 1730, North Carolina won the right to export its cotton direct to European markets. But Virginia and Maryland, centres of the richest of all colonial agricultures, tobacco, were held firmly to the letter of the trade acts. Almost seven-eighths of American tobacco exported to Britain went on to the

Continent – having been subjected first to the crippling taxes which, already in the seventeenth century, home Government heaped upon the smoker.

To their genuine grievances as time went on the Virginians and Marylanders added grouses which they had dreamed up for themselves and troubles which were of their own making. Glasgow, they complained with a shameful lack of conceit, 'from being a poor, small, petty Port' had become 'one of the richest Towns and trading Ports in his Majesty's Dominions, and all by Fawning, Flattery, and outwitting the indolent and thoughtless Planters'. British merchants, they said, used their monopolistic position in colonial trade to dump worthless merchandise and such as was not 'genteel, well manufactured, and fashionable' in the Southern colonies. The same merchants gave short measure and rigged tobacco prices to suit themselves. Worse still, these villainous Englishmen and even more villainous Scotsmen seemed without appreciation of the honour that was done them when Southern planters borrowed their money or overdrew against tobacco-credits in Britain. That they themselves had forced their factors from mere agents into commission merchants and bankers never affected the Southerners' distaste for their self-created financial masters.

In this relationship and in the whole economic imbalance between the tobacco colonies and the Home Country lies much of the cause for the eighteenth-century paradox: that the colonies which were traditionally most openly Royalist were first and loudest in animosity to Britain.

In this, too, and from the end of the seventeenth century in the rapid growth in the use of slave labour, as in the geographical isolation of the Southern colonies, lies much of the reason for the fast-developing division of habit between South and North.

The growth to full flower of the 'Southern tradition' is an eighteenth-century development, but already by the end of the seventeenth century the *mores* were enshrined which gave to the South its peculiar flavour.

Elsewhere in America towns were growing, but in 1700

Virginia had only its newly-created capital at Williamsburg and Maryland only its newly-created tiny seaport-capital at Anne Arundel's Town (Annapolis). North Carolina could not even boast this much. The great-planter typification of the Southern tradition had not yet appeared. The large colonial plantations, Nomini Hall, Rosewell, Cartoman, Wakefield, and Carter's Grove among them, were not yet built. William Fitzhugh, one of the wealthiest Virginians at the end of the seventeenth century, had twenty-four thousand acres of land, but only three hundred acres were under cultivation and in all his schemes, which included a mill, two stores, and a cattle-farm, he could only find room to employ twenty-nine slaves and a few apprentices. Yet, though there was still in the South a great number of holdings worked by the owner and his family without slaves or apprentices, the risks for such smallholders were increasing rapidly. Against the advantages of his powerful competitors (credit, labour power, large acreage, and the facilities for direct shipment to the British market provided by private wharves) he could pit only his sweat. Soon many of the smallholders who had not worked, schemed, or married their way to larger properties, moved westward, became tenant-farmers, abdicated the land for some other trade or profession, or else degenerated into 'poor white trash' fighting hopelessly on the labour market against the competition of black slaves. Socially unwanted both by whites and blacks, they lived a Negro existence among black men, only their faces and their needs proving their race.

But the 'successes', the great planters who, retrospectively, have made the Southern tradition, who were they? Never so many as their nineteenth-century descendants pretended, and few so rich in goods, spirit, or romantic qualities as the tradition would imply, they contributed nevertheless to colonial life a colour and a manner which amounted to aristocracy.

The same conventional tradition-weaving has gone far to explain this by assuming that the Southern planters were in fact the Episcopalian descendants of displaced Cavaliers, whilst their Northern countrymen were the sons of Puritans and Roundheads.

In fact, as we have seen, whilst Parliament and King matched forces, Virginia, like many agricultural districts in England and the British West Indies, had leant towards the Royalist cause, and when Charles the First was executed many Cavaliers fled to the Southern colonies. But, at the Restoration, many of them returned home to be replaced by officers of Cromwell's army who found three thousand miles of water a convenient buttress against the anger of their powerful and newly victorious enemies. All through the seventeenth century there were a few sons of the nobility who by dint of influence at Court contrived to secure large grants of land in the South, but it was the sons of merchants who could afford to purchase the greatest patents, and men from the middle-classes who had the taste for work and the skill to make their lands prosper. The Burwells, Carrolls, Nortons, Fitzhughs, and Nelsons were all from mercantile families. William Byrd, in 1688 the greatest of them all, was nephew and heir to a London merchant who had settled in Virginia. The first American Ludwells and Washingtons were younger sons of English squireens. Only the Calverts, the De La Warrs, and the Fairfaxes could claim to be of the nobility, and even the name of Fairfax has none of the Cavalier accents beloved of the myth-builders.

It was then from the merchant class that there grew, in the South, an aristocracy – not an English aristocracy, but an aristocratic society dimly reconstructed from the folk-memory of a people who in England had been one degree or more below the aristocracy. It is significant, and a little pathetic, that, in their new-found elegance, these Southern aristocrats frequently named their houses, not after their own English homes, but after the great estates in the localities from which they had come, the estates which they had coveted from a respectful distance. Even in their renewed contacts with Great Britain, most Southerners had little chance of moving among the *élite*, and in America they had no opportunity to freshen their knowledge of aristocracy from any source but each other. (In Virginia, for example, even the Governors, except Berkeley, Botetourt, and Dunmore were, like those they governed, products of a bourgeois environment.)

The First Families of the Chesapeake had come to America because there they expected to find opportunities unstifled by the traditions and the snobberies of England; once in America, abetted by the peculiarities of the plantation system, they recreated a very fair copy of the same traditions – and the same snobberies.

Some were indolent, most worked hard, and in their little spare time played hard at horse-racing, billiards, dancing, drinking, and wenching (an easy sport for the master of slaves). They travelled little, except to the colonial capital for the Season and to each other's plantations. They went to church regularly but they were hardly religious. They had their portraits painted by itinerant painters (a tradition continued well into the first years of the Republic when, with Copley and West absent in greener pastures, John Wesley Jarvis made and lost a small fortune among the Southern gentry), but they cared little for and knew less of pictorial art. Music was for elegant young ladies to perform and elegant young men to admire in the decent moments before more rumbustious pleasures, such as dancing; it was not a subject for study or intellectual appreciation.

It is in their attitude to books that one finds the greatest variation among the planters. Much can be made of the fine libraries of the few, and it is undoubtedly true that as the eighteenth century wore on the Southern gentlemen became more and more interested in certain realms of literature, particularly in legal and political philosophy. But, whereas it is estimated that already before 1700 some ten thousand different titles had made their way to New England bookshelves, and whereas Boston had, by the end of the century, fifteen booksellers for its seven thousand inhabitants, the bookishness of the South was by comparison weak. Most Southern planters had some books about the house to proclaim their gentility, but with the exception of a few eccentrics like William Byrd II of Westover (who, at all events, had been educated in England) they read little and wrote less. In an age abounding with minor poets, the South produced no poet, certainly none to compare with New England's Edward Taylor. In an age which was much given to theological speculation, the South produced no theologian, certainly none of the calibre of New England's Jonathan Edwards. On their visits to town the Southern planters enjoyed playgoing. By 1716 Williamsburg had a theatre and in 1736 the students at William and Mary were producing Addison's *Cato*, while in the same year Charleston's Dock Street Theatre opened with a performance of Farquhar's *Recruiting Officer*. But in the whole history of the pre-Revolutionary South there appeared no playwright of any consequence. Only a few cabinet dramas, written for private amusement, came out of the area, and of these it is significant that far and away the best were Robert Munford's *The Candidates* and *The Patriots*, both in their different ways plays with political themes. For such literary enthusuasm as the South possessed showed itself generally in the forms most closely connected with political effort: in oratory, in didactics, and in the exposition of legal problems.

To these quasi-literary skills must be added one other: a genius for writing the record of action.

William Byrd II was, in this respect, incomparably the greatest writer produced by the Old South, and his *History of the Dividing Line Betwixt Virginia and South Carolina* incomparably its greatest product, just as his more personal *Secret History* comes closest to the stricter rules of literary achievement.

Byrd spent most of the years of his literary apprenticeship in England, and in England he attempted most of the art forms then common to young writers: poetry, burlesque, character sketches, essays à la Steele, epigrams, and translations. But not until he returned to Virginia and had experienced physical effort was his apprenticeship of much value to him. Then, and only then, could he touch the derivative forms with something peculiarly American, and take it out of the rut of conventional early eighteenth-century amateurism.

This derivation of inspiration from the limited source of action encouraged also the occasional skills of Southerners in two sciences eminently suited to an agricultural and still pioneering people, in botany and in cartography. But even here such exponents as John Custis and, later, John Beale Boardley of Maryland, had to turn for stimulation to correspondents outside the South.

At a time when English domestic architecture was at its finest, the Southerners worked admirably upon English models to create for themselves a typical colonial manner, at once convenient and aesthetically satisfying. Not only the great homes of the First Families of the Chesapeake, but also the simpler homes of the bourgeoisie showed taste and the elements of architectural skill, but even in the glories of Williamsburg and Annapolis there is evidence of creative sterility, inevitable in a society that had little time and little patience for the artist.

The long-loved scheme for providing education within the colonies had come to fruition in Virginia in 1693, when William and Mary College was opened, and in 1696 in Maryland when the King William School held its first session, but neither institution could boast education of high intellectual content, and, although it was no longer strictly necessary, many of the planters, seeking not so much mental training as social polish, continued to send their sons to England for schooling, to Oxford and Cambridge (but above all Oxford) and to the Inns of Court. The College of William and Mary itself based its education upon an English pattern; even its early buildings were grouped like an Oxford college reduced in scale.

Qualities there were in this Southern society, a desire to emulate something worthwhile which in time produced, of its own accord, something that was for itself worthy. And occasionally from these qualities came the full flower of genius. Later, in the time of necessity which was coming to all the colonies, the South could translate its agricultural skill and its masculine code of physical activity and of chivalry into military ability which was to serve the colonials well. Its political aptitude and its nice conviction that law was the one intellectual pursuit respectable in a gentleman was later to give the colonies their revolutionary leadership, and in such as Washington, Jefferson, and Edmund Randolph the planter aristocracy came close to inspiration. But to see in the Southern planter society a bright light cast from medieval chivalry and Renaissance civilization, to imagine Williamsburg or Annapolis as Paris or London transplanted, is to inflate a very simple parish pump to the size of the Palace of Versailles.

Of all the developing differences between North and South none was so great and none was to have such far-reaching and disastrous consequences as the existence in the South from the last years of the seventeenth century of a slave labour-force, almost entirely composed of African Negroes.

The slave system adopted by the Southern colonies was not created by Southerners out of callousness towards the rights of their fellow-men, nor yet worked out by them as essential to their agricultural economy. For almost the whole of its first century the South had managed its agriculture without Negro slaves and almost without Negroes; for another century, since the Emancipation Act, the South has maintained its tobacco–cotton economy without slavery.

The enslavement of a large segment of society was in fact a European tradition which lasted longer in the Southern colonies than in Britain or the North. Only when the institution was threatened did white Southerners begin to believe and to protest that without it neither their economy nor their civilization could survive.

Villeinage, a condition of complete servitude passed on from father to child, had been part of the English social system for centuries before the American colonies were discovered and if in England it had fallen into desuetude, in Scotland it persisted well into the eighteenth century. (And, of course, in some other European countries, notably Russia, until the twentieth century.) Nor when villeinage disappeared from the English scene did it take with it other forms of involuntary servitude forced upon the victim of misfortune or the perpetrator of crimes both minor and major. Debt, vagrancy, poverty, all these were liable to lead the individual into 'slavery'. Moreover, under the human but inhuman custom of sixteenth- and seventeenth-century Britain, a husband was, under certain circumstances, entitled to sell his wife into service, a father not only permitted but at times forced by statute so to dispose of his children. And the voluntary servitude of indentures, sometimes for life but usually for a limited period of years, was no less slavery for being voluntary; yet it was this system, more than any other, which peopled all the colonies, North and South.

The first Negroes in America, though they came, most of them, against their will, were slaves only in the same sense that so many whites were slaves – and so many American Indians. When the terms of their indentures were up they were free to establish themselves as free labour, as artisans, or even, in a few cases, as landowners and employers. Nor did the Southern planters (or the West Indian) show at first any marked inclination to prefer Negro to white labour. On the contrary. The constitution which John Locke drew up for South Carolina in 1669 included a system of white villeinage, and Shaftesbury's colony at Locke Island actually attempted to put this system into practice as late as 1674, while even in Barbados the planters kept importuning London not for Negroes but for more white servants. But the Negroes suffered disadvantages unknown by whites and from these grew his greatest disadvantage: slavery. His appearance in America was almost always involuntarily occasioned. He was not a Christian; good enough reason for denying him common Christian treatment! He was inevitably simple, stupid-seeming in an environment so utterly unlike anything he had ever known. Above all, he had no means of communication with his homeland.

In the early days of settlement all the colonies had moderated terms of servitude towards those people they regarded as most desirable: the English first, then the Scots, and so on down to the Irish and 'Infidells'. By 1640 both Virginia and Maryland had set limits to the terms of service of servants 'of our own nation' without indentures, and as the attractions of other colonies, such as Pennsylvania, increased (colonies where servitude of this kind did not exist) they felt bound to make similar concessions to other Europeans in the hope that such concessions would induce more emigration. But no enticement could change the flow of Negro labour, nor were the Negroes even so fortunate as the American Indians who could at least move westwards.

So it was that in 1660 the Maryland Assembly took the inevitable step of declaring that 'all Negroes and other slaves shall serve *Durante Vita*', to be followed by Virginia in 1670 with the declaration that 'all servants not being Christians' brought in by sea were to be regarded as slaves for life. It only remained for the Southern colonies to insist that conversion to Christianity was not a prelude to inevitable manumission and the full institution of Negro slavery was established.

From then on, cheap labour ensured to them, the Southern colonies raised the status of white service and correspondingly submerged the status of the blacks. When Africa was freed to trade in 1698 the sudden increase in the rate of influx of Negro slaves forced upon the colonies the necessity for even more stringent police measures; and with these measures the division was completed – not between free and slave, but between white and Negro.

As other colonies, South Carolina and later Georgia, turned to a plantation economy, so the Negro slave system spread. As plantations grew so did the need for strict discipline. As it became obvious that Negroes were not merely units in the production of agricultural profits but also, as chattels to be bought and sold, in themselves the source of profits, so did the callousness of the system increase. The South, no less than the North, was in the eighteenth century much concerned with the problems of human rights, but by the time that this concern was translated into speech and action Negro slavery was so much part of the Southern social and economic system that it was generally assumed by Southerners that such concern could not, need not, and, indeed, must not, be applied to Negroes.

There followed, but only at this late stage, the unsubtle argument that Negroes were, after all, rather less than human, and the more subtle justification that their subservient status had been predefined by Holy Writ.

CHAPTER 7

QUAKER SETTLEMENT

WHEN Charles the Second returned from exile to the dubious comforts of his throne, he returned also to an American empire which had grown, haphazardly but definitely, since the days of his father. After the Dutch were hustled from New Amsterdam, Charles could claim at least nominal possession of all Tidewater America from the boundaries of New France in the North to the vague limits of Spanish Florida in the South. Nor was his authority challenged by any of the one hundred thousand or more inhabitants of the American colonies, except perhaps by a few disgruntled Dutchmen who took the oath of allegiance as it were with their fingers crossed and hoped for the day when they could break it.

Dilettante though he was, and in an elegantly amateurish way interested in remote places and novel ideas, Charles's knowledge of these small jewels in his crown was slight enough. 'You will have heard,' he wrote to his sister, 'of our taking of New Amsterdam, which lies just by New England. Tis a place of great importance to trade. It did belong to England heretofore, but the Dutch, by degrees, drove our people out and built a very good town, but we have got the better of it and tis now called New York.' But Charles loved a jewel, however small, and loved giving jewels as gifts, particularly when they had cost him nothing. His years of wandering and his ultimate Restoration had placed him under obligation to many; his empty exchequer, and his own poor training in economy, gave him little but honours and colonial lands with which to repay his debts. To his brother went New York, to Lord Berkeley and Sir George Carteret a splinter province from New Netherland to be known as New Jersey, and also rights over the revived project of settlement in Carolina.

But Charles and his ministers were not altogether naïve in

their attitude to colonial possessions. As his father had
extended royal prerogative in the colonies, so did Charles the
Second reinforce these policies by adding military force to
the power of statute. In the commission of Colonel Richard
Nicolls, who took New York and governed it on behalf of
the King's brother, Charles sowed for his successors a seed
that was to give bitter growth in the next century. Here
power was vested not in the will of the people, not in the
authority of a proprietor, nor yet in the charter of a company or the association of a group of eminent and energetic
colonials, but in the supremacy based entirely upon a
garrison.

The presence of armed strangers, however amiable their
intentions, is always more immediately suspect by those who
are garrisoned than any amount of autocratic government
wielded by individuals out of uniform, or by remote authority. The fact that Charles chose thus to emphasize his
strength at the moment when it seemed as if the monarchy
had won for ever its battle with republican philosophies had
little immediate recognizance from English-Americans, but
it was to remain alive for over a century as a certain memory,
a justification of discontent. (The most distinguished, and
probably the most able, of all the English republicans,
Algernon Sidney, was still a god in America long after he
had become forgotten clay to the English, and when eventually, in 1775, Massachusetts reorganized its government,
it was Sidney's motto that was chosen for the State seal,
Ense Petit Placidam Sub Libertate.)

Immediately the effect of Charles's colonial policy and the
intervention of Nicholls and his professional soldiers, which
Charles attempted to use not only in New York and New
Jersey but also up in New England, was to arouse opposition
from the jealous rulers of Massachusetts.

Linked by dogmatic ties with Parliamentary Calvinism,
Massachusetts had been throughout the English Civil War
naturally inclined towards the Parliamentary cause, and
even after the Restoration, Massachusetts and Connecticut,
though prepared to accept the inevitable, were not prepared

to regard any increase of royal authority as among those things which are inevitable. A few bushels of wheat for the King's commissioners, a few much-needed masts for the King's navy seemed to the governors of the two most powerful colonies of the North sufficient demonstration of their dutiful allegiance to the Throne; and at the same time regicides, who in England were not safe even after they were dead, were in New England made welcome. To the King's Navigation Laws and to the King's demand that the Church of England be tolerated in Massachusetts, Massachusetts paid no heed. Pompously – and almost respectfully – they explained that their real interest was in 'the continuance of our precious liberties without interruption, through the Lord smiling upon our endeavours'. And when the King attempted to break New Hampshire from Massachusetts, Governor Bellingham went so far as to urge the men of New Hampshire to ignore the King's letter, 'surely it cannot but be accounted a figg-leafe', and arrested, for their tumultuous and seditious practices, those few citizens of New Hampshire who wished to have rule from London rather than rule from Boston.

Even in Maine, where the predominance of Anglican leanings – and the threat from Acadia which followed the 1667 treaty with France – might have encouraged the inhabitants to look favourably upon the idea of direct dependence upon the King and his soldiers, the Governor of Massachusetts would have none of it and actually went so far as to expel, by threat of force, magistrates appointed by royal command.

Strangely enough, and entirely by accident, one of the results of Charles's colonial policies was paradoxical with his use of military power: the settlement in America of that most pacific group, the Quakers.

Berkeley and Carteret had their hands full in Carolina and were happy to sell out to John Finnick and Edward Byllyng in 1673 their claims in New Jersey. When Byllyng went bankrupt the Society of Friends, much persecuted in England, seized upon the opportunity to purchase refuge in

America for its members. Between 1676 and 1688 shares in the project were bought out by a number of influential Friends, and, at the time of the Glorious Revolution, all but one of the one hundred and twenty shareholders in New Jersey were Quakers, and of the fourteen hundred settlers who had come out to the province the membership in the Society was in almost exactly the same proportion.

The New Jersey Quaker Settlement, though it soon lost to Pennsylvania its attractions for Quaker settlers, to the Crown (in 1702) its proprietorship, and to Presbyterians its hold over the direction of New Jersey culture, shares with Pennsylvania a significance in the pattern of Colonial America that is too often ignored in the consideration of eighteenth-century events. In Western New Jersey, the area of Quaker settlement, members of the Society were in absolute majority only in the first generation of immigration, though for a century they formed the largest religious community. Here, as elsewhere, there was a falling-off from the high ideals of the founders, a readiness to accept the chase for prosperity as an alternative to living by principle. 'Friends in early time,' wrote the best-known Jersey Quaker, John Woolman, 'refused on religious principle, to make or trade in Superfluities; but for want of Faithfulness some gave way, and thus Dimness of Sight came over many.' But the close-knit organization of the Society, the Monthly and Quarterly Meeting, the demand upon the Meeting to supervise not only worship, but also such secular matters as registration of births, deaths, and marriages, the extension of educational facilities, sumptuary regulations ('some came into this country with Fashionable Apparel and Great Wiggs, whereby they are an Evil Example'), and the settlement of debt, all these things contrived to give Quaker colonies the rudiments of discipline and efficient local government, and to train up for those colonies a body of experienced administrators, not, by any means, all of them Friends, but all profiting from Quaker effort. Nor, in more abstract considerations, can the fierce communal spirit of Quakerdom be denied as contributing much to Americanism. The family and the Meeting were the centres of Quaker life. Tolerant, in the sense that they would not practise intolerance, the Friends were nevertheless highly exclusive: in their marriage regulations, in their care for those of their number 'thought to be going backward in their worldly estate', even eventually in their unified front against the civil authority's taxation for the upkeep of the military establishment. Such exclusiveness, such Society-centred habit, weakened drastically that dependence upon outside authority which is part of the foundation upon which all political authority is built. The dogma – better, the absence of dogma – in the Society, has always been compatible with radicalism, the discipline of membership in the Friends encouraging to the sturdy defence of personal and political freedom. But nowhere, except in New Jersey and Pennsylvania, have the Quakers had the opportunity of originating the social and political habit of a State, nowhere else has their testimony been first in the field – and foremost. That, even in the time of their numerical supremacy, this testimony was not always of such quality as George Fox would have demanded is undeniable, and that the 'pagans' around them did not always accept even the best of Quaker example. But proper pride was the heart of the Society ('when the Lord sent me forth into the world,' wrote Fox in his Journal 'he forbade me to put off my hat to any, high or low'), proper pride went with them into the making of New Jersey and Pennsylvania, and in the steps of the proud man walks his shadow, the rebel.

If Pennsylvania was at once the most successful and the least permanent of Quaker successes, the reason is to be found in a paradox that is inherent in the nature of the Society and that was most obvious in the character of William Penn himself. The Quaker is devout but he is efficient; the Quaker is stern but he loves freedom. Therefore, while Penn's 'Holy Experiment' was attractive principally to members of the Society, their very skill in colonization and commerce soon attracted non-Quakers to their side, and their faith would not permit them the delights of religious exclusiveness which had been attempted by other colonies. Penn himself was at once an honest Friend and a loyal subject, even a devout courtier, of the two English kings who, in their personal lives, seemed to fit least the Quaker ideal: the philanderer Charles the Second and his Papist brother.

And if Penn owed much to his father, both Charles and James owed rather more. Charles, as we have seen, was ever ready to pay his debts with colonial lands, and James, whose sense of gratitude was not so far advanced, had, nevertheless, one devotion which almost equalled his devotion to Holy Rome: his sailor's love for the Royal Navy, a service in which Admiral Sir William Penn had been a sturdy leader and an efficient administrator at a time when efficient administrators were few. (Penn's work for the navy puts him almost in a class with James, Duke of York himself and with that most lovable of civil servants, Samuel Pepys. The three form a strange trinity: the duke who failed so miserably as king that England had to encourage a Dutchman to chase him from his throne; the little bourgeois who has gained immortality not for his life's work but for the private thoughts and personal escapades of early manhood which he set down so that he himself could savour them over again; and the father of the Father of Pennsylvania.)

Admiral Penn's son had become a Quaker when hardly out of boyhood. For his father's sake Charles the Second held from him the full fury of persecution which was then the common lot of the followers of George Fox. In 1680 William Penn applied to Charles the Second for a grant of land in America in which he hoped to plant a Quaker commonwealth. His request was granted, more generously perhaps than even he had hoped. The land between the Duke of York's territory and Maryland was granted to William Penn and his heirs and was called Pennsylvania; not, as is generally supposed, after the first proprietor, but after his father, the King's friend.

When compared to the power of the Calverts the power of the Penns was from the very start limited indeed. The

Lords of Trade were already at work undermining the influence of colonial proprietors and bringing the reins of government in the colonies closer to London hands. But, despite these limitations, the Pennsylvania Grant gave to the Penn family power unequalled by any commoner in the King's dominions. William Penn was required to enforce the Navigation Acts, to submit to the Privy Council all laws passed in the colony, and to recognize appeals from the Pennsylvania courts to the King's courts in England. But, nevertheless, he was himself head of the State and his was the sole right of appointing a deputy.

Penn's notions of government have been much idealized by devout historians. He has been made into a democrat after the American pattern, which means inevitably a republican. He has been credited with first seeing the American vision. It is hardly worth arguing against such fallacies. Penn was a stout seventeenth-century Royalist, an aristocrat, sensible of his own importance and arrogant to those who seemed to deny it. His eye was ever on a chance of personal enrichment, though his faith made him less selfish and less greedy than many of his powerful contemporaries. His unique quality as a colonial leader was his determined stand for religious tolerance.

'Colonies,' says Penn in the prospectus which he published in London a month after he had received his patent to Pennsylvania, 'are the seeds of nations, begun and nourished by the care of wise and popular countries, conceiving them best for the increase of human stock and beneficial for commerce.' It is a fine-sounding piece of seventeenth-century propaganda, and could have been written by any man who was attempting to lure settlers across the Atlantic, but when Penn gave 'solemn assurance of all possible freedom and tolerance', he differed from most of his rivals, for he meant what he said, even if he guarded himself carefully against charges of going back on his word by including in his promise that saving phrase 'all possible'.

The success of Penn's advertising set the systematic Quaker leader a pleasant exercise in constitution-drafting,

and on 25 April 1682 he issued his Frame of Government
with a codicil of forty laws that were to serve as a basis for
the Pennsylvania Code. Here, in an age that played Utopia-
building with the same enthusiasm that later generations
wasted upon crossword-puzzles, was a magnificent opportunity and one that Penn, the friend of Locke and Algernon
Sidney, of all people was least inclined to waste.

In certain terms he established his theory of the principle
and function of government:

> Government seems to me a part of religion itself, a thing sacred
> in its institution and end. For, if it does not directly remove the
> cause, it crushes the effects of evil, and is as such (though a lower),
> yet an emanation of the same Divine Power that is both author and
> object of pure religion; the difference lying here, that the one is
> more free and mental, the other corporal and compulsive in its
> operation.

and his theory of law:

> Any government is free to the people under it . . . where the laws
> rule, and the people are a party to those laws, and more than this
> is tyranny, oligarchy, or confusion.

He added, good Friend that he was, a note on ethics:

> I know some say, let us have good laws, and no matter for the
> men that execute them: but let them consider, that though good
> laws do well, good men do better: for good laws may want good
> men, and be abolished or evaded by ill men; but good men will
> never want good laws, nor suffer ill ones . . .

And then he proceeded to the practical arrangements. A
Provincial Council (elected by those who owned fifty acres
or paid equivalent taxes) which was to initiate all legislation.
A General Assembly (elected again under a limited franchise) of up to two hundred members.

But still Penn kept to his promise to hold freedom of
conscience in trust for Pennsylvania, and his promise was
codified by the Provincial Assembly which met at Chester
in 1682:

> No person, now or at any time hereafter, Living in this Province,
> who shall confess and acknowledge one Almighty God to be the

..or, Upholder and Ruler of the world, And who profess him,
or herself, Obliged in Conscience to Live peaceably and quietly
under the civil government, shall in any case be molested or prejudiced for his or her Conscientious persuasion or practice.

His paper preparations made, his settlers coming in fast,
Penn came himself to see that all went well. There was a
fine, a righteous conceit in his heart and a boast, not unjustified, on his lips:

I have led the greatest colony into America that ever man did
upon a private credit. I will show a province in seven years equal
to her neighbours of forty years planting.

But he had known from the start that his colony needed
one thing for completeness: a fine capital city. Memories of
the Great Plague and the Fire of London still fresh in his
mind, already in 1681 Penn had sent his instructions to his
much-instructed commissioners:

Let the rivers and creeks be sounded in order to settle a great
towne. Be sure to make your choice where it is most navigable,
high, dry and healthy. Let every house be pitched in the middle of
its plot so that there may be ground on each side for gardens or
orchards or fields, that it may be a green countrie towne that will
never be burnt and always be wholesome.

And there it was set, between the Delaware and the
Schuylkill Rivers, Philadelphia, the City of Brotherly Love;
its rectangular street plan the heir to Wren's London that
never was, and predecessor to Nicholson's Williamsburg that
was soon to be. And there it grew, not too rapidly, but
rapidly enough so that by July 1682 Penn could write:

This I will say for the good Providence of God, that of all the
many places I have seen in the world, I remember not one better
seated, so that it seems to me to have been appointed for a towne
whether we regard the rivers or the conveniency of the coves, docks,
springs, the loftiness and soundness of the land and the air held by
the people of these parts to be very good. It has advanced within
less than a year to about fourscore houses and cottages, such as
they are, where merchants and handicrafts are following their

vocations as fast as they can, while the countrymen are close at their farms.

But there were 'niggers', or rather Swedes, Germans, and Catholics, among the eighty or so woodpiles of this American Elysium. Already there was a Swedish colony along the Delaware riverfront. Although the Swedes had been naturalized – without having much of an opportunity for assent or dissent – their land was needed to fulfil Penn's obligations to 'first settlers', and the Swedes were not to be ousted, certainly not by an honest Quaker, except at a high price.

They got their high price.

The main body of the German party arrived on 20 August 1683, led by Francis Daniel Pastorius. There were among them a doctor of medicine, with his wife and eight children, a French captain, a chemist, a glass-blower, a mason, a smith, a wheelwright, a cooper, a hat-maker, a cobbler, a gardener, farmers, and seamstresses – all the makings of a compact small colony. And Pastorius was a lawyer! He wanted land for his colony in Philadelphia.

Penn gave it to him, at the expense of his own son's patrimony.

In October there arrived another group of Germans which owned warrants for several thousand acres of land. They too wanted their land in Philadelphia, and adjacent to the land of Pastorius's party, for though Pastorius was in such strong agreement with Penn's views that in his own household he boasted 'those who hold to the Roman, to the Lutheran, to the Calvinistic, to the Anabaptist, to the Anglican church, and only one Quaker', all the Germans wished to hold to their national ways and their national language.

Penn compromised by giving the Germans six thousand acres to the east of the Schuylkill, just north of Philadelphia.

Thus writes Pastorius, 'I, with the good will of the governor' – and one presumes that he means it, for lawyer that he was he admired Penn deeply and was in turn much respected – 'laid out another new city, of the name of Germantown, or Germanopolis. The First settlement consisted of only twelve families of forty-one persons, the great part High German mechanics and weavers, because I had ascertained that linen cloth would be indispensible.'

Thus, in 1692, the new town was described by Philadelphia's first bad poet, Richard Frame:

> The German Town of which I spoke before
> Which is at least in length one mile and more,
> Where lives High German People and Low Dutch
> Whose trade in weaving Linen Cloth is much.

The Catholic Lord Baltimore was not subject to bribe, concession, or compromise. According to him, and he went far towards proving his point, all Penn's work at Philadelphia was mere trespass. The new city lay not in Penn's grant of land but in the lands given to Baltimore's father in 1632.

The death of Charles the Second saved Penn the price of his high-handedness – that and the ever-lightening colonial policies of Government in London. James the Second, though a Papist, was even more of a friend to Penn than his brother had been. Government was tired of ancient patents which served to limit the function of direct control from London and to place profit and jurisdiction in the hands of refractory, self-seeking provincials. Already Charles the Second's newly created Lords of Trade and Plantations had separated New Hampshire from Massachusetts and made of it a royal province. Already they were considering the same action in Maine, and were preparing to go even further: to reunite all the New England provinces except Connecticut and Rhode Island – but under a royal Governor. (A proposal put into effect in 1686, when Sir Edmund Andros, formerly Governor at New York, was made 'Captain-General and Governor of the Territory and Dominion of New England'.) Maryland, with its exclusive proprietorship, was bound to be high on the list for sequestration. In any dispute it was unlikely that Baltimore would receive much in the way of justice from the Lords of Trade.

So it turned out. Both Penn and Baltimore went to London to argue their case, and, though it is difficult to see on what Penn rested his plea, the necessity to prevaricate was removed when one of Baltimore's principal agents killed the King's Collector of Customs in Maryland. The Lords of Trade had their excuse. Up and down the American coast the story was the same, 'it was desirable,' said the Lords of Trade, 'that these colonies be brought to a nearer and more immediate dependence upon your Majesty'. *Quo warranto*, the threat that was held over Massachusetts – and incidentally over the City of London – was invoked against Baltimore's patent, and Penn, just as much a proprietor, but a new one who had as yet given the Government little cause for jealousy or alarm, won Philadelphia by default.

Such happy circumstance was not to continue for long. In fact, from the beginning, Penn's very successes had sown the seeds of disaster. His skill as propagandist had lured to Pennsylvania not only the English Quakers and the German Pietists but also the sturdy Scots-Irish – as unpacifist a group as ever found its way to America, and not inclined to treat anyone, least of all the heathen Indians (whom Penn had looked upon with especial care) with forbearance or in a spirit of quietism.

Nor could Penn contrive to work in practice his magnificent paper-scheme of government.

Even in Pennsylvania it soon became miserably apparent that good laws could 'be abolished or evaded by ill men' and that there were not enough good men, even among the Quakers, to keep good laws.

Already in 1683, a few months after the Frame had been enthusiastically accepted by the Chester Assembly, it had been brought up again, reviled and revised, just as enthusiastically.

When Penn went to London in 1684, he left his power as Governor to eighteen temporary heirs and, apart from the inevitable disputes between them, a far more serious cause for apprehension soon developed.

Bicameral legislative organization always brings with it the problem of intercameral jealousy. Penn's patriarchal notions gave the originating power to the upper chamber but the larger voice of the Assembly was soon heard clamouring for this prerogative, and, once the Governor's back was turned, it handled with obstreperousness such laws as the Council put forward and, further, refused to approve even the body of laws for more than a year at a time!

Council and Assembly at least agreed in general in those directions which Penn would have wished to keep in dispute: their lack of eagerness to enforce taxation and their refusal to support the Navigation Acts.

Faced with such problems Penn out-Cromwelled Cromwell, ordered his deputies to dismiss the Assembly and abrogate the existing laws of Pennsylvania, and sent out a commissioner (in fact an ex-New-Model soldier and Puritan) to take over the frayed reins of government.

Wisely, the deputies disobeyed their absent governor and, after a miserable year of fruitless effort, of lonely isolation among the cantankerous Quakers, Penn's commissioner, Captain John Blackwell, returned to England grumbling that every Pennsylvanian 'prays for his neighbour on First Days and then preys upon him for the other six'.

But disaster more real than any that his obstreperous colonizers could force upon him had already struck Penn. On 4 November 1688, William, Prince of Orange, landed at Torbay in Devon, chased his father-in-law and uncle from the throne of England, and by this action automatically removed the guarding hand of the monarchy from Penn's 'Holy Experiment'. Worse still, Penn himself was immediately suspected of disloyalty.

> Treason doth never prosper; what's the reason?
> Why, if it prosper, none dare call it Treason.

Those who had conspired to bring William to the throne were now loyalists; those who, like William Penn, had long proclaimed and long profited from their friendship with the Stuarts were now subject to investigation and arrest.

At his first investigation Penn contrived to satisfy the new regime, but, in 1690, James the Second's futile effort to regain his throne set suspicion working once more and Penn, with others whose Stuart loyalties were well known, was thrown into prison. After a year he was released, and for the next three years Penn vanished from public notice – and from the knowledge of history.

The Lords of Trade, who had resented the survival of the Penn proprietorship even while the Stuarts were in power, and who had permitted it only because the Stuarts were adamant and their Lordships busy elsewhere, now seized upon the Proprietor's disgrace – and the obstinate pacifism of the Quakers in the war with France which broke out in 1689 – as good reason to remove an obstacle to their policies. In 1692 Pennsylvania received its first royal Governor.

The members of the Pennsylvania Assembly had been quarrelsome enough when Penn was the legitimate antagonist. Given government by an outsider whose power depended not one iota on their agreement, the Assembly was beside itself in the effort to find reasons for non-cooperation. Such was the success of obstructionism that, in 1694, King William was forced to accept the policies of despair; Penn, on condition that he removed himself from England and governed his recalcitrant colony in person, was restored to his proprietorial function.

But the habit of contention had set firmly upon Pennsylvania, and now there was a new party to add to the troubles of the Proprietor: the predominantly Anglican, 'Hot Church' group which, either from conviction or self-interest, preferred government from London to government by William Penn or his representatives.

Further, Penn himself had changed. His latent imperiousness had become active, the easy charm which had been his since youth was fast degenerating into something which in any one but the Quaker leader would have been called querulousness. Most unfortunate, perhaps, for a man of natural vanity: Penn was growing fat.

Nevertheless, Penn contrived to hold off utter disaster for two years, and, in 1701, conceded to the Assembly the right to amend the Frame of Government to their own liking, '. . . if there be anie thing that jarrs, alter itt', and again,

'If you want a law for this or that prepare itt'. The Assembly took him at his word, and under the new charter the Proprietor's privileges were reduced almost to extinction and Pennsylvania became the only colony to be ruled by a unicameral system. The members of the Assembly had seen to it that power should be with them, and undisputed.

In the same year, 1701, Penn left Pennsylvania, never to return. The immediate reason for his departure was not fractiousness in Pennsylvania but a renewed threat from the Lords of Trade to abolish the proprietary power which, had they but realized the fact, had been virtually abolished for them by the Pennsylvanians.

Yet the miracle remains: somehow Penn clung to his rights; somehow, and in the most literal sense, he always found a friend at court – in his later years, Sarah Churchill, and Queen Anne herself (in Stuart characteristics so much more her father's daughter and her uncle's niece than was her sister Mary). His eldest son turned rake; his enemies harried him into a debtor's prison; his former beneficiaries, strength now on their side, continued to oppose even the most nominal renaissance of the Proprietor's power, so that in 1710 Penn could write in justice and bitterness to his great secretary, James Logan:

... the undeserved opposition I meet from thence sinks me in sorrow, and I cannot but think it hard measure, that while that proved land of freedom and flourishing to them, it should become to me, by whose means it was made a country, the cause of trouble and poverty.

Yet Penn's original dream had become reality. In a remarkably short time Pennsylvania had been established and become prosperous, Philadelphia built and started towards prosperity. As for Penn himself, at least he had equalled George Calvert's achievement and had established a dynasty in America.

CHAPTER 8

NEW NETHERLAND

WHILE England settled herself more or less comfortably on the American Atlantic coast, other European nations did not give up dreams of American dominion.

The hindsight of history can see in the posturings of Spaniards in Florida, and in Spain's empty boast that all North America was Spanish empire, merely the decaying vestige of a power that had vanished. But, for seventeenth-century England, it was difficult to believe that Spain was no longer the omnipresent enemy, the dangerous, temporal arm of Catholic and spiritual might. Even from the lofty tower of after-knowledge, it is not enough to dismiss Spain with contempt. For, though her political and military strength had dwindled, still through her missionary sons Spain won and held throughout the seventeenth and eighteenth centuries a new form of empire in the remoter corners of America; even in Texas and California.

In the mission field the Catholic Church was both more active and more successful than the Reformed Churches (and this though political feuds among the supporters of Roman missions forced disastrous changes such as those which, under the royal decree of 1767, expelled Jesuits from Spain's New World possessions, and replaced them with Franciscans). As proof of the fallacy and viciousness of Protestantism, a Jesuit missionary writing of Baja California in the mid eighteenth century claimed:

> They would permit the natives, in the spirit of Luther, to practise their wickedness thousands of times a day; they would allow them to kill, and yet throw the gates of Heaven wide open for them, thanks to faith alone.

But it was the training and not the dogma of Protestantism which was at fault, the education and not the conviction alone of Catholic priests which made them so successful and, for the most part, so contented in their lonely work. Brought up to be curious – in this the Society of Jesus was particularly well equipped for the mission field – the priest could always interest himself in the natural phenomena around him and could regard his study as correcting previous misinformation and thus contributing to the future success of his Church. Brought up in an international organization, he was from boyhood trained in linguistics so that when faced with the primitive languages of the Indians he had the comfortable knowledge that even in his youth he had mastered far more complex tongues. Subject to a far-sighted but severe discipline and possessed of a sense of continuity, he had, above all, no family ties and no responsibilities except to his Superior and his religion. Loneliness of place meant nothing to him; the only fear he knew was loneliness of mind – or loss of health. Against such singleness of purpose Protestant missionaries were poor competitors.

France too was aided in the strengthening and widening of her colonial possessions by the vigour of French Catholic missions, but France, far more than Spain, was quick to follow sermons with trading expeditions, to reinforce baptism with treaty, to send military reinforcements into regions which had been claimed for France by the bearers of the Cross and the builders of the trading post. St Lucon, Jolliet and La Salle followed Père Marquette, and behind them all stood the encouraging strength of the Comte de Frontenac, Governor of New France. By the end of the seventeenth century, from their settlement along the St Lawrence, the French had explored much in the area now known as the Middle West, and, to some extent by demonstration and by declaration entirely, had established for themselves, in the heart of America, a barrier to the expansion of the English colonies on the Atlantic seaboard.

Back on the coast, Sweden, too, in the brief moment of her glory as a first-class power, sought transatlantic expansion. The greatest of her kings, the Protestant champion Gustavus Adolphus, died in victory at Lutzen in November

1632, but not before he had prepared plans to launch an American colony. It was left to his powerful successor to power, Count Axel Oxenstern, to grant to the New Sweden Company, in 1637, a charter in the name of the eleven-year-old Queen Christina, and it was under this charter that Peter Minuit established Fort Christina on the Delaware well within the boundaries of the territory which Charles the First had recently granted to the Calverts.

It was not, however, the mild protests of the English (nor the somewhat more vociferous grumblings of Dutchmen who had settled to the North of New Sweden) but the poor response of Swedes to the call for settlers which limited the success of the Swedish venture. Still, in Sweden itself there was ample scope for pioneering and, as Sweden was remarkably free from religious persecution, there was little compulsion upon Swedes to emigrate. So, despite an energetic and able Governor, Johann Printz, who did all that he could, without much help from his vacillating monarch and her uninterested ministers, to ensure the military strength of the colony and its manpower, New Sweden lasted only long enough to establish Lutheranism as a vital force along the Delaware, and, most important of all, to equip the American colonies with a style of frontier building, the log cabin, which was to provide America in the future with a symbol for national democratic mythology and a real and efficient model for frontier construction.

In 1655 the Swedish colony fell into the maw of the Dutch.

For it was the Dutch who, above all, provided active competition to English ambition.

Holland, in the seventeenth century, seemed on the point of taking over from her old master, Spain, as the premier power in Europe. In the struggle against the Spaniards her genius as a nation of seafaring men had been brought to perfection and all over the world Dutch traders settled themselves where commerce was best and sent back to Holland true and solid wealth. which, in its turn, encouraged the seemingly miraculous growth of Dutch culture.

The Dutch East India Company was founded in 1602. By

the end of the first decade of the seventeenth century the Dutch had trading stations in Amboina, Guinea, Guiana, at the mouth of the Amazon and in Japan (where until 1853 Dutchmen were the only Europeans licensed to trade). Dutch fur-traders were active along the Hudson and Dutch fishermen off the coast of Newfoundland.

The East Indies, above all, had proved a comfortable breeding ground for guilders, and the West India Company, which received its charter from the Dutch Government in 1621, was but a child of the older, and already successful, East India Company, sharing with that Company the time of directors, the experience of merchants, and the skills of ships' captains.

It is perhaps surprising that in their venturings along the East coast of America, English explorers had missed the significance of the most vital strategic harbour that that coast possessed, and had virtually ignored the commercial importance of the river which drains into the harbour. It is not surprising that the Dutch recognized the potential value of the Hudson River and of what is now New York Harbour.

Henry Hudson himself had been working in the Dutch employ, but it was the directors of the West India Company who, in 1624, first settled Dutchmen on Manhattan Island, and thereby established New Netherland.

In three centuries of overseas adventuring, which came to an end only when Japanese invasion and Oriental nationalism threw over Dutch suzerainty in the East Indies, the Netherlands never knew again such a magnificent opportunity for empire as was theirs in the seventeenth century. Yet, like the Swedes and the Spaniards, the Dutch failed to establish themselves firmly on the North American continent.

The very prosperity of their homeland was against them. From Africa, Asia, America, and the islands of the Pacific, riches flowed into Holland, and, although much of this wealth, here as elsewhere, went to the few, the many benefited from an age of commercial affluence so that deprivation, the prime force behind the desire to emigrate, was in Holland almost non-existent. Dutch merchants and Dutch craftsmen led the world; to merchant and craftsman alike the wilderness beyond Manhattan Island seemed a poor exchange for the quiet comforts of Amsterdam, Leyden or Delft. Dutch farmers and farm-labourers, who might have served as a source of supply for colonial ventures, were comfortable enough tending to the solid appetites of the cities.

Jew, Catholic, and English Puritan alike had early seen in Holland a haven for nonconformity, but this proud record of religious toleration helped to deprive Holland of a further impulse to emigration: the impulse which England used (if unconsciously) to settle New England, Maryland, Carolina and, later, Georgia.

Nor was New Netherland well served by its advertising agents. Only superb 'boosting' could have roused the Dutch from their comfort to attempt the harsh adventure of life in North America, but Hakluyts, John Smiths, Winthrops, and Rolfes were few among the Dutch, too few for their stupendous task. Missionary fervour, strong in New Holland (Netherlands Brazil) throughout its precarious existence from 1630 to 1654, was weak in New Netherland. Whereas in South America the Portuguese inhabitants were an ever-present reminder of 'Popery', in North America Catholic power was represented only by the Jesuits far away in French Canada. As for the Indians: 'We can say little of their conversion', wrote two Calvinist ministers from New Amsterdam in 1657, 'and see no way of bringing it about until they are subdued by the numbers and strength of our people, and reduced to some sort of civilization'. 'And', they added significantly, 'until our own people set them a better example than they have done so far'.

In consequence, though the Dutch of the seventeenth century were ardent, and to a point successful imperialists, ever ready to seek interests from overseas adventures, they were not colonizers. It is significant that the national hero of the Dutch is not Peter Stuyvesant, Director-General of

New Netherland, but Piet Heyn, who captured the Spanish silver fleet. Holland had torn the cloak from the shoulders of Spain – and wore it without troubling to have it altered. This year's bank-balance and next year's dividends were all-important to the Dutch mercantile classes: their undoubted shrewdness did not go so far as to give them sight of the centuries.

The United Provinces were divided in their enthusiasm for maritime power and so scanty and so dilatory was the support given by the home country to Dutch America, that from the beginning Dutch administrators in New Amsterdam had to admit into their boundaries potential 'fifth columnists': Englishmen from New England.

Even the Dutch, who were at the time so much the leaders of Europe, could not provide leaders for a colony which did not demonstrate its worth by rapid turnover. Wouter van Twiller was a fool, an incompetent, a poor administrator and, least of his many offences, a notorious drunkard. Wilhelmus Kieft was an autocrat, a ferocious Indian-slayer. A more moderate Dutch-American described with horror one of the Indian massacres he ordered:

Infants were torn from their mothers' breasts, and hacked to pieces in the presence of the parents, and the pieces thrown into the fire and in the water, and other sucklings were bound to small boards, and then cut, stuck and pierced, and miserably massacred in a manner to move a heart of stone.

Peter Stuyvesant, the best of a very bad bunch of colonial administrators – but no better – was a tyrant who attempted to force upon Dutch subjects abroad the disease repugnant to Dutch subjects at home, religious intolerance, a puffed-up demagogue who once urged against the spirit of republicanism that was at that time growing in the hearts of all Dutchmen:

We derive our authority from God and the Company, not from a few ignorant subjects.

Thus handicapped and thus led, not even the inception of

the patroon system, which gave feudal rights to any Dutchman who could settle fifty adults along the Hudson or its
tributaries (in itself a retrograde step from a people which
was beginning to sense 'democracy') could encourage
growth into the withering plant, and in 1664, after only
forty years of experiment, at a time when Holland was at
peace with England, on a whim of James, Duke of York,
and with the consent of most of the inhabitants, New
Netherland fell to England and New Amsterdam became
New York. This, at a moment when, despite a miraculous
victory, England's Admiralty was bankrupt, her ships rotting, her sailors mutinous, and her king's neckwear reduced
to three linen bands. This, only three years before Holland
was to inflict upon England the greatest indignity of her
history: a foreign fleet virtually unopposed in the Thames.

All our hearts now ake: for the news is true that the Dutch have
broke the chaine and burned our ships . . . so God help us! And
God knows what disorders we may fall into . . .

One more feeble effort was made in the next decade,
when for three months the Dutch-Americans held New York
only to be thwarted once more by pusillanimity at home,
and then the Dutch dream of American empire faded for
ever.

In the long run, the permanent effect upon American life
of Holland's forty-year adventure was slight – far less
potent than the effect of similar adventures by France and
Spain, far less important than the impact of cultures which
were not associated with colonial power: the Irish, the
Italian, the newer Central European elements which came
in during the nineteenth century.

Only one Dutch institution, the Church, maintained its
integrity after the fall of New Netherland. The articles of
surrender left to the ten thousand inhabitants of the province
the right to worship in their own way. Whilst Dutch political
institutions collapsed, the influence of the Reformed Church
spread and until the Revolution it was a dominant communion throughout the Hudson Valley. Thereafter it

received fresh blood from the homeland and is, to this day, an important if not a large group in American ecclesiastical organization. (Surprisingly the American adherents did not divorce themselves from direct dependence upon the Classis in Amsterdam until 1772 and waited until 1867 to to remove the prefix 'Dutch' from the title of their church.)

For the rest, there are vestiges of Dutch law in New York State Law, and a few Dutch names remained to recur in American history (Herkimer, Van Rensselaer, Vanderbilt, Roosevelt), but the Dutch, in the seventeenth as again in the nineteenth century (when, at all events, immigration from Holland was on a small scale compared to mass immigrations from Central Europe and Ireland), adapted themselves almost too easily to Anglo-American custom. Their influence was as individuals not as a race; their power came not from difference but from similarity. By religion, racial characteristics and education they fell victim eagerly and easily to the processes first of Colonial Anglicization and then of Americanization.

The possession of New York Harbour could have meant Dutch culture in all North America; instead, it added new blood for the success of a culture that was essentially Anglo-Saxon.

CHAPTER 9

POETS AND PURITANS

In the South, people of essentially bourgeois origins established, with conscious effort, an aristocratic society and culture; in the Middle Colonies and in New England the bourgeois habit persisted.

No less derivative than that of the South, Northern culture lacked the colour provided by God's sun reflecting man-made aristocracy, but found compensation in a greater earnestness of endeavour and enhanced seriousness of purpose, and it was this which provided New England in particular with individuals of an intellectual eminence such as no Southerner could claim.

Plastic art was in New England negligible, for the harsh restraints of Calvinism still hung over New England aspirations and prevented New Englanders from attempting artistic effort in this direction. The aristocracy of the South had at least some pretensions to the aristocratic prerogative of patronage and in this the merchants of the North, holier perhaps but even more materialistic, seldom shared. Music (*pace* Dr Percy Scholes) the Puritans regarded as worthless, not necessarily vicious but inevitably wasteful. 'Musick I had almost forgot,' wrote President Leonard Hoar of Harvard in 1661 to a nephew who had begged him for the gift of a violin, 'I suspect you seek it too soon and too much.' The nephew did not get his fiddle. Cotton Mather, who said that what children learnt at dancing school was 'scarce worth their learning', fumed constantly against songs and ballads as corruption in mind and manners and, aping Cromwell in Ely Cathedral, fought violently, and successfully, against the installation of an organ in the Boston Brattle Street Church. Until Episcopalianism became the religion of the socially eminent even in such Calvinist strongholds as Boston, the attitude of New England to music was, for more than a century, much like that of the early English Puritan, Owen Feltham:

It is a kind of disparagement to bee a cunning Fiddler. It argues his neglect of a better employment, and that hee have spent much time upon a thing unnecessarie . . . and indeed it softens the minde; The curiosity of it is fitter for Women than Men, and for Curtezans than Women.

Early in their American adventure, the Puritans were close enough to their Renaissance descent so that on occasion they could sing the Psalms well, though, as a rule and by their own confession, their performance even in this direction was so bad that 'they were made a laughing stock to strangers'. Again, late in the Colonial period, Boston produced at least one musician whose compositions, though circumscribed by their consistently sacred tones, were at least considerable when compared to the rest of colonial achievement in this art, but William Billings has little glory when compared to his European contemporaries, Haydn and Mozart, or his immediate European predecessors, Handel and Bach, even Arne and Blow. For the most part, only in the privacy of New England homes and New England beds did the Puritans burst out in song.

It is at least a happy shaft shot through the prevailing gloom to know that the early quiet of pilgrim New England was, on occasion, broken by an East Anglian folk-song, and that the oppressive peace of the seventeenth-century New England fields and woods were sometimes shattered by a rude song originally picked up in London or in Leyden. It is at least some sign of musical grace, if of eternal damnation, that there persists a good Boston legend that Mother Goose of the rhyme-book was one Elizabeth Goose, or Vergoose, or Verboyse (even the legend does not get its facts straight) of that City, whose son-in-law, Thomas Fleet, took down the nursery rhymes from her lips and published them in Boston in 1719. Unfortunately for the legend, and for Boston, Mère L'Oye was already well known in France in the mid seventeenth century, and, though gullible visitors may still see the grave of Mrs Goose, or Vergoose, or Verboyse, in the Old Granary Burying Ground off Washington Street, no copy of Thomas Fleet's song-book has ever come to light.

Even for the preservation and continuance of the English folk-song tradition, one must look farther South than Boston.

Church music, to the Puritans as to the Quakers, but for different reasons, was usually anathema. Where it survived in America the credit must be given for the most part to the Church of England transplanted, and to such sects as the Moravians, and, later, the Methodists.

Boston, Providence, New York, and New Haven, all had occasional polite recitals, after the manner of Annapolis, Williamsburg, Charleston – and London. In New England, as in Old England or the South, gentility was sometimes demonstrated by harpsichord or voice, but of art-music as a creative form the colonies were well-nigh innocent.

An age such as our own which has a decent respect for the aesthetic merits of simple geometry finds much sympathy for the neatness of colonial domestic building and colonial town-planning, and, in this respect, New England and the Middle Colonies were not so very far behind the South. The two accidents of ancestry and a plentiful supply of timber made New England particularly imitative of the architecture of the English Eastern Counties and the weather-board frame-house of Essex and Suffolk reappears in seventeenth-century New England and has become in time more American than English. But not only this style but almost every model that England could provide was in New England used sensibly and with sensibility.

Anglican Church architecture was, of course, disliked by the New Englanders. Whereas the South often copied the English parish church, New England evolved not a church but a 'house of worship', avoiding anything that smacked of Anglicanism or Popery. Theirs was a rectangular and, later, almost a square building; a steeple and platform on the front is only relief. Inside, hard benches faced the true heart of Puritan worship: the pulpit. During the seventeenth century, wood, New England's principal product, gave way to brick in house-construction, and by the end of the century not even New England could deny that in Wren and his pupils Britain had found its greatest school of architecture and New England could but compliment by imitation. The one-and-a-half-storey Flemish cottage and the two-storey medieval house with an overhang, with chimney and fireplace in the centre, gave them the model for their typical domestic architecture – and throughout the three centuries that were to follow has littered the so-called 'Cape Cod' house from coast almost to coast.

By the end of the century some deviation from the strict code of opposition to luxury had allowed into New England architecture an element of ostentation – and ostentation to the English model. The Connecticut pilastered doorway, for example, here a new-fangled luxury long after it had become general in original construction in England, was nevertheless common by the first years of the eighteenth century. But the finer extravagances frequent in Virginia and South Carolina were seldom seen north of the Susquehanna. Everywhere in the colonies simplicity gives the appearance of good taste, but creative originality is rare and only in the South can even the wildest-drawn bow pin architecture as an art in which the colonials excelled, and in the South, as even more in the North, it is rare to find technical ability touched by artistic genius.

For literature, however, the story is quite different and the wordy intellectualism of the Puritan-built Northern Colonies gave to those colonies a distinct advantage. Trained in the use of words, accustomed to the manipulation of ideas and educated by one of the Cambridges, or by New England grammar schools, to a considerable respect for bookishness, the New Englanders inevitably developed a literature of sorts when the South was still happy either without books or with books imported from England. Such intellectualism, such bookishness, did not imply any pleasure in the artistic function of the writer and prose most prosy was the general delight of New Englanders, both male and female.

Bradford, Winthrop, Higginson, Mather, and others of the second generation of New Englanders wrote histories and biographies of their New England predecessors in an attempt to prove how successful had been God's plans for his chosen people, and in an attempt to arouse in the second generation an admiration for the ideals of the first and a determination to keep from backsliding. The glory of God they published from the pulpit and then to add to His glory set their sermons into print. They took from seventeenth-century England a form of meditation – a sermon in silence – and gave their thoughts to the printer. America's first best-seller was also the first piece of literature which can be claimed entirely for New England – the so-called *Bay Psalm Book*, printed in 1640 at the newly established Cambridge Press. Far more graceful translations of the Psalms were already available to New England, but, claimed the Puritans, 'God's Altar needs not our pollishings', and so yet another version was prepared in which the emphasis was on 'Conscience rather than Elegance, Fidelity rather than Poetry, in translating the hebrew into the english language and David's poetry into english meetre'. The first edition of the *Bay Psalm Book* ran to seventeen hundred copies at a time when there were hardly twice as many families in the Northern Colonies, so it must be presumed that already the book had found its way across the Atlantic, as it was to do throughout colonial times, for before the end of the eighteenth century fifty new editions had been published in New England, in England, and in Scotland.

Of more humble books the most popular was the *Almanack*. The first, pirated from Britain and re-edited in New England, was published even before the *Bay Psalm Book* and proved a sound medium for spreading quasi-scientific knowledge to an agricultural and maritime people living still in frontier conditions.

It is illuminating to follow the bookly progress of the courtships of Judge Samuel Sewall (himself a diarist of some charm, but without the humanity or the literary skill of Pepys). When his first wife died he set his flat cap at Mrs Denison, and to support his attack gave to her '*Dr Mather's Sermons* very well bound', and a '*Psalm Book* neatly bound in England with Turkey-Leather'. Mrs Denison would have none of the Judge, so, instead of the chocolates and flowers of another age, Sewall took his books to Mrs Tilley. Here a second-hand copy, again one of Mather's books, *Ornaments for the Daughters of Sion*, was enough, but either the book or the position, both of which had belonged to the first Mrs Sewall, were too much for the second. Seven months after their marriage she was dead and the Judge was looking for a successor. Again he went out courting with books under his arm. Mrs Winthrop he tried with a copy of Samuel Williard's *The Fountain Opened* (a less successful theological work than that same author's *A Compleat Body of Divinity*) and then followed it up with the *Account of the Indians on Martha's Vineyard* and Preston's *The Church's Marriage and the Church's Carriage*. Such unaccustomed generosity had no effect upon Mrs Winthrop, so to Mrs Ruggles the Judge took a copy of *Mr Moody's Election Sermon*, again without winning her. Then Cotton Mather rescued him once more; his *India Christiana* was given to Mrs Gibbs, and she became the third Mrs Sewall.

The interest in the account is not only in the picture of a somewhat pompous lover offering suit to ladies as pompous as he. In fact Sewall was not above gifts of shoe-buckles, almonds, and ginger cake 'wrapped up in a clean sheet of paper', nor too puritanical to bribe the servants of the various ladies. The startling fact in this story is not even the general solemnity of subject-matter, but rather, though this was but seventy years after the foundation of New England, the number of New England written and New England published titles.

Yet if prose, and religious prose at that, was the principal exercise and pleasure of literate New England, the New Englanders made many attempts at poetry. The exercise that verse-writing provided was still regarded as one of the proofs of education, as necessary to Cotton Mather as to such scholars as Joshua Barnes in England, and the experience, natural and spiritual, which seventeenth-century New England provided demanded of its subjects an expression that went sometimes beyond the capabilities of prose.

The sparkling licentiousness of Restoration England had isolated the Northern Colonies from the practice and perusal of English poetry. True, New England had slipped from its original standards; even the strength of Puritanism at Harvard had so weakened its walls that, in 1701, the devout set up Yale at New Haven as a defence for orthodoxy. But New Englanders had not fallen so far into hedonism that they could enjoy Rochester or Suckling. For poetry they showed some respect, but it was because their respect was coupled with doubts as to the respectability of poetry more than because they doubted their own achievement that most New England poetry was written only to be hidden.

Judged by purely literary standards the effect of this poetic privacy was excellent because most of the work of the New England poetasters was mediocre, at best technically efficient, at worst stylistically clumsy and spiritually Pharisaical. But just like Anne Bradstreet in the generation before him, one New England poet shook off the intellectual and technical barriers of his environment. Like so many of his contemporaries, Edward Taylor regarded his verses as a private performance. He even went further than most in insisting that his heirs should not publish them, and not until 1937 was his work available. It now seems sardonic that when eventually, in the mid nineteenth century, the spirit of American independence broke through into literary criticism, its sponsors knew nothing of their finest exemplar; for Edward Taylor is one of the very few poets (perhaps the only one) of America's first two hundred years who is at once undeniably American in his inspiration and yet, in his achievement, comparable to his English rivals.

Taylor was a Puritan and a graduate of Harvard, but his poetry comes of a conflict between the Puritan theology, to which he held earnestly, and the natural sensuality of a vigorous mind and body. The severe and poetically debilitating aesthetics found Taylor in rebellion and the stern tenets of his contemporaries held him to the secrecy of his endeavours. But Taylor was fortunate in the models he chose. Writing at the end of the century, but still reading Donne, Quarles, and George Herbert, he found in them something of his own conflict between aesthetics and morals, and saw that conflict gloriously used, to make poetry and not to destroy it. Less disdainful of English example than his more pious countrymen like Michael Wigglesworth, Taylor nevertheless added something that was essentially New England: his concern with the natural world was primarily a concern with the natural world immediately around him and he was always ready to use the imagery and even the dialect of New England to express what were to him the universal and eternal verities. In the poems of Edward Taylor the paradoxical earnestness and earthiness of the New England Puritan is demonstrated most powerfully and most lovably:

> Peace, Peace my Hony, do not Cry,
> My Little Darling, wipe thine eye,
> Oh Cheer, Cheer up, come see.
> Is anything too deare, my Dove,
> Is anything too good, my Love,
> To get or give for thee?

Parent to child, lover to his love? So it would seem, and so Taylor would wish it to seem as his speaker continues, now giving comfort to his listener against the threat of a barking dog:

> And if he run an inch too fur,
> I'le Check his Chain, and rate the Cur.
> My Chick, Keep close to mee.

But the speaker is Christ, the 'Cur' Satan, and it is the believer whom Christ addresses in good New England accents.

Time and time again Taylor's simple imagery is of New England born, of honest Christianity, not over-intellectual, not too severe:

Upon what base was fixed the lath wherein
He turned this glove and riggalled it so trim?
Who blew the bellows of His furnace vast?
Or held the mould wherein the world was cast?
Who laid its corner-stone? On whose commands?
Where stand the pillars upon which it stands?
Who laced and filleted the earth so fine?
With rivers like green ribbons smaragdine?
Who made the seas its selvage, and its locks
Like a guilt ball within a silver box?
Who spread its canopy? Or curtain spun?
Who in this bowling alley bowled the sun?

Due to the cabinet nature of his work and to the fact that it is successful verse, it is impossible to place Taylor as anything but a curiosity in New England literature. Anne Bradstreet, that other good and most lovable poet of Massachusetts, had readers; Taylor had none. He was an individual without influence, and if his emotions were sometimes typical of his time and his country the direction and manner of his genius was entirely atypical.

Comparable literary achievement, with the additional flavour of public knowledge and influence, was not to be seen until the next generation. Not until then did the devotion which New England had always shown to intellectual activity – above all where the mind and the soul were close relations – give to that region, and to America, its first great philosopher and its first major literary achievement.

Jonathan Edwards was born in East Windsor, Connecticut, in 1703, and graduated from Yale in 1720. After a period of post-graduate theological study, a year or so of preaching in New York, and two years of tutoring at his old college, he went, in 1727, to share the ministry of his grandfather in Northampton, Massachusetts, and it was in Northampton that most of his working life was passed. After twenty-three years, in which he had made the Northampton pulpit the most distinguished in America, Edwards's unequivocal standards – and his willingness to accept his parishioners' accounts of their conversions as valid evidence of their salvation instead of submitting them to the rigid ministerial examination of more conservative pastors – so aroused the antagonism of his congregation that he was dismissed. For the next seven years, grandson though he was and successor to the Reverend Solomon Stoddard who had recommended in the year of the philosopher's birth that troublesome Indians should be hunted down with dogs, Edwards was a missionary on the frontier at Stockbridge, making a poor living for himself and his family by preaching to the few Indians who would listen and the few whites who were around to hear – and by painting fans. Then, in January 1758, he was appointed President of the College of New Jersey. But Edwards, the most influential President that Princeton has ever known – with one possible exception, Woodrow Wilson in the twentieth century – was President only for a few weeks. In March 1758 he died of smallpox inoculation. These are the short uneventful details of a short and not very eventful life, but the record of philosophical and literary effort is long and of great distinction. Defender of Calvinist orthodoxy against the increasing power of Arminianism, Edwards was at once the last and the greatest of the essentially seventeenth-century New England preachers, and among the first, and certainly the greatest American, of the philosophers of the Enlightenment. He followed Mather, he defended Whitfield's Great Awakening, and he had in his theological equipment weapons that were provided by each of them, but the substance of his philosophy came from the Cambridge Platonists, above all from Ralph Cudworth, whose portentously learned *True Intellectual System of the Universe* has hardly been given enough attention among English works which helped to formulate American thought, and from John Locke. From such sources, and from Newton, Edwards learnt what was rare among Yankee divines, an appreciation of logic and the ability to use it. From his own (and his wife's) mystical experiences, from the traditions of his church and from the revivalist movements of the early eighteenth century, he gathered his conviction that 'conversion', the emotional obverse to the rational front of theology, was an essential concomitant of faith.

His reactionary devotion to the old standards of Calvinism (and Edwards was in many senses struggling against the current of his age) could not hold his countrymen from the more comfortable lures of the Enlightenment, but his systematic philosophy became a bulwark to the unsystematic emotionalism of Whitfield, and so paved the way for Methodism, while his aesthetic intensity gave new heart not only to those who wished to resist the materialistic attitudes then prevalent in New England, but also to those who were faithful to Calvinism but resentful of its crabbed disdain for the beautiful:

There is . . . an analogy or consent between the beauty of the skies, trees, flowers, etc., and spiritual excellencies, though the agreement . . . require a discerning, feeling, mind to perceive it . . . There seem to be love and complacency in flowers and bespangled meadows; this makes lovers so much delight in them. So there is a rejoicing in the green trees and fields, and majesty in thunder beyond all other noises whatever . . . The beauties of nature are really emanations or shadows of the excellencies of the Son of God.

So that, when we are delighted with flowery meadows, and gentle breezes of wind, we may consider that we see only the emanation of the sweet benevolence of Jesus Christ . . . So the green trees, and fields, and singing of birds are the emanations of this infinite joy and benignity. The easiness and naturalness of trees and vines are shadows of this beauty and loveliness. The crystal rivers and murmuring streams are the footsteps of His favor, grace, and beauty.

He brought new life to what was now almost exclusively an American ideology. His sermons were magnificent and awe-inspiring. 'The God that holds you over the pit of Hell,' he thundered, 'much as one holds a spider or some loathsome insect over the fire, abhors you and is dreadfully provoked. . . . He looks upon you as worthy of nothing else but to be cast into the fire. . . . You are then thousand times more abominable in His eyes than the most hateful, venomous serpent is in ours.' Or again, 'Were it not for the sovereign pleasure of God, the earth would not bear you for one moment; for you are a burden to it; the creation groans with you; the creature is made subject to the bondage of your creation not willingly; the sun does not willingly shine upon you to give you light, to serve sin and Satan; the earth does not willingly yield her increase to satisfy your lusts; nor is it willingly a stage for your wickedness to be acted upon; the air does not willingly serve you for breath to maintain the flame of life in your vitals while you spend your life in the service of God's enemies . . . and the world would spew you out were it not for the sovereign hope of Him who had subjected it in hope.' No wonder that one who heard him preach on the subject of the Day of Judgement wrote that it was, 'so vivid and solemn . . . that he fully supposed that, as soon as Mr Edwards should close his discourse, the Judge would descend, and the final separation take place', and no wonder that such magnificent ferocity had immediate effect. His writings too were much read and much used in America (as in England and even more in Scotland) in his lifetime and in the remaining years of the Colonial Period, so that he became 'the inspirer and the logical drill-master of innumerable minds in his own country and in Great Britain'.

Because of his faith in the importance of emotional experience, this highly intellectual writer can be counted among those who elevated the position of the uneducated. But his ultimate importance to America could not be appreciated for a century, until another, and in so many ways a lesser group of New Englanders, Emerson a leader among them, set before the American people, in stolidly intellectual terms, the conviction that the Americans had come to hold in their hearts: that emotion and intuition are the mainsprings of human endeavour.

CHAPTER 10

FRANCE OR ENGLAND

By the end of the eighteenth century the American colonies had achieved independence from British imperialism, political union and a measure of cultural maturity, yet the inspiration for all these achievements was not so much oppression from without as the growth of ambition, restlessness, and vision within the boundaries of the Thirteen Colonies. It may even be said that American imperialism pre-dated by more than one hundred years the defeat of British imperialism at Yorktown, that 'Americanism' became a reality when English-Americans were ready to settle beyond the Appalachians, and that American nationhood became inevitable when the colonials first saw the whole continent as their peculiar province.

In 1700 the vision of an English-speaking continent was hardly clear to the British or to the British-Americans, and seemed but a fanciful proposition even to those who considered such things. The English language had scarcely moved from the Atlantic seaboard on which it had originally been planted. Imperial France, on the other hand, was constantly on the move and seemed bound to grasp the great American heartland, the Middle West, to increase its hold over the North, and perhaps to outflank and make untenable Spain's uncomfortable dominion in the Far West and Texas.

The Spaniards were wealthy, numerous and established in areas rich in mineral and agricultural reserves, while the few French settlers in the austere North were gripped by the promise of the grim forest regions, and, as fitted islanders by heritage, the English seemed bound to the sea-coast. But Spain frittered away the gift: as much as anything through political chicanery at home such as that which in 1767 brought about the expulsion of the Jesuits from Spanish possessions in the New World and their replacement with

Franciscans. France, particularly under the guidance of wise ministers like Colbert, added to priestly self-sacrifice lay support through merchants, *voyageurs*, and energetic colonial administrators.

Yet, by the end of the eighteenth century, the imperial power of France was shattered, the hold of Spain slipping, and almost the whole of the North American continent divided, at least by decree, and to a considerable extent in fact, between the two Anglo-Saxon nations. In studying the story of the American continental empire it seems at times that certainly the English, as frequently their American successors, hardly deserved the gains that came to them. In a century of accident and battle, of greed triumphant and confusion rewarded, the English seldom showed the constructive wisdom which would have justified their success. But the seeds of power in North America were for the most part sown not in America itself but on European battlefields; Blenheim and Malplaquet were vital to the future of America, and even the final struggle on the Plains of Abraham was in many senses but a European battle, the extension of a European war, fought on American soil. To the success of the Anglo-Saxon in North America, Marlborough, or even Clive, contributed as much as Oglethorpe, Wolfe or Robert Rogers. Similarly, but in negative terms, Louis the Fifteenth, Robespierre – and the Emperor Napoleon – were as important for the future of the American continent as Frontenac, Jolliet or La Salle.

From the very beginning of colonization the notion of the West was implicit, and at times explicit to colonials, French, Spanish, and British. 'I propose,' wrote Columbus,

to make a new map on which I shall draw the Ocean Sea and all its lands in their true positions and under their winds. And I desire to compose a book in which I will make drawings to represent everything truly, by the lattitude from the equator and by the longtitude from the west.

The desire for completeness was not for his fulfilment, nor for his successors in three hundred years, but the effort inspired the dedicated few, the opportunists – and the rejects – from increasingly civilized areas on the fringes of the continent. Hakluyt, Cartier, Gilbert, each fostered the child of wishful thinking: the idea that either by land or by water the West was near and accessible. The idea became statute in the original charters granted to Massachusetts, Connecticut, Virginia, and both Carolinas; in each case the colony, still by practical knowledge limited to a narrow Atlantic strip, was by decree granted dominion from Atlantic to Pacific – and this though at the time of the later charters the French were already blocking the way to Westward expansion.

The detailed story of the invasion of the West is both long and complicated. In 1608, when the English were recently established on Jamestown Island and the French in the process of founding Quebec, the Spaniards opened Santa Fe in New Mexico. Three years earlier Onate had reached the mouth of the Colorado, and returned across Arizona. By the time the Pilgrim Fathers landed at Plymouth, Champlain had already opened the French imperial route up the Ottawa River and into Lake Huron and the Spaniards were hard at work in the South-West. As in the mid seventeenth century the British moved up and down the East coast, the Spaniards increased their hold over the far Pacific coast and in the South-West and, for the French, Etienne Brulé reached the Sault, at the passage between Lake Huron and Lake Superior. In 1634 Jean Nicolet moved into Lake Michigan; in the next year the men of Massachusetts ventured sixteen miles from Boston to the Indian village Musketquid, settled there, and renamed the place Concord!

For almost another thirty years the three empires were, at least in the West, uncompetitive, but in the last quarter of the seventeenth century the threat of rivalry became a reality, the routes of adventure began to converge, and battle for power, ever a possibility, became instead an imminent and certain event.

In 1673 Colbert launched the project which made conflict inevitable; Colbert, whose eyes were everywhere, who alone among the ministers of the seventeenth-century colonial powers was capable of grasping and manoeuvring the direction of empire. But England was wakening. With a little prodding from a few dissatisfied Frenchmen the British launched out into Hudson's Bay. ('The Governor and Company of Adventurers of England Trading into Hudson's Bay' received a charter from Charles the Second in 1670.) Colbert and his master Louis the Fourteenth were certain of the European power of their nation and to seal it for the future the armies of France under Condé and Turenne were on the move against the Dutch and the Spaniards. If French European greatness was to be paralleled by power in North America it was clear to Colbert that France must establish the existence and direction of the great river reported by Nicolet twenty years earlier, and by Father Claude Allouez in some detail in 1665. This river flowed either into the 'sea of Florida or that of California'. Either way its conquest by the French could strengthen vastly their nation's strategic position in North America. Should the longed-for circumstance be proven and the great river find its way to the Pacific, France would have the Spanish Empire checkmated – and could afford to laugh at the feeble English freezing in Hudson's Bay and quarrelling with each other along the Atlantic seaboard. So it was that in 1673 the Governor of New France, the Count de Frontenac, sent Louis Jolliet and Father Jacques Marquette to explore 'the Great River called by the Savages Mississippi, which leads to New Mexico'. The facts they established; they proved that the Mississippi went South; it only remained for La Salle in 1682 to make the discovery firm by reaching salt water on the Mississippi; and then at long last, around the turn of the century, the dream that Colbert had dreamed, for which La Salle had explored – and intrigued – became waking truth. France established settlements to guard the mouth of the Mississippi, first, in 1699, at Biloxi, in 1702 at Mobile and finally, in 1718, at New Orleans. Canada was already French, and now to the French fell a region far richer than Canada, a latent agricultural economy of huge potentiality and surpassing by far Canada's unstable fur economy, a warm inviting land which offered wealth and comfort to settlers by the thousand who could never be lured to the harsh Canadian forest. With Louisiana in their hands the French hope of empire seemed certain.

Nor were the French slow to bolster their gains, to ensure that neither Briton nor Spaniard could trip the Frenchmen straddling the continent. As they established Biloxi, so did they make a settlement near St Louis. In 1713 they set up a post on the Red River, and in the next ten years French forts were built at many points on the Mississippi. They began to explore and to settle the Missouri River, which the Jolliet-Marquette expedition of 1673 had discovered, and which, once the direction of the Mississippi had been ascertained, had become the new hope of a North-West Passage.

Spain was quick to react to the threat. To the west of the French-held dividing line, the Spaniard pushed out from Mexico to Texas. To the east, in 1689, they established Pensacola on the Gulf-ward coast of Florida and followed it with other settlements as support to the surviving settlements on the Atlantic coast. (Settlements which faced another threat: from the English in the Carolinas.)

European events and the activities of their one sturdy American ally, the Iroquois, roused the British to some consciousness of the nature of American strategy.

Sixteen eighty-eight, and Louis the Fourteenth's unwilling ally, James the Second, became his not very welcome pensioner. In the place of James sat a Dutchman with the memories of French bullying fresh in his mind. Sixteen eighty-nine, and the formation of the Grand Alliance; the energies of the world turned to destroy the seemingly indestructible power of Le Roi Soleil. And in North America, where in 1687 the Iroquois had been roundly defeated by Governor de Denonville, where the first considerable attempts on the trade of the West by merchants from Albany had been frustrated and the three Hudson's Bay Company trading posts on James Bay seized, apparent success for France spelled eventual disaster. The Iroquois launched a

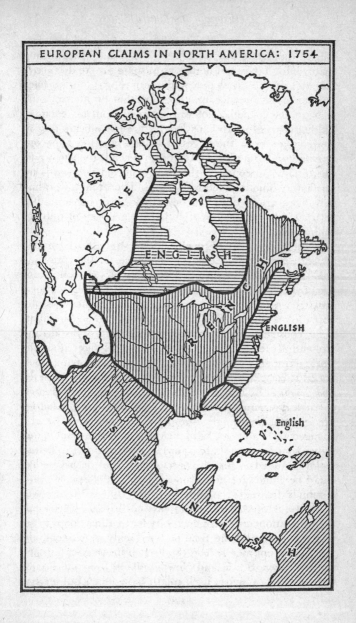

EUROPEAN CLAIMS IN NORTH AMERICA: 1754

'commando' war, harrying the outposts of French coloniza-
tion, so that trade was halted and New France thrown into
terror. King Louis had no troops to spare for the defence of
Canada; the best that he could contrive was to send back
Frontenac as Governor, and the most that Frontenac could
manage was a method of war adopted from his enemies.
Raiding parties of Indians led by French officers dug at
Iroquois power at the edges of British settlement in New
England and New York. At first to defend, then to trade,
and, finally, to conquer, the British moved westwards towards the Ohio and the Mississippi. The French who had
the advantage of time had nevertheless lost the initiative.
All that they could now attempt was a policy of military
containment.

Within a few years, French military strength was sapped
beyond renewal. Louis' covetous glances at the sprawling
possessions of Spain, the failing giant of two continents,
began the disaster from which France did not recover for a
century. For those possessions the King of France was prepared to overturn an ill-fitting alliance which he had labor-
iously constructed with the twin governments of Britain and
Holland. By forcing his grandson, Philip of Anjou, upon the
world as the successor to Charles the Second of Spain, Louis
hoped to clear the Pyrenees – and the Mississippi – from the
map. Against his design there rose up in Europe the greatest
of English generals, John Churchill, and in North America
the anger of New England and New York settlers. Bitterly
engaged on European battlefields, it was more and more
difficult for Louis to spare troops for North America, British
victories added to British consciousness that decisive effect
could be gained in the European War of the Spanish Succession by fighting it on imperial fronts, (Queen Anne's War
it was called in America) and gave to British governments
the inspiration and the opportunity for sending troops to aid
their colonials. By the time of the Treaty of Utrecht, the
British had not merely held the French in America but had
dragged Nova Scotia and Newfoundland from the French
Empire. Even Quebec itself might have fallen but for bad

direction by British commanders and, for the French, providentially good direction of storms.

At just that moment when the French established their southern positions on the chain which was to bind Britain in the East, the British were breaking off the northern links. From now on, though bold, hopeful but unorganized French expeditions might move out into the Spanish South-West, and though French explorers, missionaries and *coureurs de bois* still held the initiative of expansion to the West, France could not postpone without avoiding her conflict with the real rival, Britain. From now on the race was between French military skill and the courage of the Canadians on the one hand and, on the other, the growing military power of Britain, her rapidly developing commercial wealth, and the maturing British colonies.

One more interlude of war which settled nothing: the War of the Austrian Succession in Europe between 1740 and 1748 (in America, King George's War), an interlude which again included an attempt to invade Canada, successfully conducted by the British Navy and a British New-England army which captured the great French fortress at Louisbourg, and miserably wasted by British statesmen who, by the Treaty of Aix-la-Chapelle, gave Louisbourg back to France. A final bolstering of the British position on the East coast by the settlement of Georgia under that little-acknowledged genius of British Empire, General James Oglethorpe, and Britain was ready for the West.

Looked at from the point of view of the inevitable conflict between the imperial powers, the foundation of Georgia seems a mere interlude. Yet it was vital to the eventual success of the Anglo-Saxon, for not merely did Oglethorpe render impotent the Spanish in Florida, he aimed a knife at the French in Louisiana and built a defensive position from which the British could guard, against both French and Spaniards, the southern flank of their line of colony as it advanced across the Alleghenies.

Georgia had its origins in philanthropy. Here debtors, the indigent, and men of unorthodox religions, Jews, Catholics, Moravians and even followers of the new Methodism could find a home. Here, too, those many Highland Scots who lived uncomfortably under the Hanoverians could prove their loyalty as settlers – and, if necessary, show their vaunted military ardour in battles against French and Spaniards. Here there was to be no slavery, no fighting with the Indians, no governor, no outright ownership of land – and no rum. Here the development of the silkworm, a creature which hitherto had remained obstinately un-British, was to save the British Empire a half-million pounds a year of foreign expenditure.

Almost every one of the Utopian and commercial ambitions of the founders of Georgia had collapsed within a quarter of a century of the granting of the first charter. Slavery, rum, outright ownership of land, a royal governor, and a legislative assembly to quarrel with the governor, had all been introduced by 1755. Neither debtors nor the silkworm had enjoyed Georgia – even Whitfield and Charles Wesley had departed. With the possible exception of the fact that in Georgia nationalities and religions mixed more easily than in other colonies, Georgia was, at the outbreak of the Seven Years War, not unlike the other colonies. Its economy, close to that of South Carolina, depended upon rice, naval stores, and the Indian trade, its social structure upon slavery and inheritance.

But Georgia, in an amazingly short time, had become an established factor in the battle for empire.

Twice in a half-century Britain had won a military victory over France only to lose the battle of the conference table. The political overthrow of Marlborough and his party had caused at Utrecht the virtual nullification of his successful campaigns. Because British policy held Madras to be more important than Louisbourg, the comparative success of King George's War came to little. But after 1748 the issue could no longer be ignored or avoided; either France or England must win the way West.

The British were pushing out towards the Great Lakes, but the French still controlled communication from Canada by way of Lake Erie and the Ohio down to the Mississippi, New Orleans, and the Gulf of Mexico.

The Seven Years War, the French and Indian War of American history, differed from its predecessors in that whereas the earlier wars were colonial wars only incidentally, this was a colonial war by inspiration.

So far as any great event can be laid at the feet of one man, the conquest of Canada can be regarded as the victory of William Pitt. Favourite grandson of a 'buccaneering East Indian merchant, who began life as an interloper in India and finished as the Governor of Fort St George in Madras', Pitt gave much of the energy of his own life, both in and out of office, to the study of imperial problems. Influenced by his correspondence with William Vaughan of New Hampshire, after the capture of Louisbourg Pitt realized the importance of an attack on Canada. In the days before the outbreak of the Seven Years War his conceptions of the virtues of Canadian conquest were commercial rather than strategic. That 'the expulsion of the French would give security to British North American colonies' was only fifth in a list of reasons sent by the Duke of Bedford, with Pitt's approval, to Newcastle. Before it came the seizing of a monopoly in the fur and fish trade, the prevention of French commerce with the West Indies, the depriving of France of a market for manufacturers, and the limitation of French naval strength because France would no longer be able to build ships in America or acquire from America masts and timber. But once Pitt, as leader of the Commons, had succeeded in his attempt to secure the direction of the war with France, strategy was made an equal of trade. All over the world, off the French coasts, in the West Indies, in India, and in North America, Pitt launched operations which were designed to cripple French power and French commerce.

For the defence of Canada, the French used their Western Indian allies, the Ottawas, Winnebagos, Hurons, Miamis, Potawatomis and Chippewas, but these allies were as fierce in victory as they were unreliable in defeat. Once the tide had turned against France, the Indians swam with the tide.

The British were slow to learn, and the British colonials were hardly quicker. Already, before the War had broken out in Europe, a young Virginian officer, George Washington, out on one of those quasi-diplomatic, quasi-military expeditions which were common practice even in the unquiet days of peace, had blundered into a French-Indian stronghold at Great Meadows, had stupidly opened fire without counting the cost and, having killed the French commander, had then himself been forced to surrender. And – still before the outbreak of the Seven Years War – two regiments of British regulars on their way to Fort Duquesne, the key to the West, under Braddock, a regular commander, obstinate and inflexible, with the same George Washington as his staff officer, having ignored both the common practice of European warfare and the peculiar lessons of the frontier, were routed by the French and their Indian allies.

Each of the colonies was trying its own hand with occasional rumbling support from London. Each of the colonial governments was content at first to keep the Indians from its frontiers and, for the rest, spent its time in squabbles with other colonial governments over leadership of expeditions and appropriations.

But, in London and in North America, the British were learning from their defeats; learning that a new tactic must be developed if the Indians were to be faced, learning that some union among the colonies was both inevitable and necessary; learning, finally, from William Pitt, that the key to victory was Quebec.

Retaliation against the Indians was successful only when British and colonial troops began to imitate the Indians. Unity among the colonies was never achieved in this war, though the Albany Congress of 1754, designed originally to frame an Indian treaty to which all colonies would be a party, gave some inkling of the news that war would come in another twenty years. At Albany, the editor of the *Pennsylvania Gazette*, Benjamin Franklin, had made a case which would never be closed until the colonies had become the United States, the case of 'Join or Die'. But the strategic

concept brought to bear on British policy once William Pitt
had become Secretary of State for War in June 1757, gave
direction to British effort – and temporary unity to colonial
support – and when that policy had been brought to its
logical conclusion, Canada was Britain's.

In Europe, Prussia contained France, in India, Clive and
Eyre Coote were founding the British Raj. In North America
even the severe setback at Ticonderoga in July 1758 was of
but temporary significance, for Pitt was at work removing
incompetents from command in the Army and putting in
their place men of energy and imagination like General
James Wolfe. Pitt was in no hurry; he and his new advisers
understood well the complications of American terrain and
the supply and reinforcement of an army over the long, hard
routes of North America. Planning was essential. For American victory the blockade of France was as important as
battle successes in Canada or on the frontier. And the men
were available; not only Wolfe for North America, but also
Admiral Hawke and Admiral Boscawen to watch the coasts
of France, and the greatest navigator of them all, Captain
James Cook, to survey the St Lawrence River in preparation
for the final and decisive assault on Quebec.

The curtain went up at Louisbourg in 1758. For the second
time in the decade, this time for ever, the great fortress fell
to the British under General Wolfe. In the same year
colonials and British Highland troops drove the French out
of the Ohio Valley: Fort Duquesne was captured and renamed after the architect of victory, Pittsburg. The French
lost control of Lake Ontario when the English captured
Fort Frontenac.

In August 1759 Boscawen destroyed the French Toulon
fleet off the coast of Portugal. From 26 June to 13 September
the British Fleet and Army lay off the city of Quebec.

The story of the siege and capture of Quebec is like a
Greek myth retold. Vast implications, the shattering of an
empire, the creation of dominion and republic, all are in
those weeks in the Quebec 'Basin' and in that one night and
one day on the Heights of Abraham. But the full glory of the

story lies not with the implications but with the men who fought there.

Cook's superb survey made it possible for the British to move a large battle-fleet up the St Lawrence to within view of Montcalm, but the French, with memories of many an ancient victory achieved in this manner, set out with a squadron of fire-ships to destroy the invader. Admiral Saunders, in command of the British Fleet, answered boldness with boldness; manned his boats, grappled the approaching fire-ships with steel hooks, and hauled them off to the shallows.

Britain had won the first move, but still Montcalm was unassailable except by a suicidal frontal attack.

A few battleships with troops aboard ran past the city batteries through the narrow defile from the Basin into the river above Quebec where the cliffs rise up sheer to a height of two hundred and fifty feet.

Then, on the afternoon of 12 September, the detachment of the fleet in the Upper River set off as it were for Montreal, leaving the French concentrating on the front where the main fleet lay, the front from which they had always expected attack. Their expectations were confirmed in the dark night when every ship in the Basin opened up a furious bombardment as if preliminary to a landing. But, meanwhile, the Upper River squadron, under cover of that same darkness, had beat back for Quebec, discharged troops into boats and landed them at the foot of a goat-track from the water to the Heights above. Each soldier carried his musket and his bandolier; the Navy sent up everything else, and by dawn on the morning of the 13th a British army was on the Plains of Abraham. Too late Montcalm attempted to bring his troops to face the threat against his weakest quarter; a short and murderous battle gave Quebec to Britain. The price of victory for Britain was the death of her young general, for France defeat cost much more but this too: Montcalm, like his opponent, died at the end of his greatest battle.

The tradition that the two were close friends added to the

tragic loveliness of their story and kept the ballad-singers
busy for a century:

> He drew his army up in lines so pretty
> On the Plains of Abraham back of the city
> At a distance from the town where the French would meet him
> In double numbers who resolved to beat him.
>
> Montcalm and this brave youth together walked
> Between two armies they like brothers talked
> Till each one took his post and did retire
> It was then these numerous hosts commenced their fire.

The consequence of the battle was momentous but not
yet decisive. The final blow for Canada was struck in the
narrow seas between Britain and France.

With such a power of British ships absent in the St Lawrence, and even despite Boscawen's great victory in the
Mediterranean, Britain herself lay open to attack. An invasion had long been planned by the French and news from
the South and from the distant West made them attempt
such desperate measures even in the storms of November.
Those same storms had driven Hawke from his vigil off
Brest. When he returned the French Channel Fleet had
slipped out to rendezvous with the troop transports. The
genius of Hawke found them out, against the warnings of
his navigators chased them into Quiberon Bay and there
destroyed them, and with them the hopes of victory for
France or reinforcement for the Governor of Canada at
Montreal.

Clive in India and an heroic Anglo-Hanoverian army at
Minden had added to the certainty. 'We are forced to ask
every morning what victory there is,' wrote Horace Walpole
in that great year, 'for fear of missing one.' Time alone was
needed before France in Canada would be utterly destroyed,
and on 7 September 1760 General Jeffrey Amherst, with
an army greater than had ever before been seen in North
America, received at Montreal the unconditional surrender
of the French Governor, the Marquis de Vaudreuil.

CHAPTER II

PRIVILEGES AND FRANCHISES

THE Peace which followed the Seven Years War was not signed until three years after the fall of Montreal, and in that time much had happened to render futile the successes of the War. A young king had come to the throne, George the Third, who cared not a whit for colonial possessions but a great deal for the position of the monarch as active head of the administration. Such a one could not long stomach the overbearing practices of Pitt, and by the end of 1762 Pitt, never popular with his Parliamentary colleagues, had been ousted, and with him his nominal chief, Newcastle.

Pitt, who had realized that not only France but also Spain stood between Britain and imperial expansion, had insisted on war with Spain, and a short war fought after Pitt's power was broken, but while the habits of strategical thinking which he had engendered were still alive, went far to achieving his object. But at the Peace of Paris, signed in February 1763, at the urgent instigation of the King and his peace party under Bute, much of the advantage was surrendered. True, Canada was now British, and Florida ceded by Spain in exchange for the return of Spanish Caribbean possessions. But the French had given Louisiana to Spain in 1762, and the Bute Ministry permitted Spain to retain all of that territory west of the Mississippi except the city of New Orleans. For several years Spain made little effort to implement this decision. No Spanish governor arrived until March 1766, and even then Antonio de Ulloa had with him only ninety men. Still, in 1768, a Frenchman was in command of Louisiana's military defence, and this officer, Philippe Aubry, could write to his government:

I am still waiting for the arrival of the Spanish troops, without whom it is absolutely impossible that Ulloa should take possession of the colony. In the meantime, affairs are conducted as much as possible as if it had been effected.

And, in these years, when French power in Louisiana seemed broken, the arrival of French refugees from Quebec and Nova Scotia strengthened the possibility that in future the culture and social habit of the colony would remain French.

But whether France or Spain controlled the mouth of the Mississippi, Britain, who had defeated both, had at that end of the great river gained nothing at all. Without such gains the strategic battle was incomplete.

Yet never before had England appeared so powerful as she did at the time of the Treaty of Paris. India seemed bound for English dominion, the Atlantic had become an inland water in the British Empire. Not France, not Russia, not Prussia, not Spain could now compete with British power, and there began a short period of colonial energy, of inspired exploration, such as Britain had not seen since the days of Elizabeth and James the First. But in achieving world power Britain had won enemies everywhere and built up for herself an unprecedented national debt; in making such vast increase in her colonial territories Britain had stretched beyond her capabilities the area which she was bound to finance, administer and police. The Parliament of Britain, said Burke, now owned 'an imperial character in which as from the throne of Heaven she superintends all the several inferior legislatures, and guides and controls them without annihilating any'. But the heavenly nature of British imperialism was more apparent in Britain than in the colonies. Above all, the North American colonials were beginning to wonder if it was not the very opposite of heavenly, and were becoming more and more certain that their legislatures should not remain 'inferior'. Britain had obligingly removed one of the strongest knots which bound the colonies to the English throne: the fear of France. In her new-found power and its accompanying threat of bankruptcy the British Parliament quite naturally assumed that the colonials, relieved by Britain of the menace of France, should pay for the maintenance of their security against the surviving menace: the Indians, and launched a policy of taxation and of closer control from Westminster which after-knowledge shows to have been inflammatory.

From the beginning of American history such policies had been attempted, and resented and resisted by the colonials, but neither English politicians nor even American quite realized the changes that had come over America, the difference between the colonies in 1760 and the colonies at the time of the Restoration of Charles the Second, the comparative maturity that now existed in each of the colonies. Resistance to Britain was real, able, and vocal; all that it needed to make it dangerous and active was some sense or reason for unity between the colonies. This only personalities and British folly could provide.

Still the majority of Americans were Anglo-Saxons – but the majority was slight and time had frayed the bonds of sentiment and social connexion which linked even the aristocrats among the Anglo-Saxon Americans to an English heritage. The immigration pattern of the eighteenth century was quite different from the pattern of the preceding century. Then, to the many English, the Dutch of New York, the Swedes of Delaware, the Swiss of North Carolina, the Jews of New York and Rhode Island, and the Huguenots who, after the Edict of Nantes, flocked to New York, Massachusetts and South Carolina, added their various faults and qualities, but none of them was inherently antagonistic to English institutions. Now came the Scots-Irish in their thousands, men who had already mastered frontier techniques in Ulster, religious, hard-working, lovers of liberty but not particularly lovers of England. In the back-countries from Georgia to New York they founded their homes and found the independence they coveted. No Englishman could interfere with their security. To support them came, in 1715 and 1745, a few Scotsmen, victims of mistaken loyalty to a Scottish king, and natural haters of the German family which now lorded it over Britain. (Time would be when, even of these, many would choose loyalty to a 'Hanoverian' king in preference to loyalty to an American President.)

No colony, with the exception of Massachusetts, had done

much to assist the victories of the French–Indian wars. The 'Quaker' colonies added to a worthy religious objection to all war a somewhat less worthy objection to this particular war on the grounds of the damage that it might do to the trade of New Jersey and Pennsylvania. New Hampshire, Georgia, and North Carolina pleaded poverty; Rhode Island turned its back upon a business that did not touch its own frontiers. Most of the colonies found one excuse or another for avoiding the financial responsibilities which they had accepted during the period of crisis.

So jealous were the colonies for their trade that they had never regarded the war as a reason for abandoning their comfortable commerce with the French West Indies. Pitt claimed that the French–Indian Wars lasted three years longer than they need have done because of American smuggling to the enemy.

Out of all these activities and evasions, naturally as praiseworthy to the Americans as they were objectionable to Englishmen, came a series of Westminster actions that were to drive the Americans further from Britishness. Even during the War, Britain had been forced to issue 'writs of assistance' or general search warrants to hunt down smugglers, and colonial merchants had responded by sending James Otis, the Attorney-General of Massachusetts, to Britain to plead that such measures were invasions of their rights as Britons. But, with the War over, and with it the economic good times that went with war, British statesmen began to seek means to facilitate a tightening of imperial control over American affairs.

From the earliest days of colonization there had been pressures towards unity in the colonies – from within the New England Confederation of the mid seventeenth century, for example, 'a firme and perpetual league of friendship and amity . . .', and, enforced from without, the Dominion of New England of 1686, but the failure of the Albany Congress and the colonies' miserable record during the French–Indian Wars gave considerable authority to the view that was held by many Englishmen and some

Americans, that what the colonials could not, or would not, organize for themselves, Britain must organize for them.

As the British conception of empire was primarily economic, so most of the measures designed to strengthen imperialism were given economic accents. The Americans must pay for the safety that Britain had provided.

Throughout the last fifty years of the seventeenth century and the first fifty years of the eighteenth, English policies in the colonies had been based on certain economic assumptions: that it was the function of the colonies to provide the basic raw materials needed by English industry and trade; that it was the duty of the colonies to buy the surpluses of English manufactures; that it was the responsibility of the colonies to tie their currencies to the pound sterling. The Acts of Trade and Navigation passed under Cromwell and Charles II had laid the foundation-stones of the system, the Acts of 1706 and 1721 had strengthened it by enumerating the lists of raw materials produced in the colonies which were to be exported to Britain alone. The colonial businessman was by these Acts limited in his business ventures; he could neither make what he wanted nor sell it wherever his fancy, or the possibility of a good price, dictated.

Yet the colonies had developed much the same system of merchant capitalism as the Mother Country; both were operating in the same economic sphere, and thus an economic clash was well-nigh inevitable. The Northern colonies, for example, had few staple goods which they could trade for England's manufactured goods. New England's fish, lumber, rum, and flour, even much of New England's timber and shipbuilding services, had to find a market in such places as Newfoundland, Africa and the West Indies so that New Englanders could obtain exchange with which to buy British merchandise. The merchants' bases, the port towns, could but compete with their British counterparts – and in the same markets. In the South, where commerce in tobacco and rice was temporarily in a bad way, some effort had been made to turn over to wheat and cattle, already over-produced in the British Empire, and to the manufacture of products such as textiles, ironware, and barrels. Both North and South hoped that the West would provide the market which Britain refused to provide overseas. But the Home Country, too, had its eyes on the West.

When the Board of Trade was established in 1694 it had, with certain political powers such as the instruction of colonial governors, the supervision of the judiciary and the review of colonial legislation, several functions which were primarily economic., The Board considered the requests of British companies seeking investment openings in the colonies – and granted them but seldom. It used its powers of 'disallowance' of colonial legislation to limit the function of colonial manufactures, by advising the Privy Council or governors in the colonies to veto such acts as the colonies had designed to encourage local manufacture, for example, the Pennsylvania shoe-making laws of 1705, the New York sail-cloth legislation of 1706, and the 1756 linen laws in Massachusetts. It advised such generally limiting legislation as that included in the Woollen Act of 1699, the Hat Act of 1732, and the Iron Act of 1750.

The principle of mercantilism was specifically stated by the Board in 1756 when it declared that 'the passing of laws in the plantations for encouraging manufactures, which any ways interfere with the manufactures of this Kingdom, has always been thought improper, and has ever been discouraged'. But with restraint went encouragement – where it suited British commerce. Special privileges were offered and bounties given in an effort to direct colonial activity into production in which English growers either could not compete at all, such as naval stores, wine, and silk, or could not compete with much chance of success, such as tobacco. The tobacco growers of Gloucestershire were driven out of business in order to give the tobacco growers of the Southern colonies a greater chance of prosperity.

Tied to the English currency, forced locally into the use of paper and commodity currency, the colonies found themselves faced always with inflation. In the middle years of the eighteenth century the value of sterling to paper money reached, in Massachusetts, the ratio of eleven to one, in Connecticut eight to one, in North Carolina ten to one, and in Rhode Island as much as twenty-six to one. Only in New York and Pennsylvania was depreciation held within sensible limits by legislation.

But, during the period of the Seven Years War, the colonials had evaded with great success many of the disabilities thrust upon them by mercantilism. With the end of the War the Acts of Trade and Navigation were tightened and enforced. The navy in colonial waters became virtually a customs patrol. Sinecure holders in the colonial customs service were ordered to their posts in 1763 and 1764 and a Vice-Admiralty court was set up for all the colonies to try offenders against the Acts of Trade. Informers were encouraged, the salaries of the colonial judges were freed from dependence upon provincial assemblies in 1768, and a board of five resident customs commissioners was set up.

The list of enumerated commodities was extended in 1764 and in 1766 it was provided that all goods still off this list – principally fish and flour – must be landed in England first if destined for European ports north of Finisterre.

The Sugar Act (calculated as usual to restrict the spheres of colonial business enterprise and, as usual, to encourage colonial capital from trade into raw material production) put new customs duties on sugar and molasses, and forbade entirely the importation of foreign rum. No new conception, but based upon the old Molasses Act of 1733, the Sugar Act was different from its predecessor only in the severity with which it was enforced. American merchants, no longer free to trade with foreign possessions in the West Indies, saw themselves faced with disaster and the 'utter impoverishment of His Majesty's colonies'.

The Sugar Act had implications far beyond the economic, and implications that were immediately recognized as obnoxious to colonial liberties. Under its terms, customs' officials were exempt from suit and the burden of proof of innocence was placed on such colonial merchants as were accused of violation of the Act. The local courts were deprived of their authority to judge offenders against the Act, and their place taken by a general court of the Admiralty.

Also in 1764 Parliament struck at currency evasions. The Currency Act of 1751, which had been limited to the New England colonies, had forbidden the creation of land banks and declared that bills of credit could not be recognized as legal tender. Now the Act was extended to all the colonies. Credit, already weak, began to totter, and was further reduced by the regulation that all customs dues had to be paid in specie. Hundreds of American merchants faced bankruptcy.

In yet another field, at once economic and military, London set out to restrict and regularize colonial function. When war with the French came to an end England found herself the nominal master of many Indian tribes which had long looked to France for leadership. Irked by the high-handed treatment which they received from colonial merchants and British officers, in 1763 the Indians began a highly organized policy of attrition along the Western Frontier. Central organization had never been an Indian virtue and though historians, following Parkman's romantic exercises, have fathered the unique features of the Frontier Wars of 1763 upon Pontiac, the chief of the Ottawas, it is more likely that the hand of France was still active in the West. Whatever the organizing power, the Frontier was helpless to defend itself, the colonies either refused to unite in the face of threat or else would not agree about the mechanics of unity. All the frontier outposts except Fort Niagara, Fort Pitt, and Detroit fell to the Indians, hundreds of frontiersmen lost their lives, and the rebellion was finally quelled only by the intervention of British regular troops.

As this situation developed, the Board of Trade decided to provide for the security of the West by declaring that all lands west of the crest of the Alleghenies should be reserved for the Indians, that political control should be taken out of the hands of colonial governors and placed under imperial agents, and that further settlement should be controlled from London. The policy of the 'Proclamation Line', though amply justified by the events of the moment, was a powerful blow at the charters of the older colonies, at the fortunes of merchants in Philadelphia, Boston, and Albany, and at the Southern planters who had turned to land-jobbing in the West and to the fur-trade in an effort to compensate for the temporary recession in the tobacco trade.

In 1768 a report of the Board of Trade suggested a gradual but tightly controlled westward movement by the colonials, and in the same year the Indian Boundary Line made the provisions of the proclamation line more rigorous; its objectionable nature became even more obvious to colonial merchants when the Board of Trade used its powers and its cunning to sabotage American effort to encourage westward expansion through the offices of such American organizations as the Vandalia Company.

In 1765 Parliament passed the bill which of all the acts of mercantilism most aroused colonial animosity and set the colonials closer to the road of cooperation than ever before in their history. Previous revenue acts, however stringently enforced, had failed in their main purpose: to raise enough money to reduce appreciably the British national debt. Grenville, the new Chancellor of the Exchequer, whose knowledge of American sentiments was even less than that of his royal master, but who in this particular effort seems to have had some justice on his side, had the notion of imposing a general tax to be collected by means of stamps on all newspapers, bills, and legal documents. Such legislation seems unexceptional in our times when it has become a recognized form of governmental money-raising, but it aroused the colonials to objection more vociferous than had any previous act of Parliament. Previous revenue acts had been directed principally against New England and against New England merchants in particular; the Stamp Act affected every man of property in every colony, and affected above all those who were especially skilled in the methodology of politics and public persuasion, the lawyers and the journalists.

It could be regarded, and may have been in part designed, as an attempt to stifle the cheap press which was increasing its strength as the voice of American merchants and politicians addressed to the ears of the American common people. Openly a revenue act, it was also an anti-subversive act in thin disguise. Heavy fines could be imposed if a publisher failed to give his real name and, presumably on the theory that Americans who could afford to be subversive at length were not likely to be subversive at all, the tax went up steeply according to wordage.

Virginia, virtually unaffected economically, had naturally been content to register mere formal complaint against earlier acts such as the Sugar Act; it now took the lead in urgent objection to the Stamp Bill. Edward Montague, the colony's agent in London, was instructed to persuade the agents of the other colonies to press their objections strenuously. Grenville met them with sweet reasonableness. His was the task of managing the national revenue, but could they suggest a better way than the Stamp Bill for allotting to Americans their proper part in national financial recovery he would be glad to consider it. One agent suggested the 'usual constitutional way' of demands from the King and responsive votes from the colonies. Would the colonies agree upon their respective shares? The evidence of the past few years hardly led Grenville to suppose that they would, and the agents could not promise that their countrymen would behave better now than in the past.

The agents thrust their opposition upon the British Parliament and people, but their opposition was by Parliament and people unheeded. In the early spring of 1765 what Lecky has called 'one of the most momentous pieces of legislation in the history of mankind' was passed through a half-empty House and on 22 March received the King's assent. (Incidentally, by commission, George the Third having just had his first attack of insanity.)

The Bill was now an Act, and many distinguished colonials felt that the moment for protest was over; that as James Otis declared it was the 'duty of all humbly . . . to acquiesce in the decision of the supreme legislature', Richard Henry Lee, later no mean American patriot, thought of applying for the post of stamp-distributor. In England Benjamin Franklin, though he was still working for the repeal of the Act, began to look for a similar job for his nephew. But in Virginia, Patrick Henry, young, excitable – and a lawyer – brought into the House of Burgesses five bold resolutions on the 'privileges, franchises, and immunities' of the Colony, and thus rang the alarm for the whole of America.

'Tarquin and Caesar each had his Brutus, Charles the First his Cromwell, and George the Third may profit by their example. If this be treason, make the most of it!' Thus Patrick Henry against the Stamp Act, and even if the Speaker of the Virginia House of Burgesses, and many members, felt that it was treason, even if Governor Fauquier was so enraged by the 'rash heat' of the Virginia Assembly that he ordered it to be dissolved, it was not before four of Henry's resolutions had been adopted by the House.

From Virginia's lead, but without a representative from the momentarily non-existent Virginia House, the other colonies gathered the courage to call a meeting in New York. Once there, boldness faltered; the submissive tone of the 'Stamp Act Congress' hardly matched the anger that still blazed in the colonies. The courts either declined to act in matters requiring stamps or else continued business without stamps on the grounds that there were no stamps available. The judges in Northampton County, Virginia, even went so far in defiance as to hand down an opinion:

That said Act did not bind, affect or concern the inhabitants of this colony, inasmuch as they conceive the same to be unconstitutional, and that the said several officers (the Clerk and other court officials) may proceed to the execution of their respective offices, without incurring any penalties by means thereof.

Such policies of non-cooperation alarmed British business interests and the Act was repealed. In their rejoicings at victory and reprieve the colonials hardly noticed the ominous wording of the Parliamentary declaration which went with the repeal:

The Parliament had, hath, and of right ought to have full power and authority to make laws and statutes of supreme force and validity to bind the colonies and people of America, subjects of the Crown of Great Britain, in all cases whatsoever.

Here was the old subject of debate explicitly stated. Economic differences between the colonies and the Mother Country had brought into the open the fundamental political question: should Parliament reign supreme, or should it govern only through the *consent* of the colonials as represented by their own Assemblies? It was not, as it was later made out to be, a debate over 'taxation without representation'; thinking colonials knew well that the concession of a few seats at Westminster would leave them worse off than before, victims of the overwhelming vote that would still be in the hands of home-based members and yet deprived, by apparent concession, of their most cogent argument, 'the rights of a British subject'. It was their contention that the colonies had established their own parliaments – and established them by royal charter. By these, and by these alone, they argued, should the internal policies of the colonies be decided.

'Power abstracted from Right,' wrote the Virginian, Richard Bland, in *An Inquiry into the Rights of the British Colonies* (published in Williamsburg in 1766), 'cannot give a just Title to Dominion. . . . Rights imply Equality in the Instances to which they belong. If the Colonists . . . are deprived of their Civil Rights . . . their Remedy is to lay their Complaints at the Foot of the Throne.'

Thus was laid down once more a theory which was to win a measure of general acceptance among Americans in the next ten years – the colonies equal with Britain under the Crown – a theory which was to become after a hundred and fifty years the major constitutional principle of the British Empire. And with it Bland set down another dogma which Americans had frequently felt but had so far seldom stated:

The Colonies upon the Continent of North America lie united to each other in one Tract of Country, and are equally concerned to maintain their common Liberty. . . . Bodies in Contact, and cemented by mutual Interests, cohere more strongly than those which are at a Distance, and have no common Interests to preserve.

CHAPTER 12

PLEASURES AND NECESSITIES

In the extra-Parliamentary debate over the passage and implementation of the Stamp Act, as later in the whole furore of the American Revolutionary War, public sentiment in Britain was by no means anti-American. In the popular cartoons of the times, for example – and cartoons are often more accurate as weathervanes to sentiment than any verbatim reports from the House of Commons – the general trend is against Grenville and his Act. A description of one cartoon in the British Museum collection is enough to give the sentiments of many. It is entitled 'The State of the Nation, An. Dom. 1765' and in it Britannia comforts an angry and frightened America who is being threatened with Grenville's rod; Pitt grasps Grenville's hand and says, 'You have no right'. On the other side, Lord Mansfield, urged on by Bute, attempts to stab Britannia but is prevented by Lord Camden. Into Camden's mouth is put the caption, 'No general warrants'. In the background, two ships, representing British trade, are driving fast on to a rocky promontory.

The coherent imperial system which Grenville had contemplated seemed to founder on the failure of the Stamp Act. Those who had proposed an Imperial Western plan, the American landowners whose holdings would decrease in value with the opening of the West, the colonial governors who wanted for themselves many acres of back country, and the energetic groups of land-speculators, had all united with humble Americans and with many in Britain, both humble and powerful, who saw in the Stamp Act a threat to liberty, to local government – or to their private purses. But though Grenville had not created the centralized imperial structure of his dream, he had gone far towards making it a possibility by uniting Americans in opposition. In the dispute over the Stamp Act a conglomeration moved far towards becoming a nation, thirteen colonies came one step nearer to being united colonies and therefore one step nearer to being the United States. But on the way to becoming a nation these thirteen colonies had first to go through the process of learning to think of themselves as one American colony. In the actual physical and mental structure of the colonies there was as yet little encouragement for the sentiments and activities of unity. Travel between them was difficult and uncomfortable. There was as yet no metropolis, no centralized colonial culture or education, no centralized press, no simple means of getting information from one colony to another.

Yet, at least in the coastal districts, America was no longer a wilderness, and the American people no longer pioneers settled down uncomfortably on the edge of forest and disaster. The streets of Boston had been paved since 1715, at night they were lighted and patrolled by night-watchmen; New York, its streets still unpaved until 1775, had, nevertheless, a well-established police service. Philadelphia, by the middle of the eighteenth century, had grown into a city of almost forty thousand, with four hundred shops and six thousand houses; a city considerably bigger than New York (approximately thirty thousand), Boston (approximately eighteen thousand), or Charleston (approximately fifteen thousand). But Charleston could claim a public library of sorts, thriving bookstores, excellent newspapers, 'easy manner clubs', a racecourse, dancing assemblies – and milliners in touch with the latest Paris fashions. Down in Georgia, two cities, Savannah and Augusta, even had golf-clubs before the Revolution.

For the most part, the streets in the colonial towns were dusty or muddy with the seasons and, in this like their English provincial counterparts, as much the province of farmyard animals as of human beings. The elegant street planning which was beginning to touch Europe was seldom imitated in America; among colonial main streets only the Duke of Gloucester Street in Williamsburg, wide and long, from the College of William and Mary at one end to the provincial Capitol at the other, had any claims to refinement.

But the houses which lined the streets of the colonial towns were liveable and, at their best, dignified and beautifully proportioned. Variations there were from colony to colony, from region to region, but of all aspects of colonial life the buildings of America were the most indigenous. Here was functionalism suited to the American setting, simple and solid, but well-proportioned, and at times even stately and gracious. The age of memory in which American builders had drawn upon their own recollections and upon the folk recollections of British buildings had given way to the age of architectural books, and, inspired by the publications of Wren and Inigo Jones and of James Gibbs, American architects had spread English patterns throughout the colonies transposing them into an American idiom that hardly differed from colony to colony, whether the material used was the frame of New England, the stone of Pennsylvania, or the brick of Virginia.

For their pleasures the people of North American colonies followed the general lines set by their English contemporaries. There are many stringent accounts of the habits of the time but few can be more direct than that written by Thomas Gwatkin, who sailed to Virginia in 1770 to teach mathematics and languages at the College of William and Mary. Gwatkin's five-year stay at Williamsburg was eventful. Since he strongly opposed the establishment of an American episcopate he was at first popular among Virginian patriots. But by 1774 with revolutionary fervour growing among his neighbours, his loyalty to Governor Dunmore and to the King had made him so universally disliked that he was subjected to the vilest treatment by the Virginians. His account of social customs in Virginia appears to have been written before his life in the colony became unbearable, but it is nevertheless severely critical even in its apparent moderation. On the subject of alcohol, Gwatkin says:

I would not be understood to insinuate that the Virginians are remarkable for excessive drinking. On the Contrary I never saw so much liquor consumed at a sitting as I have at entertainments in England. But everyone the least acquainted with the practice of physick must have observed the pernicious Effects of the constant use of Spirituous liquors 'tho taken in the greatest moderation. A convincing proof of their tendency to shorten human [life] may be brought from the Ladies of this Colony who generally live to a much more advanced age than the men. The longevity of Women in comparison of Men is apparent every where. Their common drink is water, except a small draft of toddy just before a single Glass of Madeira after dinner. This and the same quantity at supper is rarely exceeded.

And with drinking went a tendency to gluttony that was notable even to an immigrant from Britain, a country not without its failings in that respect. 'That they eat larger quantities of animal food and are permitted to indulge in it even from their infancies is certain,' writes Thomas Gwatkin. 'It is no uncommon thing to see meat, both cold and harshed, served up in conjunction with tea and coffee for breakfast at houses of persons of the first rank in the country.' And later, Thomas Gwatkin offers his unknown correspondent a short account of the gustatory habits of the Virginians:

I observed above that the natives of Virginia eat greater quantities of animal food than the Inhabitants of Britain. A short account of their manner of living may afford you some entertainment. Their breakfast like that of the English consists of tea, coffee and chocolate; and bread or toast and butter, or small cakes made of flower and butter which are served to Table hot, and are called hoe Cakes from being baked upon a hoe heated for that purpose. They have also harshed meat and homony, Cold beef, and hams upon the table at the same time, and you may as frequently hear a Lady desiring to be helped to a part of one of these dishes as a cup of tea. Their tables at dinner are crowded with a profusion of meat: And the same kind is dressed three or four different ways. The rivers afford them fish in great Abundance: and their Swamps and forests furnish them ducks, teale, blue-wing, hares, Squirrells, partridges and a great variety of other kinds of fowl. Eating seems to be the predominant passion in Virginia. To dine upon a single dish is considered as one of the greatest hardships. You can be con-

tented with one joint of meat is a reproach frequently thrown into
the teeth of an Englishman. Even one of the fair Sex would be
considered as Gluttons in England. Indeed I am inclined to believe
more disorders in this Country arise from too much eating than
any other cause whatsoever. In the Afternoon tea and Coffee is
generally drank, but with bread or toast and butter. At Supper you
rarely see any made dishes. Harshed and Cold meat, roasted fowls,
fish of different kinds, tarts and sweetmeats fill up the table. After
the Cloth is taken away, both at dinner and supper; Madeira and
punch or toddy is placed upon the table. The first toasts which are
given by the Master of the family, are the King; the Queen and the
royal family; the Governour and Virginia; a good price for Tabac-
co. After this, if the Company be in a humour to drink, the ladies
retire, and the Gentlemen give every man his Lady; then a round
of friend(s) succeeds; and afterwards each of the Company gives a
Sentiment; then the Gentleman of the house drinks to all the friends
of his Company and at last concludes with drinking a good Afternoon or good Evening according to the time of day.

Nor was gluttony the only American excess. At least for
the South Thomas Gwatkin could add another:

But the principal Cause of the brevity of life of the Virginians
has not yet been mentioned. Their Constitutions are frequently
destroyed before they arrive at Manhood; and a young Man of
twenty with all the infirmities of Sixty is no uncommon spectacle.
This flows from their early connections with the Negroe Wenches,
who find their Interest too much concerned and their vanity too
much flattered in bestowing favours on their young masters. By
this means their health at the time of Marriage is generally so much
impaired as to render the condition of their Wives little better than
that of nurses. Their Offspring (as may be reasonably supposed) is
weak, and puny; thus the human Species in this Country suffers a
continual degradation, insomuch that were it not for the Supplies
they receive from other countries; and their intermarriages with
the inhabitants of the Upland Counties, whose manners are very
different from those of the Lower parts of Virginia, I cannot help
thinking they would scarcely be able to support any given degree
of population during the space of fifty years.

Of other pleasures in town and country, dancing was
probably the most general. A few in high-flying centres,

such as Williamsburg or Philadelphia, attempted to ape the sophistication of London or Paris; dancing-masters flourished in the big cities, survived in the small towns, and even found their way to the frontier settlements. But in general the dancing of the colonials was more robust than the dancing at home; even amidst the suave surroundings of the Apollo Room at the Raleigh Tavern in Williamsburg or Gadsby's in Alexandria, closer to the folk-dancing of the English countryside than to the refinement of Bath or Matlock. Such was the enthusiasm of the colonials for dances like 'Worse to Better' or 'Ragged Jacket' that the athletic achievement of George Washington when he danced for three hours with Mrs Nathaniel Greene must be recognized as a feat of endurance comparable almost to the famous dance of William Kempe from London to Norwich.

In 1752 Alexander Finney, the keeper of the Raleigh Tavern in Williamsburg, announced that there would be a ball held there 'one every week during the sitting of the general assembly in the court'. And, while a student at William and Mary in 1753, Thomas Jefferson wrote to John Page, 'last night as merry as agreeable company and dancing with Belinda in the Apollo could make me, I never could have thought the succeeding sun could see me so wretched as I now am'.

Nor should it be without note that long before the Negro had set his mark on American music his betters and masters were already imitating his jigs and reels.

In the South, for rich and for poor, for wise and for foolish, horse-racing was the most popular of outdoor activities, and even such pompous and correct ministers as Commissary James Blair were prepared to serve as the eighteenth-century equivalent of the twentieth-century track steward.

Philip Fithian, the tutor at Nominy Hall, the great Carter estate in Virginia, describes with enthusiasm the sporting activities of his charges:

Bob, ever at twelve o'clock is down by the riverside with his gun after ducks, gulls, etc., – Ben is on his horse ariding, Harry is either in the kitchen or at the blacksmith's or carpenter's shop. They all find places of rendezvous so soon as the bell rings and all seem to choose different sports!

And for the five girls of the family – 'All dress in white and are remarkably genteel' –

The two eldest are now learning music, one to play the harpsichord, the other the guitar, in the practise of which they spend three days in the week . . . the young ladies tell me that we are to have a ball of selected friends in this family – but I, hard lot, I have never learnt to dance!

To game-hunting and horse-racing the North added skating in season. In the South, cock-fighting was so popular that it was expressly forbidden to the students of William and Mary. Bowls and golf had a large following. Of indoor games, billiards and backgammon were the most popular and the most respectable. Chess lost favour during the eighteenth century, but card games and dice-throwing were enthusiastically followed by all classes and in all sections. And everywhere for the men there were clubs, 'for a social time, the interchange of ideas and the generous absorption of liquor'.

The habit of quasi-social, quasi-intellectual club, which was developing in England from such organizations as the Royal Society, had its imitators in America. The oldest of the college clubs, the Flat Hat Club at William and Mary, was founded in the middle of the century, to be followed there just before the Revolution by the first of the Greek letter fraternities (and still the greatest) Phi Beta Kappa. Brown University, founded in Providence, Rhode Island, in 1764, soon established a 'pronouncing society' for its students. There were 'literary' societies in Philadelphia, in Boston, and in New York. Annapolis had its Tuesday Club, a weekly gathering of twenty-five gentlemen who wrote burlesques about each other and their friends, who wore a metal badge on great occasions, gave an annual ball to the ladies and were so gallant that the first toast of every evening was always 'To the ladies' – this even before the toast to the King. Their rules forbade the serving of anything more exotic than a gammon of bacon, but their language was more elaborate; even a handshake was officially referred to as a 'manuquassation' and the manners of members were so refined that they decided, by a formal vote, to carry their sandboxes with them to their meeting so that when they spat tobacco it might not dirty the floor of their host's 'withdrawing room'. Just outside Annapolis stood (and still stands) the club which vies with the Fish House Club of Philadelphia for the glory of being the oldest in America, the South River Club. Already, in 1746, when the loyal members sent a congratulatory message to King George the Second on his victory over the Young Pretender, they referred to themselves as 'the ancient South River Club', and their rules provided (and still provide) for membership by heredity alone.

From the earliest days of the colonies, the colonials of the unpuritanical provinces had waited eagerly for the arrival of strolling players to liven their routine existence. The first theatre performance recorded was staged in Accomac County, Virginia, in August 1665, but the right to boast the erection of the first playhouse is a matter of dispute between Williamsburg, Annapolis, and Charleston. Williamsburg seems bound to win, for in a contract dated 11 July 1716, William Levingstone, merchant, released a dancing master, Charles Stag and Mary his wife, from indentures by which Stag was employed 'in the preparation and acting of plays for the joint benefit of himself and the said William Levingstone' and undertook 'with all convenient speed to cause to be erected and built at its own proper costs and charge in the City of Williamsburg, one good substantial house, commodious for acting such plays as shall be thought fit to be acted there'. And it would seem that his obligation was soon fulfilled, for, writing in 1733, Hugh Jones referred to a large area in Williamsburg 'for a market place, near which is a playhouse and a good bowling green'. From that time until the Revolution, Williamsburg was seldom without a playhouse and seldom without plays. The Charleston Dock Street Playhouse was not built until 1736; in Annapolis, though there are records of plays, there is no firm record of a playhouse until the New Theatre was built in 1771. In 1724 the *Philadelphia American Weekly Mercury* reported performances by a band of itinerant acrobats on the outskirts of the City, and already, a year earlier, the Mayor of Philadelphia had expressed alarm because a group of wandering players had set up a stage just outside the City limits, which 'the sober people' wished him to suppress, but which Governor Sir William Heath was inclined to encourage. But Philadelphia's theatre owes its true origin to the advent of Lewis Hallam's company which in 1754 presented the tragedy, *The Fair Penitent*, and, anticipating trouble, passed round in the streets a pamphlet setting forth the virtues of the stage and called by the all-embracing description, *Extracts of Several Treaties Wrote by the Prince of Conte with the Sentiment of the Fathers, and some of the Decrees of the Councils, Concerning such Places, Recommended to the Perusal and Serious Consideration of the Professors of Christianity in the City of Philadelphia.* Theatres followed in Newport and Providence; small towns such as Chestertown and Marlborough in Maryland adapted tobacco warehouses for the performance of plays by touring companies. New York had no theatre until 1767, but, as always, when New York finally decided to initiate an experiment, it did it on a grand scale, and the box-office takings of the first New York theatre amounted to a regular eight thousand dollars a night.

Plays were even better known in print than by performance. Lillo's *George Barnwell*, for example, first acted in England late in 1731, was serialized in *The New England Weekly Journal* a few months later. In 1760 Salem imported plays by Lillo, Gay, Mrs Centlivre, Steele, and Farquhar for its Social Library. William Byrd of Westover, like almost every American of justified or unjustified pretensions had *The Beggar's Opera* on his shelves. *She Stoops to Conquer* was published in New York in the year of its first London performance.

Still Timothy Dwight, the Connecticut poet, could pontificate that 'to indulge a taste for play-going means nothing more or less than the loss of that most invaluable treasure, the immortal soul', but the old puritanism was shattered, and even Cotton Mather thought of 'sending some Agreeable Things to the Authors of the Spectator'. Daniel Boone read *Gulliver's Travels* in the wilds of Kentucky and called a stream Lorbrulgud, after the capital of Brobdingnag. Although in 1731 Bradford's bookstore in Philadelphia sold nothing but religious books, five years later his advertisements included only one religious book and, in the place that they had once filled so completely, such works as *The Spectator*, *The Tatler*, and Steele's *Guardian*. By the time of the Revolution, when that arch-hater of America, Dr Johnson, in a pre-echo of Sydney Smith remarked 'the Americans! What do they know and what do they read?' an American friend could answer with justice, 'they read, Sir, the *Rambler*'.

Jonathan Edwards who was, as we have seen, the last of the great American Calvinists as he was, despite himself, the first of the great American rationalists, read *The Spectator* as avidly as his religious texts. Not Edwards, not Mather, not even Wesley or Whitefield could hold the American people to the delights and frenzies of regeneration – far more exciting were almanac revisions of Newton's Theories on an universal natural law, and Locke's *Essays Concerning Human Understanding* with its enlightened thesis that man's own experience and reason could lead him to understand his place in the universe, broke violently into the orthodox notions of scriptural revelation and dealt a vicious blow to Calvinist ideas of predestination.

Locke's words were everywhere and read by everyone, his influence upon the deistic thinking of American readers such as Jefferson, Franklin, and Adams greater possibly than that of any other thinker, British or American, with the exception of Tom Paine, and Paine was, at all events, in so many things his pupil. Harvard, William and Mary, Yale, and Princeton had all been founded with the notion that in part at least they were to be forcing-grounds for the ministry, but the new colleges of the middle of the century, the College of Philadelphia founded in 1751, and King's

College in New York founded in 1754, had no such inspiration. Parson Weems writing in the last years of the century for books that were to stock his Virginia bookstore, described the movement thus:

> Let the Moral and Religious be as highly dulcified as possible. Divinity for this climate should be very rational and liberal.

As an ally to the English scientists and philosophers in their work upon the American mind came the writings of the French *philosophes*. Voltaire, applying his sharp common sense to vigorous criticism of Church and State, and Montesquieu (particularly his *De l'Esprit des Lois*). Fénelon's *Télémaque* was particularly welcome to a people for whom the execution of Charles the First and the enforced abdication of James the Second were still matters of close memory and whose minds were already beginning to turn upon the iniquities of the House of Hanover in American affairs.

The principal American exponent of this new age of reason, whose life and activities were in this like a miniature history of American eighteenth-century society, was Benjamin Franklin, born in 1706 in Boston, the son of a Puritan soap-maker.

At the age of seventeen he had already helped his brother, the publisher of the *New England Courant*, but he ran away to become a jobbing printer in Philadelphia, and by the age of twenty-three had his own newspaper, the *Pennsylvania Gazette*.

In 1732 he began his immensely popular *Poor Richard's Almanac*. In 1736 he established the Union Fire Company, and in the same year became Clerk to the Pennsylvania Assembly. A year later he was Postmaster of Philadelphia. Seventeen forty-one saw him issuing the second magazine in the colonies, *The General Magazine and Historical Chronicle*. He followed it by inventing the Franklin stove and entering the American Philosophical Society in 1744. His were the proposals behind the foundation of the University of Pennsylvania and his the plan of colonial union which was adopted by the Albany Congress in 1754. He was colonial agent for

Pennsylvania from 1757 and, as such, a mild opponent of the Stamp Act. He proved the identity of lightning and electricity and invented the lightning-rod. He was elected to the Royal Society and awarded its gold medal. He helped frame the Declaration of Independence, the Treaty of Alliance, The Treaty of Peace, and the American Constitution. He was a member of the Continental Congress, United States Minister to France and President of Pennsylvania (1785). He wrote his autobiography, a number of essays, many political and economic tracts, and a long sequence of brilliant letters. He had a mind ever ready to consider the importance of nature and society but was nevertheless quick to make significance out of trivialities. The same man who could attack an empire with Swiftian zeal in *Rules by which a Great Empire may be reduced to a Small One*, could show equal enthusiasm for tackling the minor disadvantages of mankind such as gout or smoking chimneys.

His style he modelled on Addison; the very first words in the *Courant* echoed the introduction to the *Spectator*. But such was Franklin's multiplicity of interest that it is impossible to draw from his life and activities either the sources of his inspiration or a clear notion of the direction of his influence. He was in most respects a typical son of the age of reason, practical and humane, yet his determination to improve himself had in it much that came from Puritanism, and it is because of this combination, even contradiction, that Franklin is so typical of Americanism. Since he was a colonial he was opposed to mercantilism and shared with Adam Smith a belief in free trade, but since he was typical of his times he could not trust the opinions of the mob. The world, in his view, was ruled by a Divinity, but a Divinity who shared the prejudices towards order of the eighteenth-century rationalists. His thinking was comfortable, but he wished to share the comfort with others – and thus became a revolutionary. He was a pagan who believed in God.

Franklin has become in retrospect America's greatest prophet. It may seem at times that the measure of his genius is exaggerated, for his was not a great mind as was Jonathan Edwards's. Edwards looked to man to mould himself according to a vision of the Almighty. Franklin looked to improve man's temporal lot. Edwards was a philosopher; Franklin was an aphorist. He made some considerable and original contributions to the study of electricity but he was, for the most part, a technologist, an ingenious inventor, a good mechanic and a provider of gadgets. He had wit, wisdom, humanity, but little poetry. All his genius was directed towards communication and all that he wrote and said in his long life was followed avidly by a circle of admirers greater than that which had ever before been given to an American. Above all Franklin symbolized for his American contemporaries their ideals and hopes by being an eminently successful human being operating within the intellectual framework as they knew it. To them – as to a large extent to their successors – the qualities of manner and mind he displayed are the pre-eminent typification of the Age of Reason, American version.

Travel, though in the South particularly a necessary prelude to pleasure, was hardly of itself pleasurable, and few colonials savoured tourism except to Europe or the West Indies. The roads within and between the colonies were little more than clearings through the woods. There were few bridges, and such as there were were rickety affairs as likely to damp the enthusiasm of the traveller as the more normal method of crossing rivers by fords. Many of the colonies passed road maintenance laws in the early years of the century, but few of them were kept, and, as a rule, a few logs thrust into the mud was the best road maintenance that was attempted. Some of the great families vied with the English aristocracy in the elaboration of their coaches, the upper-middle class in chaises and sulkies. There was, by the middle of the century, a regular stage-coach service between New York and Philadelphia. The journey, which today takes a few minutes by air, took three days by stage-coach in 1756, and in the 'Flying Machine' of 1777 the time was reduced to one and a half days. But most men stayed at home and if they had to travel went by horse, by boat, or on foot.

As in England, this was an age of inns, taverns, and ordinaries, which sprang up along all the principal highways. The North, with its closer concentration of population, was better served than the South, but the South, with its greater tradition of luxury, had the finest taverns of all. Williamsburg, which at the height of its fame as colonial capital could claim no fewer than fifty-six taverns, twenty lodging-houses, eight ordinaries, as well as many private houses which took in lodgers at 'public times', could boast in the Raleigh Tavern an inn finer even than Boston's Green Dragon, Baltimore's Fountain Inn, and Philadelphia's Indian Queen. Henry Wetherburn, the first known keeper of the Tavern, brewed such fine arrack punch that William Randolph of Tuckahoe sold two hundred acres of frontier land to Thomas Jefferson's father in exchange for 'Henry Wetherburn's biggest bowl of arrack punch'. In Williamsburg, as in many another colonial city, the principal Tavern was the heart of commerce, political and social activity. 'I now have got a store exactly opposite the Raleigh Tavern,' wrote Catherine Rathel in 1772 to John Norton, a merchant of London and of Yorktown, 'which I look on as the best situation in Williamsburg, where I hope to do three times the business I ever did.' 'Before the door of the Raleigh' were held auctions of slaves, houses, land, harness, horses, and cattle. Within the Tavern, lottery and theatre tickets were bought and sold; the proprietor acted as a lost-property office and here lost articles could be returned for a reward and 'no questions asked'. In 1769 the Apollo Room at the Raleigh first accommodated the dissolved House of Burgesses, who reconvened there as a meeting of 'the late representatives of the people', following their protest against the Revenue Act, and there passed their agreement not to import British goods. Again, in 1773 and in 1774, trouble with Royal Governors adjourned formal gatherings in the Capitol, and informal gatherings took place beneath the motto carved above the mantelpiece in the Apollo Room,

Hilaritas Sapientae et Bonae Vitae Proles – 'Jollity the Child of Wisdom and Good Living.' Of these occasions Thomas Jefferson wrote:

Not thinking our old & leading members up to the point of forwardness & zeal which the times required, Mr Henry R. H. Lee, Francis L. Lee, Mr Carr & myself agreed to meet in the evening in a private room of the *Raleigh*, to consult on the state of things. There may have been a member or two more whom I do not recollect. We were all sensible that the most urgent of all measures was that of coming to an understanding with all the other colonies, to consider the *British* claims as a common cause to all, & to produce an unity of action; and for this purpose that a committee of correspondence in each colony would be the best instrument for intercommunication; and that their first measure would probably be to propose a meeting of deputies from every colony, at some central place, who should be charged with the direction of the measures which should be taken by all. We therefore drew up the resolutions. . . . The consulting members proposed to me to move them, but I urged that it should be done by Mr Carr, my friend & brother-in-law, then a new member, to whom I wished an opportunity should be given of making known to the house his great worth & talents. It was so agreed; he moved them, they were agreed to nem. con. and a committee of correspondence appointed, of whom Peyton Randolph, the Speaker, was chairman.

Something of the importance of the tavern in colonial life can be gathered from the famous quotation ascribed to Benjamin Franklin:

My name is Benjamin Franklin. I was born in Boston. I am on my way to Philadelphia and I have no news. Now what can you give me for dinner?

Tavern-keepers were the best-known men in town and the strongest of them wielded influence beyond that of many of their seemingly greater neighbours. A few of them attempted to reduce the violence of colonial living. Cato, for example, at his roadhouse in New York, set aside a sitting-room for ladies and forbade the common practice of lifting sleeping occupants from their beds and usurping their places in the middle of the night. But, for the most part, tavern-keepers were content to make money as fast as they could – and the fastest way they knew was by pouring an excess of rum into ever-thirsty visitors.

In addition to its purely social activity the tavern acted as a clearing-house for gossip and for varied news, but its place as such was gradually taken by the newspaper. At the time of the Revolution every colony, except New Jersey and Delaware, had at least one newspaper, Boston and New York had four each, Philadelphia had seven. Circulation was not much though it could be wide; although William Goddard's *Pennsylvania Chronicle* had only a little more than one thousand subscribers he employed subscription agents in Delaware, New Jersey, Maryland, and Virginia as well as in the State of origin. Hugh Gaine claimed that his *New York Mercury* went to all the 'capital places' and to many rural communities in the colonies and West Indies as well. A colonial newspaper was tabloid in shape and in make-up as much a magazine as a newspaper. The whole of one page would be given up to a poem or essays, another to European items, to news from other American colonies and to West Indian activities. There would be many shipping notes, many advertisements, and some account of social life. Much handicapped by slow communications, the editors found it difficult to provide fresh news and as time went on gave more and more space to editorializing instead of news report. The *Pennsylvania Gazette* of 6 December 1765 gave nearly half its space to the Stamp Act controversy, and this argument, which was directly affecting newspaper proprietors, was the first on which editors throughout the American colonies showed some measure of unanimity. Government, from time to time, attempted to muzzle the growing opposition from the press, but as the movement towards revolution developed, 'the chief threat to free discussion came from the Radicals rather than the Conservatives, and through extra-legal methods'. Already in 1770 the *Boston Chronicle* was forced out of existence because of its violent Toryism. Yet it is only in retrospect that politics seem the most interesting item in colonial newspapers:

Tis truth (with deference to the college)
The general source throughout the nation
Of every modern conversation.
What would this mighty people do
If there alas were nothing new?
A newspaper is like a feast,
Some dish there is for every guest:
Are services you can't express
There's not a want of human kind,
But we a remedy can find.

(*New York Journal*, 19 April 1770)

The criminal code of the American colonies was neither more nor less vicious than that of the Mother Country, but though statistics are not easy to come by it seems possible that England's generous custom of emptying its prisons into the colonies gave to those colonies a larger criminal population than ever England could boast at the time. Slavery too (which was in Great Britain non-existent) added to the record of crime, for desperate and escaping slaves faced with vicious penalties were apt to exercise vicious acts in order to achieve freedom. In New York, robbery, burglary, housebreaking, and forgery were all punishable by death. Delaware had no less than twenty capital crimes. Not until the 1760s was the practice of witchcraft abolished as an offence subject to the death penalty in all colonies, though anyone who could read Latin could, until 1770, still claim the old medieval right of benefit of clergy. For less serious offences, for treason, for blasphemy, perjury, cheating, forgery, dicecogging, even for issuing false invitations to dinner, offenders could be nailed by their ears in the pillory. Slander, idleness, and stubbornness made offenders liable to be placed in the stocks, scolding and gossiping wives were washed of their habits in the ducking-stool. Whipping-posts and the cat's-tail were in frequent use. Adultery was thrice punishable: by whipping for both parties, by fines and by enforced wearing of the scarlet letter 'A'. Blasphemy, viciousness, drunkenness, and forgery were all proclaimed in the offender by his being made to wear the initial letter of his crime.

(Even this was a great improvement on the earlier habit of branding it on to his body or face.) Some offences against public opinion but not against the law, were punished by the mob with an uncomfortable application of tar and feathers – not by any means an exclusively American custom, but one increasingly practised as the century wore on towards revolution. Already in its quest for liberty the American people had begun to define freedom according to the wishes of the majority.

Every major city had its 'strong, sweet prison', always strong but seldom sweet. Gaol was, as a rule, but a temporary lodging-house on the way to great discomforts. The eighteenth century preferred violent punishment and profitable fines to long imprisonments as a deterrent to crime, and only debtors and lunatics stayed for a considerable period within prison walls.

Perhaps no single factor demonstrates so clearly the changing nature of the colonies as the growth of the imporance of the lawyer. In the seventeenth century the leaders of the colonies had been, for the most part, ministers, merchants, or, to define by the indefinable, 'gentlemen'. By the time that revolution became the urgent gossip of Americans, the place of these leaders had been taken by colonial lawyers. A rapid survey of the list of those who led and inspired America between 1760 and 1781 shows that, with the exception of George Washington and Benjamin Franklin, almost all of them were trained in the practice of law. Already before the Revolution more than one hundred and fifty Americans had passed through the Inns of Court in London. Hundreds more with no training but that which they had given themselves, or with the indifferent training provided by their seniors, set themselves up to advise the new class of wealthy merchants. Here and there a distinguished legal scholar of the calibre of George Wythe provided true legal discipline for his students, and it was appropriate that Wythe held the first chair of law established in America.

The apprenticeship system, still predominantly the system by which English solicitors are produced, had the advantage of example, but many of the best lawyers viewed it with critical eyes and, Jefferson among them, felt that, as with all apprenticeship systems, the student was apt to be exploited by his senior as a mere unpaid clerk. Jefferson, who himself received an excellent classical education and had the fortune to study his law under Wythe, argued to the end of his days that the best equipment for a legal career was to engage independently on a course of reading. Inevitably the books that he himself had read were the books he recommended to others: writings in world history and the physical sciences and philosophy, the Greek and the Roman classics and, thereafter Coke's *Institutes of the Laws of England*, Matthew Bacon's *Digests of English Law*, Kame's *Principles of Equity*, and Blackstone's *Commentaries on the Laws of England*.

Until Blackstone appeared, between 1765 and 1769, Coke and Bacon were the principal authorities of young American lawyers. Jefferson recognized Blackstone as 'the last perfect digest'of English law, but felt objection to his Torydom; 'Old Coke', on the other hand, that sturdy supporter of constitutional rights, was his love through life. Some there were among the first great generation of American lawyers who were content to train themselves, and Patrick Henry, for example, spent only six weeks before presenting himself to the examiners to be truly examined 'into his capacity, ability, and fitness'. His ignorance of municipal law was such that George Wythe flatly refused to sign the licence, and both Peyton and John Randolph felt some doubts about his ability. It was not until Henry demonstrated his skill before John Randolph and showed 'the laws of nature and nations, on the policy of the feudal system and general history . . . to be his stronghold', that his certificate was signed.

The business of a colonial lawyer, particularly on the frontier and in the thinly populated districts, was arduous and varied. Much of Henry's reputation was built on his success in collecting debts for merchants, but as a criminal lawyer it was necessary for him to travel from court-house to court-house in distant counties. Waightstill Avery, of

North Carolina (whose greatest fame is that he fought a duel with Andrew Jackson) tells, in his journals, something of the difficulties and hardships of the lawyer in such countries. In the days immediately before the Revolution, when he was first practising in North Carolina, the Regulator Movement was demonstrating by violence the identification which the pioneers had established between the lawyer and the government official, and in 1771 Avery himself was captured by the Regulators in Rowan County, and testified later that his captors had exclaimed:

The Governor is a friend to the lawyers, the lawyers carry on everything, they appoint weak Justices of the Peace for their own purposes, they had worsted the Regulators in making laws for fees, but they, the Regulators, had sworn that they would not have them – there should be no lawyers in the province, they damned themselves if they should.

Superficially, it would seem that from law no lawyer achieved great wealth in Colonial America, but the real rewards of the profession were in the magnificent opportunities open to lawyers to speculate in land and to find their way into political office.

The mob and the *élite* might resent the power of the legal profession, but, as Sir Charles Grant Robertson has written, 'one is almost tempted to conclude that lawyers are always the real makers of revolution'. So it was that the American Revolution, and the success of the revolutionary movement, depended to a large extent upon the skill and opportunity of colonial lawyers.

CHAPTER 13

TRANSATLANTIC DEBATE

THE spread of civilization in the colonies did not of itself strengthen colonial unity. Nor indeed was there much that could be called unity within each colony, and certainly there was little of what later came to be described as American democracy. In Pennsylvania, for example, only eight per cent of the population qualified for a vote, and in Philadelphia itself only two per cent. (If, as now seems probable, more citizens voted than the percentage would appear to justify, the excess of voters over qualifications was created, in eighteenth-century America as in eighteenth-century England, by the necessities of politics and also by the looseness and flexibility of frontier society.) Provincial assemblies, girding for the struggle against the Crown, were by no means champions of popular rights; Virginia was ruled by the great planters of Tidewater, New York by the heirs of the patroons, and New England by merchant aristocrats; it was the Royal Governor and not the colonial patriots who called upon the Crown to end the system whereby 'any one or two families should be able to return so large a proportion of the members of our assembly'.

Colonial oligarchs, fattened with royal favours, desired 'an approachment of what is called English principles in America in order to hold in check the rising anger of the masses and of the bourgeoisie'. Had there been enough favours to go round among the aristocracy, the revolutionary movement might have been denied many of its foremost leaders. Richard Henry Lee, for example, an honest and, on the whole, unambitious Virginian aristocrat, was nevertheless ambitious for office under the Crown, and had his ambitions been satisfied his hot Americanism might have been damped before it burst into flames.

Long before the Revolution a popular party was forming in the North under the leadership of men like James Otis and Sam Adams, but its animosity was directed primarily against the American aristocracy and only by implication against the Crown which held that aristocracy in power.

Between colony and colony rivalries existed which at times reached depths of bitterness seldom plumbed in the disputes with the Mother Country. Such a sensible cleric as Jonathan Mayhew could still write of York Staters in 1763 that 'the clothes of some of our people, butchered by them (the Indians) have been amicably sold at Albany *with the blood upon them*'. Each of the colonies suspected the manners and the motives of all the rest, and within those colonies which had made considerable Western accessions another division existed: between the old-established and the new, between the oligarchic and the opportunistic, between aristocracy and potential democracy. The Eastern Seaboard and the Frontier despised each other; indeed they were almost at each other's throats. The colonies which had access to the West were the object of the jealousy of those with no such outlet.

Only the follies of home government could have united such diversity of interest as existed in America in the twenty years before the Revolution, but the folly was amply provided after the fall of the Whigs in 1762, and the unity supplied by the battle against the Stamp Act and against the policies of mercantilism was virtually unbreakable once it had tasted its first success: the enforced repeal of the Act. The struggle and the victory had given to the American Colonies something more powerful than constitutional union; in the debate over the actions of the Government at Westminster, the Americans had discovered – almost despite themselves – a new ideology. In their efforts to achieve home rule, natural law and its certain corollary 'the rights of Englishmen' had become the battle-cry of Americans. 'We claim nothing,' wrote George Mason of Virginia, 'but the liberty and privileges of Englishmen, in the same degree as if we had still continued among our brethren in Great Britain.' The words of Locke ran from the pens of the American polemicists as if he had been one of their number;

If anyone shall claim a power to lay and levy taxes on the people by his own authority and without such consent of the people, he thereby invades the fundamental law of property and subverts the end of government.

Taxation was the first battleground of the American Revolution: the British forces were routed and the Americans discovered that the forces they had temporarily beaten were the forces of Parliament. A battle with Parliament was almost more than they could face, for though they resented its authority it took time and courage to break away from the notion that Parliament still had supervisory rights over colonial policy. Even James Otis considered that the notion of a Commonwealth of independent assemblies united only by the Crown was treason to the Constitution and anathema to every American. Sentimental, even to the very moment of the Revolution, the Americans looked with veneration towards Britain, and while they were attempting to destroy such impudent reminders of British authority on American soil as customs officers, they still held from their minds the thought of active breach with Britain.

American leaders attempted two major compromises in order to resolve the confusion in their minds. The British Parliament was supreme, on that they agreed, yet their own assemblies could not be subservient: accordingly, they built up with William Pitt a fiction of divided taxation. Parliament, they argued, had the right to tax colonial trade even though Americans were not represented in Parliament; therefore, Parliament could levy port dues. But Parliament could not tax Americans without their consent; therefore, Parliament could not enforce such internal taxes as the Stamp Tax.

The second compromise was potentially of greater consequence, for by making a hero of the monarch American thought divorced itself inevitably from a considerable body of opinion in Great Britain which would otherwise have been sympathetic to the American cause. 'Whoever insinuates that Americans can be disloyal to the Brunswick Line,' wrote an American patriot in 1769, 'may such a damned rebellious villain be banished from our peaceful land.' In attempting to establish a constitutional reason for undermining the power of Parliament, the American leaders seized inevitably upon the ancient Royal Charters of the colonies and encouraged their followers to exorbitant reverence for the person of the King. Time was to make George the Third into an anti-American demon, but before this could be achieved time had to make a hasty *volte-face*. The most radical provincials wrote and orated of George the Third in such effusive terms as to terrify many good Whigs. Bute, North, and Grenville, these were names of mere humans. George the Third, on the contrary, was 'a Prince of heaven-born virtues and ever tender to the cries of injured innocence'; the Whigs had no love for Bute, North, and Grenville, but even less love for rule by royal prerogative.

Yet English Whiggery could not resist the attempt to undermine the ministry by throwing another terror into American hearts; the terror of an English episcopate established in America. It is possible, and indeed probable, that such intentions were never in the minds of any British government, but the fear of them was much in the minds of Americans. It is one of many sardonic twists that the course of Revolution towards democracy in America was much aided by growing religious toleration in Britain. The decline in anti-Catholic persecution and the passage of the Quebec Act persuaded many an American dissenter that rumours of the impending arrival of an Anglican bishop foretold horrors even more horrific, for in their minds Anglicanism was the twin sister of Popery.

There were divisions more profound than any represented by politics, religion or economic policies. Their very remoteness made Americans into outmoded Englishmen and, for the moment, the mode in an England 'victorious in four parts of the world' was far from the nobility which loyal Americans read into what they regarded as their own history. This was not the England of Magna Carta, Hampden or the Petition of Right.

To Tory Grenville and his Stamp Act succeeded Whig

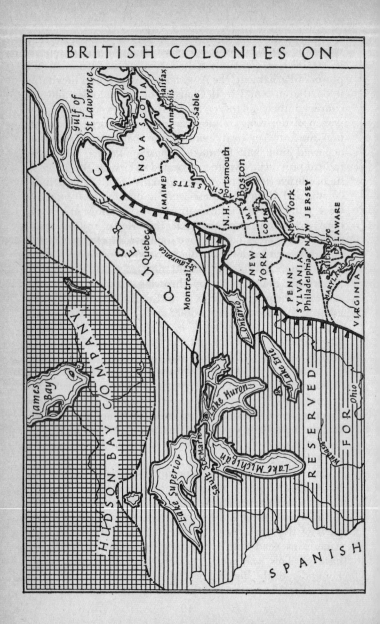

BRITISH COLONIES ON

THE EVE OF REVOLUTION

Richmond
Norfolk
C. Hatteras
Wilmington
NORTH CAROLINA
SOUTH CAROLINA
Charleston
GEORGIA
Savannah
St Augustine
EAST FLORIDA
INDIANS
Cumberland
Tennessee
Mississippi
WEST FLORIDA
Mobile
New Orleans
LOUISIANA
GULF OF MEXICO
Bahama Islands
CUBA

Rockingham and repeal, but neither Pitt nor the King could be happy under a ministry which threatened to tax the landed gentry in an effort to make up for the one hundred and thirty thousand pounds lost by the repeal of the Stamp Act. Therefore, in August 1766, the King rid himself of Rockingham and put in his place 'the illustrious Mr Pitt, under God, and the King, the Saviour of Britain, and the Redeemer of America'. Nothing could have been more pleasing to the colonists, but no pleasure could have been so short lived. As Pitt moved from the House of Commons to the House of Lords, so did he move out of the rays of American affection. Pitt had been loved, Chatham was soon hated. Not that he himself had much changed his views, nor yet, however much they pretended, had the Americans learnt not to love a lord. But Pitt was faced with the inevitabilities of finance, and though he had helped to make his own new position difficult by forcing the repeal of the Stamp Act it was still necessary for him, or for any British Premier, to find some way of making the Americans pay for their own safety. He had inherited the Mutiny Act, by which the colonies were required to provide quarters and supplies for British troops in North America. Some concession had already been made to American sentiment with the excision from the Bill of 1765 of the provisions which gave British officers in the colonies the right to quarter troops in private houses. But even Chatham could not expect the violence with which the colonials greeted the modified Mutiny Act.

Massachusetts moved first. In 1766 two companies of artillery were forced by storms into Boston harbour; the commanding officer applied to the Governor for supplies; the Governor forwarded the request to the Council; the Council accepted the order; and then Massachusetts went mad. James Otis announced that he 'would as soon vote for the devil as such Councellors as were bettering the principles of their country by inserting acts of parliament into the provincial law books'. The House of Representatives followed Otis's lead and refused to vote supplies. General Gage, Commander-in-Chief of British forces in North

America, said, with some justice, that this action had 'near annihilated all the authority of the British legislature over the colonies', and Gage's conviction was strengthened when defiance spread to the province in which his own head-quarters was established, for New York went further than Massachusetts and proclaimed the Mutiny Act unconstitutional. Other colonies indulged in opposition that was no less forceful even if it was shifty rather than direct. New Jersey appointed commissioners to deal with the quartering of soldiers and instructed them to act according to the custom of the province. South Carolina showed its independence by refusing to include salt and beer among the supplies provided. Only Pennsylvania kept to the letter of the law. Chatham sighed at the ingratitude of the Americans; the Stamp Act, he complained, had 'frightened those irritable and umbragious people quite out of their senses'. He himself, and many in England, believed that patience and moderation were alike incomprehensible to Americans.

At this moment, when only a political genius could have brought about a rapprochement between two parodoxical sets of logic, the one political genius Britain owned lost his touch. Chatham was in Bath, ruined physically by gout and hovering on the edges of delusion. The leadership of his Ministry was in the hands of a wit without wisdom: Charles Townshend, the Chancellor of the Exchequer, who could outdrink and outspeak any politician, British or American, whose most brilliant speeches were made when he was most drunk, but whose one real incentive was his love of popularity. Chatham was ready to 'act with vigour to support the superiority of Great Britain over her colonies'; Townshend, no less than his opponent Grenville, only cared for the approval of the British squirearchy and the London hostesses. In January 1767, without consulting his ostensible chief, he promised the House of Commons that the Americans would be made to help relieve taxation at home. Naturally, the first of his supporters was George Grenville.

It took time for Townshend to produce the rabbit from the hat; indeed it is doubtful if it was ever there; but soon efforts on behalf of the stockholders of the East India Company helped to deprive Parliament of some of the revenues which might have made the lack of American money less noticeable, and eventually Townshend announced his plan for America.

Fundamentally this plan was based on a notion which in retrospect seems not without sense; the expenses of empire were to be reduced by cutting the size of the British forces in the colonies and by posting them in regions far from the frontier, where their maintenance was less of a drag on the British taxpayer.

But no threat of positive action could have exasperated and terrified the colonials so much as this threat to withdraw protection. Western settlers had long grumbled that neither Parliament nor provincial assemblies realized to the full the dangers and horrors of Indian raids, and this charge formed one of the principal causes of complaint levelled by those who inhabited the frontier regions against those who sat comfortably in Boston, Albany or Williamsburg. Now Parliament promised to remove the regulars. Horror and fright made for anger and disgust. Frontiersmen who cared little for philosophies or economic policies united in violent disapproval of acts which seemed to bring scalping-knives closer to their heads.

At the same time Townshend proposed a series of new duties upon the colonies: taxes upon tea, lead, paint, paper and glass. These, he argued, were all external taxes, and therefore all agreeable to Americans and 'perfectly consistent with Dr Franklin's own arguments while he was soliciting the repeal of the Stamp Act'. Americans naturally did not see it that way, nor were they grateful for Townshend's refusal to use a military force against them, which they found nullified by his decision that one of the colonies at least – New York, the most violent against the Mutiny Act – should lose its Colonial Assembly until such time as it chose to recognize the sovereignty of the British Parliament. The obvious implication was there, and was taken – even by colonies which did not much love New York. The authority of provincial assemblies would be rendered nugatory by the very suggestion that Parliament could at will suspend their activities.

On the whole, the Townshend policies united British opinion, and when 'Champagne Charlie' died unexpectedly in the autumn of 1767, his passing was almost unanimously mourned in Parliament. But Townshend had also united the colonies, for he had gone one step further towards making Parliament the real and obvious enemy of Americans. His Acts had been designed to defray 'the charge of the administration of justice and the support of civil government' – a motive laudable enough to the British and logical enough to provide relief from the argument which the Americans had used against the Stamp Act and the Mutiny Act. But the Americans were no longer concerned with logic; they realized full well that if the Townshend duties were successfully collected and used according to the law, Parliament would profit at the expense of the Crown and, in America, colonial administrators and the hated oligarchy would become the undoubted creatures of Parliament.

The edict against the New York Assembly was successful for the moment – by a one vote majority the Legislature agreed to supply the troops, though only by indulging in the usual pretence that this agreement was a free gift – but not until excited patriots of other colonies had shown how wide the gap had grown between the colonies and Great Britain by talking, almost for the first time, of battle and blood.

Opposition to the Townshend duties took longer to organize, but once organized it provided an effective precedent for the years to come. The Massachusetts Circular Letter of 1768, drafted by a group of Massachusetts Whigs with Sam Adams as their flaming sword, and the *Letters of a Pennsylvania Farmer*, published by John Dickinson of Philadelphia in colonial newspapers, inspired the colonies to unite in the preservation of colonial rights. Virginia debated the Circular Letter in April 1768, and in turn sent out a letter to all the Colonial Assemblies supporting the Massachusetts plea for alliance against British taxation. Only Pennsylvania stood against the movement. All this was mere paper debate, but now the Ministry took up once more its seemingly constant role of acting against its own best interests. Supervision of the colonies was centralized in a new office, that of Secretary of State to the Colonies, and to that office was appointed Lord Hillsborough. Of Hillsborough even George the Third said that he had never known 'a man of less judgement'.

No sooner was Hillsborough in office than he began to implement the generally fatuous policies of his predecessors by finding a way of antagonizing even the most moderate opinion in the colonies. His method was simple: he drafted a circular letter of his own as an answer to the Massachusetts Circular Letter. Instead of ignoring what might have been considered beneath him, instead of compromising or conciliating, instead of reasoning or cajoling, Hillsborough attacked and thereby proved that the worst fears of the colonials were justified. Colonial governors were ordered to pass on to colonial assemblies Lord Hillsborough's instructions that the Massachusetts Circular Letter should be ignored, and, further, that any which refused obedience were to be dissolved immediately. The Massachusetts General Court was required, on penalty of dissolution, to rescind the Circular Letter. No Massachusetts Assembly was to be permitted until it had announced its disapprobation of that rash and hasty proceeding.

This was tyranny indeed. Hillsborough had played into the hands of American extremists; now they could write:

One spirit animates all America, and both the justice and importance of the cause is so plain, that to quench the spirit, all the colonies must be absolutely destroyed.

Sam Adams rubbed his hands with delight, even the Pennsylvania Legislature came to its American senses; other colonial legislatures, already incensed by government policy, allowed their anger to show by approving the Massachusetts Circular Letter – and were promptly prorogued. Individuals who had been moderates and who had urged patience with Parliament and overriding loyalty to Great Britain, now found themselves unwaveringly sympathetic towards the colonial cause. Down in Virginia a loyal soldier and servant of the British Government, Colonel George Washington, who had hitherto preached to others his policy of loyalty, now declared that if necessary he would take up arms rather than allow British freedom to vanish from the American colonies.

Under the Townshend duties, British tyranny became physically identifiable through the persons of the Commissioners of Customs and their customs-houses, and when Hillsborough underlined, by his stupidity, the apparent harshness of the Townshend duties, America replied with boycott. The mercantilists had long hoped for self-sufficiency within the British Empire, the Sons of Liberty now turned their own hopes upon them and looked for self-sufficiency within the American colonies. America, they urged, would have to develop its own industries. Americans must abhor imported luxuries and necessities. It became a patriotic virtue among colonial doctors that they should prescribe medicines compounded of American herbs. Benjamin Franklin urged his countrymen to turn from tippling rum – made from imported molasses – to the consumption of home-distilled whisky. 'That disagreeable noise made by the rattling of the foot-wheel was accounted fine music,' it was said, 'and preferred to the music of a violin that was imported from England since the non-importation agreement.' In tones beloved of a later age 'buy American' became the order of the day, and if Northern merchants and Southern planters saw in the boycott a useful means of relieving themselves of their habitual debt to British creditors, they could at least demonstrate in the process their patriotism and virtue. The whole of America was dressed in homespun; the minds of Americans were now as homespun as their dress.

It is probable that the Grafton ministry which succeeded to Chatham's would have liked to repeal the Townshend duties, if on economic grounds alone. Certainly Grafton himself argued that the disastrous effect of boycott upon British manufacture rendered the Townshend duties 'so uncommercial' that he was prepared to repeal them. But politics and pride outweighed economics and expedience. Lord North, the new Chancellor of the Exchequer, was so hot to teach the Americans a lesson that he forgot that though the responsibilities of his office might have justified him in any attempt to secure to Britain revenues from the colonies, it was not his duty to drive the colonies into out-and-out antagonism. Pride and anger, the fool's substitutes for wisdom and policy, drove him towards extremism, and the extremist (when he is, as North was, an able Parliamentarian) can invariably win leadership from men of moderation who have, nevertheless, no policy. 'Upon my word,' grumbled North, 'if we are to run after America in search of reconciliation, in this way, I do not know a single Act of Parliament that will remain.'

It was North's intention to divide the colonists one from the other by giving with the right hand and striking with the left. He would repeal some of Townshend's duties, but he would make it clear that he did so only because they were damaging British commerce, and, at the same time, he would continue authoritarianism in America. The most important of the Townshend duties, the only one which provided substantial revenue to the Home Country, and almost the only one which the Americans could not circumvent by boycott, was the tax on tea; this, North insisted, would never be repealed.

Some indication of the closeness of British opinion can be gleaned from the fact that the retention of the tea tax passed through the Cabinet by a majority of one, and though North's bullying voice struck up with that of Hillsborough – an unfortunate duet which was to echo in the ears of Americans for the next ten years – even some who were inclined to favour the colonial view felt that he had right on his side. Shelburne was among them and the Duke of Richmond, the most extreme of American partisans who nevertheless admitted to Burke that if Britain once gave up her sovereignty, she gave up everything. 'A peppercorn in acknowledgment of right is of more value than millions without' was the general argument of the House of Parliament, and the King himself spoke for most Members of Parliament when he declared that 'distant possession standing upon equality with a superior State is more ruinous than being deprived of such connections'.

Across the Atlantic the Massachusetts Speaker cried that 'if Parliament could bind the colonies they were all slaves'. Goodwill and compromise were now out of the reach of possibility.

CHAPTER 14

TRANSATLANTIC QUARRELS

THE economic breach between the Colonies and the Mother Country had grown over the years. The tobacco and rice planters of the South had resented all the acts of trade and navigation which forced them to export only to England. They had objected to the Staple Act of 1663 which had made it mandatory to buy in England. They had hated, though with less reason, the mortgaging of their trade to British merchants which had fastened on to them the burden of debts. They had objected to taxation from Britain which added much to their production costs and nothing to their profits. And they objected now to the Sugar Act, the Stamp Act, and the Townshend Acts which took away so much and gave nothing back.

Similarly the merchants of America had seen their profits cut, the cost of their imports increased by taxes, their trade in foreign markets restricted, and their possibilities of gaining credit reduced by currency policy. They could not speculate in Western land, nor could they set up joint stock corporations without Parliamentary permission. Instead, in certain areas of trade, they found themselves blocked by British monopoly.

The small farmer of America was taxed into debt and then, victim to currency policies, was unable to obtain cheap money to pay either tax or debt. When he could no longer keep up his Eastern farm, land policy forbade him to move West.

The labourer or the artisan, suffering bitterly from the depression years of 1764 to 1770, found the trade in which he had made his living destroyed by restriction, and as the restraints of new enterprise meant that there were few new jobs available, so did the restraints on Westward movement, after 1763, bring home to him the heightened competition for such jobs as there were in the cities. All classes in America were affected by the general rise in prices.

But if the economic pinch was felt by all Americans, such difficulties could never alone produce the unity of objection which now sprang readily from political deprivation: from the sense that liberty was threatened.

At about the same time that North was arranging to bring Americans to their knees for 'so paltry a sum in the eyes of a financier, so insignificant an article as tea in the eyes of a philosopher', the citizens of Boston were doing their part to make struggle bloody and inevitable. Up in arms against the customs officers, they hustled them with such vigour that the poor men, not altogether innocent and yet not altogether worthy of the abuse and violence that was meted out to them, had to appeal to General Gage, the new Governor of Massachusetts. An army of occupation was sent into Boston – an army that, because of the greater demands of India and of home defence, was hardly representative of the best elements in British soldiery.

Such was the behaviour of the British troops in Boston and such the advantage taken of this behaviour by Sam Adams and his colleagues, that the situation in Boston amounted to civil war even before a shot was fired. But, on the very day that North stood up in Parliament to announce that until the Americans behaved themselves they would win no further concessions from Britain, civil war became real. A small body of British soldiers, taunted beyond endurance, opened fire upon a mob of toughs on the Boston Rope Walk. The subsequent trial proved, even to many Americans, that the action had been taken in self-defence, but Sam Adams had his watchword, 'Remember the Boston Massacre!' In a sense 5 March 1770 was the first day of the American Revolutionary War, and by one of those strange quirks of history, the first martyr to the cause of American freedom was a Negro called Crispus Attucks. Those who were held responsible for the Boston massacre, the British forces, were exonerated, and rightly exonerated, by a civil court of law, and it is noteworthy that before this court of law the defence was conducted by John Adams. But the true responsibility for the massacre lay at the door of the man who now took greatest advantage of it. Sam Adams it was who had spent his time and political vigour upon stirring up trouble between the populace and the troops, and Sam Adams it was who leapt at the chances created by the Boston massacre and grasped them with the strength of the master publicist.

Revolution was in his bones; he was a rebel by nature and conviction came with nature. At everything else he had tried – at the law, at business, and even at tax collecting – he had been an utter failure, but he had a flair for political organization and for propaganda almost incomparable in American history. It is impossible to see in Sam Adams an addition to the calendar of American saints. He had neither the integrity of a Washington, the courage of a Patrick Henry, nor the philosophical genius of a Jefferson. In him there was none of the wisdom and learning that inspired his cousin John. Sam Adams was an opportunist, an intriguer, a political 'boss' to father generations of American political bosses; these qualities, if qualities they be, were just what America needed if the dispute with the Mother Country was to be turned from conflict over high political, high economic and high philosophical concerns beyond the interest of the common man, to those regions where the common man can be excited into action. Times were hard in America. The country was in ferment and the ferment was not all directed against Britain. Sam Adams took it upon himself to see that the embittered relations between the old and new sections of Pennsylvania should be forgotten in general anger against Britain; that the frontiersmen of North Carolina should lose their ire against the tax-collectors of the Eastern counties in general animosity towards Britain; that the poor should be made to ignore their natural jealousy of the rich and should turn instead to hatred of the British; that the rich should be befuddled into thinking that they did not really want peace with Britain and should instead stand up as leaders of the common people whom they despised.

For all his tinder-box quality Adams was an efficient organizer of revolution. More than Pym, Hampden, or even Cromwell, more than Marat or Robespierre, he was faced with a major organizational problem, in embryo the problem which was to face the makers of the American Constitution: how to unite in interest and action groups not yet united by habit, philosophy, economic consideration, tradition and separated above all, by geography and by the difficulty of communication.

The Committees of Correspondence, not unlike the 'Committees of Safety' and the 'cells' of a later date, but far more practical than either, were a stroke of genius, and the genius who gave the stroke was Sam Adams:

At a meeting of the freeholders and other inhabitants of the Town of Boston, duly qualified and legally warned, in public town meeting assembled at Faneui Hall, on Wednesday the 28th day of October 1772 ... it was moved by Mr Samuel Adams that a Committee of Correspondence be appointed, to consist of twenty-one persons, to state the Rights of the Colonists and of this Province in particular, as men, as Christians, and as subjects; to communicate the same to the several towns in this Province, and to the World, as the sense of this Town, with the infringements and violations thereof that have been, or from time to time may be made – also requesting of each Town a free communication of their sentiments on this subject.

The request was met; in each town, in each colony, similar Committees were set up with the means of communication between them. Before long intra- and inter-colonial conventions of committees were organized; the machinery for revolution was keeping pace with the urge to make revolution.

By the time that Sam Adams came to the fore as a leader of revolution, it was clear to him that rebellion against Britain need not necessarily confine itself to the intellectual movement, a form of considered opposition; it was to Adams's advantage that he was able to take over and to strengthen emotional and unreasoned objection to British rule, the objection of the less educated masses. Even in this he could find support and precedent in the feeling, already well developed in Britain itself as well as in America, that the popular cause was not safe in the hands of orthodox Whigs.

To those in America who came to support Adams's belligerent policies, the outstanding politician of Great Britain was not Grenville or Townshend, North or Pitt himself, but John Wilkes the radical. It is significant that between 1768 and 1771, though Wilkes was out of office, his activities received more press comment in North America than in Britain and were certainly more fully reported than those of any other British political figure. The articles of some of the small London political societies which were formed to stand by Wilkes in his 'martyrdom', were drafted in almost identical terms with those of the North and South Carolina Regulators; one of these London groups actually borrowed Sam Adams's name for his own group and called them 'Sons of Liberty'. Wilkes himself, like Adams ever ready to seize upon distant grievance to feed the flames of present discontent, was never averse from casting an eye over his shoulder to the political hardships of those in America and Ireland, and so in both America and Ireland became a hero of causes with which he was not much concerned. In the whole battle between Wilkes and his king, Sam Adams, as eventually a majority in the colonies, was able to appreciate the hopelessness and the political folly of attempting to differentiate between King and Parliament, of attempting to resist the power of the Commons and the overweening authority of the Ministry while still bending a respectful knee towards the monarch. In the days of the Stamp Act the Americans still held to the view that the nice balance of the British Constitution demanded that George the Third guard colonials against excesses of Parliamentary authority. 'The Parliament which represents the people of England,' wrote a New York newspaper in 1766, 'have no right of sovereignty over us; but the King has a constitutional right, and that we always have submitted to and always shall.' The proof that this optimistic prophecy was soon proved fallacious lay as much in George's personal animosity towards Wilkes and the British Radical Party as in his failure to stand up for the rights of his colonial peoples.

Wilkes fell from grace as a radical leader into the comforts of the City of London, but the radical movement continued in Britain as an example and as an inspiration to American rebels, and the growth of anti-monarchism in British political life was paralleled by the growth of anti-monarchism in America. By 1770 the writings of Junius, that brilliant, if mysterious, radical commentator, were being reprinted in many colonial newspapers. Even five years before they would have been considered not merely objectionable but also positively antagonistic to the conviction then held that American principles would and should be guarded by the King.

Pitt and his moderate Whigs were alive to the excessive power of the throne. 'The influence of the Crown,' said Pitt, 'is become so enormous that some stronger bulwark must be erected for the preservation of the Constitution.' But theirs was the awareness of political philosophers; the Radicals expressed their convictions in terms more readily comprehensible to everyman, for theirs was the language of rebels. To them, as to Sam Adams, George the Third was nothing but a tyrant; to each of them (and by 1771 it was almost possible to regard the English and American radical movements as one) his tyrannies were deliberately directed against the peculiar principles by each most beloved. 'You may depend upon it,' wrote Arthur Lee of Virginia to Sam Adams on the question of the Townshend Act, 'that the later American Act of Revenue moved from the throne with the insidious view of dividing American opposition.'

Nevertheless the course towards revolution was erratic indeed, and for almost three years after the Boston Massacre it seemed as if America might be forced back into decent subservience. For this apparent change of heart, which satisfied neither North on the one hand nor Sam Adams on the other, each of whom wanted definite but contradictory conclusions, the fears of the American oligarchy were responsible, and here once more can be seen at work the inevitable conflict between Whig and Radical. The merchants of New York, for example, the colony of all colonies most subject to class struggle, were almost unanimously opposed to the repressive economic policies of the House of Commons; in the early days of the struggle, New York merchant aristocrats, like the Delanceys and the Livingstons, were opposed to each other only in their eagerness to head the opposition to Britain. But soon, in New York, as all over the country, such men wakened to the realization that there could be tyranny from below as well as tyranny from above. 'It is high time a stop was put to mobbing,' said the voice of the merchants speaking through the mouth of the *New York Gazette* and *Weekly Mercury* in July 1770, 'without which property will soon be very precarious, as God knows where it will end.' Interests of purse and pride came together in the hearts of the merchants. They could not afford to stand by the non-importation agreement, they could not abide the company they were forced to keep in opposition to Britain, nor the fact that the wishes of 'men of liberal education' should be 'dictated to by illiterate mechanicks' and by 'every insignificant Whiffler that can scarce spell his name'.

New York, which had for a while held more rigorously than any other colonial port to the terms of the agreement, was forced out of it by its merchants. Elsewhere, even such ardent rebels as the author of *Letters from a Farmer in Pennsylvania*, found convenience more important than convictions; for John Dickinson had now settled with his rich Quakeress wife in a glorious country house near Philadelphia. Virginian aristocrats – and most Virginian aristocrats were merchants of one kind or another – found themselves, for the first time for several years, with a thoroughly aristocratic governor, Lord Botetourt, and liked what they found, with the inevitable consequence that there was a noticeable diminution in their animosity towards the country which had sent such grandeur among them. In South Carolina, Christopher Gadsen found the need for 'a receipt effectively to cure supineness'. Everywhere, except among those few devoted to Sam Adams and his activities, the middle classes and the aristocracy were only eager to return to making money, and everywhere they felt that making money and making politics could not coincide.

George Mason of Virginia wrote that 'there are not five men of sense in America who would accept of independence if it were offered; we know our circumstances too well; we know that our happiness, our very being depend upon our being connected with our Mother Country'. As in 1770 the trade between Britain and the American colonies totalled almost eight million pounds and was estimated as one-third of all the trade in the Empire, there were many, both American and British, who agreed with him.

For a few months, while American Tories came into their own, American Whigs attempted to achieve a compromise between their economic interests and their political desires, and American Radicals struggled miserably to keep the fires of revolution burning. In opposition to Britain it seemed that there could be no unanimity in America; although Americans might cry loudly against British oppression, those who had most power in the colonies had no intention of sacrificing their own right to oppress. But the Radicals were still at work, determined that the buried hatchet should be uncovered, and in 1773 when he passed the Tea Act North gave them the opportunity for which they longed.

The history of the approach to revolution is full of strange contradictions, but none is stranger than the fact that one of the prime causes of the final outbreak was this Act which, in so many ways, gave to the American colonials all that they had long asked. The East India Company was in great distress and there was in America much sympathy for the Company. Americans saw its future as a symbol of the future of all royal charters, including the charters of the American colonies. They had themselves contributed considerably to the difficulties of the East India Company by refusing to drink tea as a protest against the Townshend Acts. Now North made what was for him a great concession. He eliminated the English middle-men who bought their tea at the Company's auctions in London and resold it to American merchants: the East India Company was given the right to export tea directly to America. As a result of this, East India Company tea could be sold in America at a much lower price than it was sold at in England itself. But to preserve the appearance of authority, North insisted that the tea should still bear a threepenny tax. And with a natural eagerness to ride both horses, the East India Company arranged to market its tea in America through the offices of men who were known to be favourable to the Government, rather than through the great merchants who had in recent years shown their patriotism by making large fortunes out of smuggling.

This threepenny tax gave the radicals another stick with which to beat the British Government; the cheap price of tea, undercutting as it did the prices charged by the smugglers, aroused one group of merchants, and it was John Hancock, the 'Prince of Smugglers' (who within two years was to be on trial before the Boston Admiralty Court for a hundred thousand pounds penalties incurred as a smuggler), who raised the cry of monopoly. If the Tea Act were accepted, said Hancock piously, 'We soon should have found our trade in the hands of foreigners . . . nor would it have been strange, if, in a few years, a company in London should have purchased an exclusive route of trading to America.' The threat of monopoly aroused virtually all businessmen – even those who had not been engaged in smuggling. The Sons of Liberty urged their wives and daughters to resist the great temptation that was before them. 'Do not suffer yourself to sip the accursed STUFF, for if you do the devil will immediately enter into you and you will instantly become a traitor to your country', and such was their success that when tea was found to be in the possession of a citizen of Bedford, Massachusetts, radicals of that town gave him the alternative of giving up his tea or being turned over to the women of Bedford. The choice was no choice, and instead of tea and misery he received 'three cheers from the Sons and a glass of American wine from the Daughters of Liberty'.

Faced with such unanimity, the consignees of tea looked for a moment to the British Government for protection, found none, and promptly resigned their privileges.

In December 1773, three tea-ships arrived in the port of Boston with cargoes valued at some one hundred and fifty thousand pounds. Sam Adams and John Hancock had the chance they needed. On the night of 16 December they gathered together several thousand colonials in Old South Meeting House and demanded that the tea-ships return with their cargoes to England. Governor Hutchinson refused to give way, believing as he did that another retreat would be fatal to British sovereignty. Elsewhere in America, tea had been prevented from being landed but no violence had been used. Here, in Boston, fifty Bostonians, painted and dressed as Indians, rushed to the docks and poured the tea into Boston Harbour. The Americans had done with tea, had done with it almost for ever, and in this moment of excitement Sam Adams made a point which for years he had failed to make: he had made calmness an impossibility.

The news of the Tea Party reached England in mid-January; it could hardly be expected that such wanton defiance, when coupled with a blow at commerce, could pass unpunished. The whole British nation was agreed that Boston should suffer for its impertinence, and the first measure in its suffering was the Boston Port Bill, drafted by Dartmouth, who had hitherto shown himself to be a genuine friend of the Americans. The Port of Boston was to be closed and the customs transferred to Salem until such time as Boston made compensation to the East India Company and gave guarantees for future good behaviour. There followed a Government of Massachusetts Bill under which the Government would have power to appoint all officers exercising civil authority and to nominate the members of the Council, and a bill to reform the magistrature which also followed the precedent of Scotland thirty years earlier, at the time of the Forty Five, by empowering the Governor to send accused persons to a neighbouring colony or to England for trial.

Just as at the time of the Townshend Act many American colonies which had hitherto shown little sympathy with New York had learnt sympathy from the suspension of the New York Provincial Assembly, so now ports which had scarcely loved Boston saw their own liberties and wealth threatened by the Boston Port Bill.

That all these acts would in turn inflame American opposition seems not to have deterred Parliament, which passed all three bills by a formidable majority. When finally the news did reach America, not even the terms of these three acts aroused so much anger as the fact that a soldier had been given the task of enforcing them. By transferring Thomas Gage from his post as Commander-in-Chief of the British Forces in America to the post of Governor of Massachusetts, the British Government, it seemed to Americans, had proclaimed its intention of using force where persuasion could not succeed.

Force or persuasion, Gage was hardly the man for the task. When, in 1754, Thomas Gage landed in North America for the first time, he was already thirty-four years old. Family tradition and the hearty support of his father, the first Viscount Gage – 'a petulant, silly, busy, meddling, profligate fellow' – had failed to foist him upon the electors of Tewkesbury, but he was a Lieutenant-Colonel, battle-tested at Fontenoy and Culloden and, for a professional soldier who could support his dreams with an adequate income and a powerful connexion, North America held promise of advancement unequalled elsewhere in the British service.

Measured by simple chronological progress, the promise was amply fulfilled: in 1760 Gage became military governor of Montreal; in 1763 Commander-in-Chief of the British Forces in North America, and in 1774 Governor of Massachusetts. His catalogue of active service has a more shameful ring: Fort Duquesne, Pontiac's War, the Boston 'Massacre',

Lexington, Bunker Hill; always he was associated with disaster or empty victory. But historians, looking upon the past with supercilious wisdom, for ever seeing the consequence before the event, judge him principally for his inability to sense the development of revolutionary ideology and, for his ineffective antagonism to American independence, discard him as a shambling incompetent. More than that of most failures his reputation has found history uncharitable, for the interpretation of his career has been left to American historians who are slow to reject the prejudices of revolutionary propaganda, while the few British interlopers who have trespassed in this field of British colonial history, overeasily depressed by its plethora of mediocrities, have not exerted themselves on behalf of a man who did his duty by his own dim lights. Coincident death and victory secured the fame of Gage's friend, James Wolfe; George Augustus, Lord Howe, fell before Ticonderoga in 1758 and is granted, even by American historians, the quality of his courage; Gage muddled his honest way to power when the loyal disagreement of Americans was turning to violent rebellion, and not death nor success compensated for his offences.

Gage was neither hero nor genius, but the obstacles that stood before him make it obvious that his faults were stumbles and not vicious kicks at progress. He had served for twenty years in America, married an American wife, and bought American estates. He belonged, in a sense, to the American tradition but to such a small part of it as was now vanishing from the American scene. From Gage and his colleagues the conservative strain in American life might have taken new inspiration, and had he been more competent in expressing his convictions, the Loyalist movement might have found in him the leader that it had not found elsewhere.

But the pattern of Gage's career was one that is tragically familiar. A trained soldier, he was expected to play a role that defied the skill of trained diplomatists. When he acted he was abused by his neighbours in America and repudiated by his masters in England; when he hesitated he was casti-

gated with equal energy by Whig, Tory, Loyalist, and
Patriot. His vague instructions from above were always so
worded that, for failure he would be the scapegoat, and for
success the Government could claim the honour. His stolid
loyalty led him to forward to London advice that was worthless when he gave it and fatal by the time that it was finally
implemented. Ruthlessness was his panacea; he struck
blindly at apparent ingratitude, was bewildered by uncom-
prehended treachery, and was utterly confused when his
cure spread the germs of the disease he was fighting. Devotion to George the Third was by 1774 a virtue utterly
unrecognized by Americans.

CHAPTER 15

THE LAST OF PEACE

ON 13 May 1774 General Gage arrived in Boston to supplant Hutchinson as Governor of Massachusetts. On the same day, in Boston, a town meeting called for a renewal of economic sanctions to force the repeal of the Coercive Acts, and almost immediately the Bostonians put into effect Sam Adams's eighteen-months-old plan for a Committee of Correspondence; a plan which he had designed for just such a purpose as this: to pass on to the other towns of America his conviction that Boston was the front-line of liberty.

Paul Revere rode out to New York and Philadelphia with appeals for aid and with the suggestion that all colonies should subscribe to a new non-importation agreement. Individuals responded valiantly. Down in Virginia George Washington realized that the matter of greatest moment was whether his countrymen would sit 'supinely, and see one province after another fall to despotism'. But the colonial leaders proved their lingering Britishness even in their opposition to Britain: they were prepared to act but not until they had had a meeting to discuss their action. On 17 May, Providence, Rhode Island, issued the first of many calls for an inter-colonial congress, and though Boston's Committee of Correspondence drew up a solemn league which bound all subscribers to end all mercantile dealings with Britain on 1 October, the pressure for discussion was too great even for Massachusetts, and in mid-June the affair was moved from the realm of private action to the realm of legislative discussion. It was then that the Massachusetts House of Representatives suggested that a congress of all the colonies should be held in September at Philadelphia.

Once more it seemed that the moderates among the patriots had won a victory over the radicals and that, with the Tories clinging to their hems, opponents of Adams and action would win time for discussion and compromise.

Benjamin Franklin grumbled from London that the Bostonians had gone too far, that they should waste no time before offering apologies and compensations to the East India Company, and apologies, with concessions, to the royal Government.

All the colonies but Georgia agreed to send delegates to Philadelphia, yet it was apparent from the very beginning that there was little agreement about the purposes that the Congress was to fulfil. Even the implementation of the Boston Port Act, though, on the one hand, it came near to making the Bostonians martyrs to the American cause, and thus, on the other hand, increased the sympathy felt towards Boston by colonials of more conservative tendency elsewhere, did not bring about the unity which the very fact of inter-colonial congress seemed to imply.

Of those who came to Philadelphia in the first week of September 1774 there are many whose names seemed even at the time a promise of great things to come. No less an authority on statesmanship than the great Chatham himself is said to have described it as 'the most honourable assembly of statesmen since those of the ancient Greeks and Romans in the most virtuous times'. But John Adams, who was there and who himself added much to the composition of statesmanship, called it with less kindliness a gathering of 'one-third Tories, another Whigs, and the rest mongrels, with Trimmers and Time-Servers on the other side'.

Whatever their quality of statesmanship, these delegates to Philadelphia could hardly pretend to represent the common people. They were the American aristocracy; the merchants, the lawyers, and the great planters of the South.

Had the leadership of the Radical wing remained with Sam Adams it is possible that fear and despising of Boston violence of extremism might have given an opportunity to those of conservative views to win the day, but the radicals played well the political game and, in Philadelphia, seemed content to work behind the scenes and to leave the appearance of political leadership to the unexceptionable delegates from the Southern colonies. Even the non-importation and non-exportation agreement was passed on a motion by Richard Henry Lee of Virginia. Thus it was that 'Adams, with his crew of haughty Sultans of the South, juggled the whole conclave of the delegates'. On 17 September a series of resolves, which had originally been adopted a week earlier by a convention in Suffolk County, Massachusetts, and brought to Philadelphia by the indefatigable Revere, were endorsed by the Congress. These resolutions declared the Coercive Acts unconstitutional and, therefore, not worthy of obedience, they urged the people of Massachusetts to refuse taxes to the royal Governor until the repeal of the Acts, and they recommended sanctions against Britain. Most significant of all, they advised the people to arm. To ensure that the resolutions would be enforced an Association was set up to deal with offenders against the common wish.

Finally, the Congress drafted and sent off appeals to George the Third and to the people of Great Britain. The conservative element in the Congress was still strong enough to add tactful frills to pointed accusations; there were, even now, references to 'affection to our parent state' and the delegates described themselves as 'Your Majesty's faithful subjects'. But the frills were woven by habit, and by habit alone.

Rumour, always a fine ally to revolution, shattered the last hope of compromise, and the story which spread by the winds of gossip and the fans of the Sons of Liberty, that General Gage was slaughtering Bostonians (though it may have given a moment of pleasure to mere New Yorkers or Virginians) could but arouse 'the awful genius of America'. Blood was up; conciliation was now impossible; if necessary the Americans would fight. And many of them believed with Patrick Henry that 'the next gale from the North will bring to our ears the clash of resounding arms'. Some even listened, as did Henry, in the hope that the gale would blow soon.

But the Americans, like their not-so-distant cousins the British, believed that trade was more powerful than war. With great enthusiasm they planned more and more econo-

mic sanctions and boasted cheerfully to each other that
bankruptcy for Britain would bring victory without battle
to America. The Pennsylvania Association, closely modelled
upon a Virginia Association which had been drawn up in
August, consisted of a pledge by each province that within
six weeks it would cease all importation from Britain, that
within the same period it would discontinue the slave trade,
that by 1 March 1775 all exports to Britain, Ireland,
and the West Indies would cease. These were stern economic measures and their implementation would have spelt
disaster indeed for many in Britain as for many in the
colonies, but the delegates of the Continental Congress were
not satisfied with practical severity. To the North lay the
great new British possession, French-speaking and Catholic,
and yet sensibly held to its new-found allegiance by moderate legislation. It is one of the wonders of history that the
Quebec Act should have been passed in the very same year
that saw the passage of the Coercive Acts, but the American
delegates at Philadelphia held firmly to their view that all
must agree with them that Britain was a tyrant. And so they
passed a high-sounding *Address to the Inhabitants of Canada*,
which can but be regarded as one of the most stupid documents drafted in the whole history of the world by a body of
distinguished politicians. Not only were the Canadians invited to renounce George the Third, but they were also
informed that the British had forced on them the tyranny of
Catholicism. The Quebec Act was a vicious papistical,
monarchical, imperialistic document. If only the Canadians
would join the American cause, they could be free from
Westminster and from Rome.

The realities of the Canadian situation were apparently
never clear to American leaders. Fearing the Pope only
slightly less than they feared George the Third, the stupidities of their anti-Canadian activity at the Congress and in
the next few months did much to secure the position of
Britain in Canada. Within twenty years after the defeat of
Montcalm, French troops were again on American soil
fighting alongside the Americans against the old enemies of

French Canada. Yet, because the French-Canadians disliked and despised the American provincials far more than they could ever despise or dislike the new rulers of French Canada, few French Canadians went over to the side of the Revolution.

During the winter of 1774 hotheads in Massachusetts, both among the Sons of Liberty and among the British officers, waited eagerly for an opportunity to break the false peace. Neither side wanted to fire the first shot, but both sides were eager to load the musket. The winter passed and most of the spring, and then suddenly the American Revolution, which had been inevitable for so long that it almost seemed as if time might prevent its outbreak, flared into life.

In origin, as in implications, the War of the American Revolution was a civil war. On one side of the Atlantic Briton argued against Briton over rights and wrongs, hopes and frustrations – and no blood was shed. On the other side of the Atlantic some Britons, living thousands of miles from Britain itself, fought against their neighbours and against the professional soldiers who were sent out to police them – and thousands lost their lives. In the bloody and in the bloodless war, the terms of the dispute were one. The character of the disputants was changed only by the shedding of blood. Even Americanism need not have been antithetical to Britishness, and in the long years of the War there were still many on both sides who would have welcomed a victory for their own side which would not necessarily have involved complete defeat for the other.

The relationship between the Colonies and England during these years was complex and curiously ambivalent. The colonists, especially in the flush of patriotism that followed the victorious wars with France and Spain, were loyally British. Francis Hopkinson, who ten years later signed the Declaration of Independence, wrote in 1766, 'We in America are in all respects Englishmen, notwithstanding that the Atlantic rolls her waves between us and the throne to which we all owe allegiance.' Much of this genuine loyalty lasted beyond the verge of revolution. The

Virginia Convention of 1774, rebellious as it was, nevertheless vowed 'inviolable and unshaken fidelity and attachment' to England, and Jefferson, two months after Bunker Hill, wrote that he looked 'with fondness towards a reconciliation with Great Britain'. President Ezra Stiles of Yale, an avowed rebel, nostalgically recalled even in the midst of the war 'the ancient national affection we once had for the parent state, which we gloried in being part of the Empire'.

Yet at the same time the American colonist for some years had thought of himself as an Englishman with a difference. The years after the French and Indian War witnessed the development of a sense of colonial solidarity that marked the first stages of what would become an American nationalism. A conflict was beginning between a set of colonies that – though colonial loyalties were strong – was beginning to feel like a nation, and a central government that was determined to knit its empire together after a long, weary war. After 1763 the colonies unconsciously began to close ranks against British authority and to think of themselves as 'American' Englishmen, and even 'Americans'. It is impossible, of course, to point to a particular year or incident and say, 'Here Americanism begins', but it is certain that by the seventies the colonists conceived of themselves as a special kind of Briton, possessed a common outlook and a sense of relationship that could best be described as American. The term seemed to have a meaning distinct from 'British' or 'English' that the term 'West Indian', for example, did not have. It was normal for Franklin's Poor Richard, who was no revolutionary, to speak of his countrymen as 'American patriots', or for Dr William Smith of Philadelphia, long before the Revolution, to speak of the colonies as 'our nation' with no sense of disloyalty to England.

The American colonist after 1760 considered himself to be as loyal as any Englishman living in England, but he had a distinct and separate regard for his native colony and how it fitted into the imperial frame. There were two English societies – his own and the one centred in London – and by insisting that both be equally recognized he widened the rift already opened by the French wars. Some colonists were careful to emphasize their dual allegiance: Franklin did not call himself a British subject, but 'an American subject of the King', and young Alexander Hamilton argued with his Loyalist opponent Samuel Seabury that 'we are a part of the British Empire, but in this sense only, as being the free-born subjects of His Britannic Majesty'. The growing national spirit provided a wider dimension to the arguments with Britain over colonial policy, and contributed eventually to the decision of independence. This is no doubt what John Adams meant, in part, when he remarked later that 'The revolution was effected before the war commenced. The revolution was in the hearts and minds of the people.'

The intervention of France gave an international accent to a private squabble, but at least in the early years of the War it was possible to assume that America was the scene of two separate struggles; the struggle within an empire and the struggle between empires, and that only because it was convenient for the Americans to have allies, and for the French to seize any excuse to belabour Britain, did these struggles come into coincidence.

In international war it used not to be difficult to decide who had fired the first shot. Civil war is always another matter; a brawl in the streets, a stone from a mob, a trooper's horse ridden carelessly or deliberately into a crowd: these are the things which start civil wars and these the things which it is difficult for an historian to establish. Blame here or blame there; no one can say. Previous events and previous conflicts predestine battles; the moment for the beginning of battle is unimportant, the responsibility for its commencement an intriguing puzzle, but hardly an important problem.

Thus it is that 'the shot that was heard round the world' may have come from Briton or from colonial and the decision as to who actually fired it depends almost entirely upon the nationality of the decider.

The shot was fired on 19 April 1775, at Lexington, Massachusetts, but even to disentangle this event from the mass of causation which made the War of the Revolution it is necessary to go back to 1 September of the previous year, when British troops from Boston marched out to Charleston and Cambridge and seized arms and ammunition belonging to the province. Then it was that the militiamen first turned out in force and then it was that General Gage faced the threat by fortifying Boston Neck against the hostile provincials. On 7 October the Massachusetts House had met in Salem and constituted itself for provincial congress. John Hancock, arch smuggler and principal ally of Samuel Adams, was given the control of the Committee of Safety with power to call out the militia. Special groups within the militia stood by to be called out at a moment's notice and, just before Christmas in 1774, on the warning that the British garrison at Portsmouth, New Hampshire, was being strengthened (a warning given, as usual, by Paul Revere, who should have won glory as a silversmith, but had secured his fame by riding hither and thither as stirrer-up and messenger of trouble), the minute-men broke into the British fort and carried away both arms and ammunition, though without causing or receiving casualties.

Meanwhile, in England, wiser statesmen than North were attempting to avoid or postpone the inevitable. On 19 January 1775 petitions of the Continental Congress were laid before Parliament, and on the next day Chatham moved an address from the Lords to the King requesting the immediate removal of troops from Boston. This was roundly defeated, as was the attempt at reconciliation put forward by Chatham two weeks later. Instead, on 9 February, both Houses deemed Massachusetts to be in revolution. Some grudging concessions were allowed by Lord North, but were nullified by a bill, introduced late in February, which forbade New England colonies to trade with any nation but Britain and the West Indies and barred New Englanders from the North Atlantic fisheries.

To the side of Chatham came another great Parliamentarian, Edmund Burke. It has been said of these two that 'Chatham supplied his hearers with motives to immediate action. Burke furnished them with reasons for action, which might have little effect upon them at the time, but for which they would be the wiser and better all their lives after.' It has been said too that Burke was no orator, but certainly, in reading his various speeches in this crisis of imperial history and, above all, his speech against the New England Restraining Act, addressed to the House of Commons on 22 March 1775, has all the power of logic, passion, and poetry which, together with power of voice, go to make up great oratory:

We are indeed, in all disputes with the colonies, by the necessity of things, the judge. It is true, Sir, but I confess, that the character of judge in my own cause, is a thing that frightens me. Instead of filling me with pride, I am exceedingly humbled by it. I cannot proceed with a stern, assured, judicial confidence, until I find myself in something more like a judicial character. I must have these hesitations as long as I am compelled to recollect, that, in my little reading upon such contests as these, the cause of mankind has, at least, as often decided against the superior as the subordinate power. Sir, let me add too, that the opinion of my having some abstract right in my favour would not put me at my ease in passing sentence; unless I could be sure that there were no rights which, in their exercise under certain circumstances, were not the most odious of all wrongs, and the most vexatious of all injustice. Sir, these considerations have great weight with me, when I find things so circumstanced, that I see the same party, at once a civil litigant against me in point of right, and a culprit before me; while I sit as criminal judge on acts of his, whose moral quality is to be decided upon the merits of that very litigation. Men are every now and then put, by the complexity of human affairs, into strange situations; but justice is the same, let the judge be in what situation he will. . . . All this, I know well enough, will sound wild and chimerical to the profane herd of those vulgar and mechanical politicans, who have no place among us; a sort of people who think that nothing exists but what is gross and material; and who therefore, far from being qualified to be directors of the great movement of empire, are not fit to turn a wheel in the machine. But to men truly initiated and rightly taught, these ruling and master principles, which, in the opinion of such men as I have mentioned, have no substantial existence, are in truth every thing, and all in all.

Magnanimity in politics is not seldom the truest wisdom; and a great empire and little minds go ill together. If we are conscious of our situation, and glow with zeal to fill our places as becomes our station and ourselves, we ought to auspicate all our public proceeding on America with the old warning of the church, *Sursum corda!* We ought to elevate our minds to the greatness of that trust to which the order of Providence has called us. By adverting to the dignity of this high calling, our ancestors have turned a savage wilderness into a glorious empire; and have made the most extensive, and the only honourable conquests; not by destroying, but by promoting, the wealth, the number, the happiness of the human race. Let us get an American revenue as we have got an American empire. English privileges have made it all that it is; English privileges alone will make it all it can be.

But against the obstinacy of men hurt in their pride the combined brilliance of Chatham and Burke was of no avail. The New England Restraining Act came into force on 30 March, and on 13 April, when news of the ratification of the Continental Association had reached London, its provisions were extended to include New Jersey, Pennsylvania, Maryland, Virginia, and South Carolina.

On 1 February the second Provincial Congress had met at Cambridge, Massachusetts, and had framed measures to prepare that colony for war. At the end of February British troops landed at Salem to seize military supplies, but were turned back without violence. Down in Virginia, there still seemed some hope that that colony, as ever with Massachusetts a keystone to colonial organization, would not go the whole way to resistance. The royal Governor, Lord Dunmore, who appears in American history as a shambling figure, half villain and half fool, had done his utmost to avoid the worst effects of the actions of Parliament and had, in fact, reasoned with courageous and intelligent casuistry to circumvent one Act of Parliament which seemed likely to make Virginians active rather than passive in their support of Massachusetts: the Act which closed the Western lands to settlement. But hustled from London and harassed in the colony by extremists on both sides, Dunmore was forced to prorogue the House of Burgesses.

In its place there met, at St John's Church in Richmond, the second Virginia Convention. Still drawn from the substantial group in Virginian life, the Convention included such leaders as Bland, Harrison, and Pendleton, who disliked indulging in acts which would bring about a recourse to arms, and Patrick Henry's resolution calling for the embodiment of the Virginia militia was strongly opposed. But the fire and logic of the greatest orator in America were too much for the forces of moderation. In the minds and hearts of Virginians there were the words of Patrick Henry, 'I know not what course others may take; but as for me, give me liberty or give me death!' There was no British force quartered in Virginia except the small ceremonial guard at the Governor's Palace, but by mid-April the Virginian militia was out to fight the troops who were not there. Dunmore retaliated by bringing sailors from the ships at Norfolk to seize the powder in the powder magazine at Williamsburg, but without force to support him his action was nugatory, and Dunmore, his wife, and his children left the capital in June for the comparative safety of one of His Majesty's ships of war.

In Richmond, Patrick Henry had predicted that the news of the outbreak of fighting in New England would be received almost immediately and his prophecy proved only too true.

On 14 April a letter from Lord Dartmouth reached Gage ordering him to use force if need be to support the Coercive Acts. (Gage also had orders to arrest Adams and Hancock and send them to England for trial.) Gage moved troops immediately towards Concord, a major supply depot for the provincial milita. Out went the ever-ready Paul Revere to warn the minute-men, and at Lexington, on the morning of 19 April 1775, British and American troops faced each other. To two comparatively junior officers, Major John Pitcairn for the British and Captain John Parker for the Americans, must be left the responsibility for starting the American Revolutionary War. Someone gave an order, someone fired a shot, there were more orders and more shots. The American empire was in rebellion.

Still, in a sense, the fight was between Massachusetts and Great Britain, but Lexington destroyed the reality of British authority over all the American colonies. The first excitements had given to the revolutionary cause its first encouragement. In most of the colonies, Committees of Safety took over executive power; there was, as yet, no American government, and even the second Continental Congress, which met in May of 1775 – and its successors until 1781 – had no centralizing authority except that of conducting the war.

Nor did the shots at Lexington turn all Americans suddenly to violent rebellion; there were divisions between colonials and colonials just as there were between colonials and British, and between British and British. The Revolution was partly a class conflict with most of the poorer classes fierce against British power. But the planters of Virginia and the South who resented British economic control stood firmly on the American side with only an occasional distinguished exception, such as Sir John Randolph, to prove that like could call to like even against the interests of the pocket.

On the other hand there were areas of New Jersey, Delaware, Maryland, Eastern Pennsylvania, and on the frontiers of Georgia and the Carolinas where economic interests or local political squabbles held much of the population to the British cause. Throughout the War, in every community there were secret Loyalists, and in every community there were Loyalists who came out with each British victory. There were more Loyalists in New York than any other colony and fewer perhaps in Virginia. In Pennsylvania there were so many that Timothy Pickering described it as ' enemy's country ' and John Adams himself produced the surprising comment that New York and Pennsylvania were so nearly divided – 'if their propensity was not against us, that if New England on one side and Virginia on the other had not kept them in awe, they would have joined the British '. It was Adams, too, who gave, much later in his life, his opinion that at least one million of the three million colonials could be classed as Loyalists, and a prejudiced Loyalist historian, writing only a few years after the events, vowed that if only the issues had been put to the vote, the Loyalist cause would have won the War.

Between Loyalist and Son of Liberty there was a large gap and in this gap still, in 1775, there stood the majority of the American people. For them, many of the doctrines which were eventually implicit in the American Revolution were doctrines that were established *ex post facto*; grievances unrequited forced them on to the side of Revolution, but almost until the moment of Revolution, although they accepted the need for indignation, they accepted no other philosophy of revolution. Until the last moments, leaders of such independent frame of mind as John Adams and Benjamin Franklin sought after means of securing satisfaction without violence. 'We are a part of the British Dominions,' wrote John Adams as late as January 1775, 'that is of the King of Great Britain. And it is our interest and duty to continue subject to the authority of Parliament in the regulation of our trade, as long as she shall leave us to govern our internal policy and to give and grant our own money, and no longer.' And a month later Franklin wrote, 'I would try anything, and bear anything that can be borne with safety to our just principles rather than engage in a war with such relations unless compelled to it in dire necessity in our own defence.'

The final *Declaration of Causes of Taking Up Arms*, drafted in part by Thomas Jefferson and issued over the signature of John Hancock on 6 July 1775 still held to the belief that war did not mean the dissolution of the empire:

We have not raised armies with ambitious designs of separating from Great Britain and establishing independent States . . . with an humble faith in the mercies of the supreme and impartial Judge and Ruler of the universe, we must devoutly implore His Divine Goodness to protect us happily through this great conflict, to dispose our adversaries to reconciliation on reasonable terms, and thereby to relieve the empire from the calamities of civil war.

A civil war, a class war, a war based on economic differences, but hardly at first a war for ideals. Not until the ideas which Sam Adams had been pouring out for ten years or more coincided with the expressions of Thomas Jefferson's thought in the Declaration of Independence did the 'rights of man' and notions of freedom or equality play much part in the American revolutionary urge. The pattern of American society was still unsettled in 1775; in 1776 Jefferson's dream was put into words, and throughout the Revolution, not suddenly, not obviously, but gradually and almost without self-knowledge the American people worked out their political future.

During the Revolution the State capitals of Virginia, North Carolina, South Carolina, Georgia, and not long after, the capitals of Pennsylvania and New York, were moved inland, and the movement symbolized the decline of the seaboard aristocracies. There was a general recognition of the importance of the Western regions; a recognition which Britain had never given; a general willingness to recognize an agrarian democracy. Only in Massachusetts, Virginia, and South Carolina did the wealthy classes retain some control when those states adopted their new constitutions. Even in Virginia a back-country lawyer, Patrick Henry, took over as Governor of the State.

State governments found themselves possessed of the estates of departed Loyalists and of Crown lands; such were broken up into small farms and either sold or given as bounties to soldiers. Most of the states abandoned principles of primogeniture – a further attack on the aristocracy. The privileged position of the Church of England went by the board and with it, everywhere except in New England, the connexion between church and state.

'We hold these truths to be self-evident,' wrote Thomas Jefferson long before they were self-evident even to the Americans who supported his words, 'that all men are created equal.' In the next seven years the weight as well as the sound of his sentence won general approval among Americans.

There is an awful and thrilling moment in the lives of nations as of men. What has been long feared, long hoped for or long thought inevitable happens at last, the dreams and the nightmares become daylight reality and are followed by an excited pause in which few men can tell whether their own excitement is terror or exhilaration. Thus it was as the news of Lexington and Concord spread through the Thirteen Colonies.

The Committees of Correspondence met, argued, planned. The militia drilled, and at last their drill had fearful purpose. Planters, frontiersmen, farmers, apprentices, turned overnight into soldiers. Moderate men lost overnight their moderation, bragged of what they would do to the Redcoats, and because they could find no Redcoats, vented their fears and their ambitions on the enemy within the gates. Loyalist homes were broken into, at first for guns and ammunition for the rebel cause and then for gold and silver for rebel pockets. As John Adams pointed out – his wisdom as ever far in advance of his cousin's, but his thinking as ever less in tune with the thinking of his countrymen – many of the rebels were hopelessly in debt and so licensed stealing had the added attraction of patriotic approval and the sudden achievement of solvency. Their pockets filled, the rebels took to breaking in for the sheer joy of breaking in. Loyalists were badgered, harried, bullied, made to look foolish, tarred and feathered, driven from their homes.

One example can stand for all the rest. It is an account written out of family tradition, first some fifty years later and then again some eighty years later, by an English writer of eminence and radical conviction, who but for these few hectic and brutal days in Philadelphia at the beginning of the Revolution might have been the first great American critic. Leigh Hunt's father, Isaac Hunt, was a Philadelphia lawyer, a graduate of the University of Pennsylvania, and of King's College, New York. His first political writing, written under the well-worn pseudonym of Isaac Bickerstaff, had appeared in 1765, and in the next year as Jack Retort, constant in scurrility, he had written various satires on the

Pennsylvania authorities which were sufficiently successful to delay for five years the receipt of his master's degree. In 1776 he wrote, and in 1777 most inopportunely published, a plea for union with the Mother Country, *The Political Family*, which made his Tory politics obvious.

'Then,' writes his son, 'his fortunes came to a crisis in America. Early one morning a great concourse of people appeared before his house. He came out, – or was brought. They put him into a cart prepared for the purpose (conceive the anxiety of his wife!) and, after parading him about the streets, were joined by a party of revolutionary soldiers with drums and fife. The multitude, some days before, for the same purpose, had seized Dr. Kearsley, a staunch Tory, who on learning their intention had shut up the windows of his house, and endeavoured to prevent their getting in. The doctor had his hand pierced by a bayonet, as it entered between the shutters behind which he had planted himself. He was dragged out and put into the cart, dripping with blood; but he lost none of his intrepidity; for he answered their reproaches and outrage with vehement reprehensions; and, by way of retaliation on the "Rogue's March", struck up "God Save the King". My father, who knew Kearsley, had endeavoured to persuade him not to add to their irritation; but to no purpose. The doctor continued infuriate, and more than once fainted from loss of blood and the violence of his feelings. My father comparatively softened the people with his gentler manners; yet he is understood, like Kearsley, to have had a narrow escape from tarring and feathering. A tub of tar, which had been set in a conspicuous place in one of the streets for that purpose, was overturned by an officer intimate with our family. The well-bred loyalist, however, did not escape entirely from personal injury. One of the stones thrown by the mob gave him such a severe blow on the head, as not only laid him swooning in the cart, but dimmed his sight for life. At length, after being carried through every street in Philadelphia, he was deposited, as Dr. Kearsley had been in a prison in Market Street. The poor doctor went out of his mind, and ended his days not long afterwards in confinement. My father, by the means of a large sum of money given to the sentinel who had charge of him, was enabled to escape at midnight. He went immediately on board a ship in the Delaware, that belonged to my grandfather, and was bound for the West Indies. She dropped down the river that same night; and my father went first to Barbados, and afterwards to England, where he settled.'

But the harrying of Loyalists brought advantages to the rebel cause beyond its merits, and probably beyond its intentions. Taken aback by the fury to which they were subjected and almost unprotected by government forces, the Loyalists found no way of uniting what might otherwise have been their powerful opposition to rebellion.

The second Continental Congress met at Philadelphia in May. Gone were the voices of moderation and gone the hopes of compromise; this was a Congress of war. Up in Massachusetts, colonial troops under Putnam, Ward, and Benedict Arnold were continuing their successes against British troops. Boston was under siege; Arnold had even crossed the Canadian border, and on 10 June John Adams proposed to the Congress that these forces be considered as the nucleus of a Continental Army. For their command, he hinted, an experienced soldier was necessary. Undoubtedly, in the whole of the American colonies, there was only one obvious candidate for the post: Colonel George Washington of Virginia. From now on the history of the American Revolution and of the early years of the United States is in many ways bound up with the story of George Washington.

Myth that holds the sentiment of a nation for almost two hundred years takes on in that time much of the authority of history. The George Washington who lived from 1732 until 1799 would stand high in the records of any nation, but the George Washington who lives on in the minds of his countrymen has influenced the United States far more than biographical evidence could justify or actual achievement demand.

A new nation needs heroes to support its national pride against international competition. For America only Washington and Lincoln can be placed without hesitation in a hall of fame which includes, for example, Shakespeare, Cromwell, and Nelson for England, Dante for Italy, and

Napoleon for France. Even Lincoln is to some degree the hero of a section; in the purely American pantheon his place is challenged by Robert E. Lee whose actions and habits were founded so much on the myth that had grown up around his father's friend that he is almost another Washington and further proof of the pre-eminence of the first President.

A young nation needs a patron saint. Pioneer, great general, and statesmen though he was, the Virginian squire who rode hard to hounds, danced energetically, gambled, swore, drank, smoked, lost his temper – and kept slaves – may seem a poor candidate for sainthood. America was fortunate in that there was, in the character of Washington, enough of virtue to give encouragement to the orators, the poets, the playwrights, and the novelists who wished to improve upon his fame, to bring him closer to perfection, even at the expense of historicity and humanity, and the gratitude of his people, secured his reputation before a nation-wide Congregation of Rites which, once the political excitements of his last years were quietened, allowed no *advocatus diaboli*. 'Hang him!' says George Warrington of his near namesake in *The Virginians*, 'he has no faults and that is why I dislike him. When he marries that widow – ah me! What a dreary life she will have of it.' But Thackeray was an Englishman, and even so aroused the anger of American critics for involving Washington in the machinery of a work of fiction, for to Americans Washington 'was not like other men, and to bring his lofty character down to the level of the vulgar passions of living is to give the lie to the grandest chapter of the uninspired annals of the human race'.

Even in his lifetime the Republicans had been in a sense discredited and apologetic because Washington had allied himself with their opponents. When inter-sectional rivalry became the substance of American political life, the South boasted proudly that Washington was of their number, and the North compensated for that undeniable fact by transforming his character until he became, in retrospect, typically

New England and Puritan. Eighteenth-century licence was to North and South alike obnoxious, so Washington was turned into a good Victorian.

Sparing no extravagance in their attempt to create an impression of super-humanity, the myth-builders likened the 'Father of his People' to Joshua, to Moses, even to Jesus Christ. With Washington, as with Jesus, dramatists permitted him to cast his shadow across the stage, but seldom more, and if the literary turned shyly from the ultimate absurdity and used the fortunate coincidence of mothers' names as a means of contriving implication instead of direct blasphemy, the public, beguiled by literary efforts, knew no such moderation: Matthew, Mark, Luke, and John might be given credit, but no decent American would believe that the cherished Farewell Address was the Gospel according to Alexander Hamilton.

Historians have reduced Washington to the size of manhood, but not until the twentieth century did the science of scholars reach the American people: 'Who cares what the fact was when we have made a constellation of it to hang in the heavens an immortal sign?' Even now to the majority of Americans, Washington 'is not as other men', his achievement unequalled and his character unassailable.

CHAPTER 16

DRAMATIS PERSONAE

THIS army which Washington is called to command in the summer of 1775 is hardly an army at all. It has neither organization nor a sense of unity. Even when the second Continental Congress resolves to send to the assistance of Massachusetts six companies of infantrymen from Pennsylvania, Maryland, and Virginia, there is nothing that can be described as a Continental army except the New England forces around Boston, already so overburdened with officers as to make nugatory the chain of command devised at Philadelphia. But the personalities are already appearing through the mists of confusion; the personalities who will bring about the amazing success of amateurs over the professional army of Britain.

They are not among the first four major-generals appointed by Congress to serve immediately under Washington. Artemas Ward, the second-in-command, is dyspeptic, alcoholic, almost too fat to ride, and incompetent to the point of lunacy. Philip Schuyler has skill but no knowledge of men and his patroon manners soon irritate his subordinates beyond bearing. Charles Lee, an Englishman, has genius and experience. He alone, among the Continentals, might have hoped for Washington's shoes, for he is an ex-regular and has roistered his way through most of the armies of Western Europe. But Lee's ambitions are all for Lee, and the cause of American independence is important to him only in so far as it may give him the opportunity to prove himself as great a soldier as the great Wolfe under whom he had once served as an obscure ensign. His ambition will lead him to double treachery. Isaac Putnam is a conceited tough, ever ready with an amusing story about himself, seldom ready to make a decision useful to the army.

But there are others rallying to the cause whose services will be more valuable. Horatio Gates, another Englishman, and the first Adjutant-General, as ambitious as Lee but far more shrewd. Nathaniel Greene, from Rhode Island, Stirling from Scotland who called himself a lord, and another New Englander, the bravest of them all and probably the best natural soldier, Benedict Arnold.

Soon, when the Continental Congress organized a navy, it attracted to its service a Scotsman who had been in America but two years, John Paul of Kirkbean, whom American history knows as John Paul Jones. A poet at heart, and something of a poet in appearance, who had been pirate, slave-trader, and possibly murderer before he became republican Commodore, he loved fighting for its own sake – and women for theirs – but cared for little else. He had no ideological reason for serving the Americans, but became one of their greatest servants.

Soon, too, when the news of American heroism – and American opportunities – reached Europe, volunteer generals came to Washington's assistance. Von Steuben, who at the age of fourteen had served at the siege of Prague and had later been, or claimed to have been, on the staff of Frederick the Great, as inspector-general of the Continental Army, remodelled American organization, improved its discipline, and gave it the text-books without which no group of fighting-men can be moulded into an army. And Marie Joseph Paul Roch Ives Gilbert Motier, Marquis de Lafayette.

The severe reasoning of historical scholarship can be used to prove that other Frenchmen did far more than Lafayette to bring about the successful conclusion of the American Revolution – Rochambeau, the sturdy professional who forced the surrender of the British Army at Yorktown, or De Grasse, whose blockading fleet made that surrender inevitable – but sentiment, with some latter-day assistance ascribed to General Pershing, has chosen Lafayette as the everlasting symbol of the friendship between France and America.

He was young, only nineteen, when he landed in America, an aristocrat adopting the cause of democracy. Like Byron in the Greek Revolution he sank his personal fortune in the

cause. He served as an American officer, and judicious
editing of a remark he made when he realized that he was
not going to get command of the French forces in North
America has added to his legend the story, comfortable to
American pride, that he 'preferred an American division'.
Above all, the romantic character of his intervention in
revolution did not end with the American War. His later
activities made him the active link between the American
Revolution and the French Revolutions of 1789 and 1830,
and all his efforts, as Commander of the National Guard,
as a member of the Jacobin Club, and as a leader of the
Chamber of Deputies, demonstrate how much he had
absorbed the bourgeois spirit of the American Revolution;
how much in fact he had learnt, and learnt unconsciously,
of a habit in revolution which was originally British.

Nor was his life without that touch of martyrdom which
makes romanticism more romantic. His vast wealth vanished
in the service of liberty. The moderation which was his by
birth and which was strengthened by service under Washington made him into an enemy of the extremists on both
sides in the French Revolution; he escaped the attentions
of the guillotine, the weapon of 'the Mountain', only to
fall victim to the instrument of the monarchists, an international <i>lettre de cachet</i>, and he spent five years as a prisoner
in an Austrian fortress, years which turned him from a
young man of thirty-five into an old but unbroken man of
forty.

On his release, Lafayette's honesty deprived him of the
part which above all things he would have enjoyed playing,
and for which experience had so admirably equipped him:
the part of a soldier. As a democrat he could not fight for
Napoleon, as a Frenchman he would not fight against him,
and so the general who, next to Bonaparte himself, could
arouse the enthusiasm of French armies, spent the years of
France's greatest military glory farming his estate at La
Grange.

American historiography draws Lafayette in appropriate
boldness. The blacks and the whites are so firm that they

seem to betray a natural tendency to exaggerate the stature of Lafayette, particularly those moments when he is present and active whilst portentous events go forward.

It can be argued that Lafayette's greatest service to the American cause was not as a soldier – though he was gallant and energetic – but as friend to Washington. The lonely and austere Commander-in-Chief, envied by so many of his immediate subordinates and much mistrusted by them for his high-handedness, needed a champion and a friend. The friend he found in Lafayette, the French aristocrat who, almost alone among his colleagues, could be considered a fit associate for a Virginian gentleman.

He found the champion in the illegitimate son of a French Jewess and a Scotsman, a young West Indian plebeian who hankered after aristocracy: Alexander Hamilton. Brilliant, brave, and efficient, Hamilton saw to it that he went far. King's College, New York, a captaincy in the Colonial Artillery, a useful marriage, the Secretaryship of the Treasury, a nearly successful struggle for the control of the new nation; all these things were to come to Hamilton; but perhaps his greatest service to America was as private secretary to Washington in the field.

To these *dramatis personae* of American leadership must be added three names of men whose activities were not primarily military: John Adams, Thomas Jefferson, and Thomas Paine.

Samuel Adams, arch-plotter of rebellion, had served his part once rebellion became a fact. Though he lived for almost twenty years after the outbreak of war with Britain, his later activities were comparatively unimportant. But now his cousin John came to the fore.

Of all the founders of the Republic, John Adams alone seems to have few enthusiasts who are anxious to build up his reputation and hold his place in the American pantheon. His services were performed in his early years, and his personality has none of the fierce integrity of a Washington, the intellectual brilliance of a Jefferson, or the romantic energy of a Hamilton to endear him to posterity.

Prejudice against Adams started in his lifetime; in fact, so many eminent contemporaries disliked him that it is surprising that he ever became the second President of the United States. 'From the year 1761,' he wrote, 'now more than fifty years, I have constantly lived in an enemy's country.' And his sense of persecution led him to hit back at those very Americans who might have been prepared to accept him for his worth; at Franklin, at Washington, even at Jefferson, though Jefferson, alone among his colleagues, he could sometimes call friend.

It was in part Adams's conviction that there was some merit even in monarchy which made him the butt of a generation whose nightmares were filled with the brutal stamping of George the Third's boots, and that same conviction preserved for him the animosity of Americans throughout the nineteenth century when the Jeffersonian–Jacksonian influence was at its height. Even today, though the reputation of Adams has been to some degree restored, it suffers still from an obstinate conviction, held by some Americans, that America is virtuous in so far as it is republican, and that to accept some merit in monarchical institutions is, in itself, an un-American activity. But these beliefs he shared, though for different reasons, with Alexander Hamilton, and Hamilton has become the darling of one of the parties in present-day American politics, just as Jefferson and Madison are the darlings of the other.

Why then the persisting animosity towards the memory of Adams? He was able, he was an enthusiast, he did more even than Franklin to make the new United States diplomatically respectable – he even had a sense of humour. Adams was above all an intellectual; his main fault that he could always see both sides of a question, and was ready to accept the unpopular side, when to him that side seemed to have all the arguments. Fairness is never congenial amidst the excitements of revolution, and intellectuals often give the appearance of havering. Jefferson, too, was an intellectual, but Jefferson possessed all the charms of versatility, and his intellectualism was moderated by the warmth and humanity which Adams lacked. John Adams, as he himself was the first to admit, found it difficult to make friends. He was stubborn, impatient with fools, and quick to recognize foolishness.

Superficially and from a distance the American Revolution looks more political than most revolutions. The inevitable divorce between the interests of Government in London and the interests of the colonials, the stupidities of English viceroys, and the growth of economic rivalry between the Thirteen Colonies and the Mother Country seem sufficient explanation for the break of 1776. But there was, behind the growth of the revolutionary movement, a great deal of philosophical preparation, and the influence of writers like Sydney, Bolingbroke, Condorcet, and the French *philosophes* was immense. Most of the Americans who read their works seemed content to stop once they had translated foreign thought into American action; Adams went on reading and considering, and this reading and consideration made him frequently discontented with the results of American action. He was an inveterate note-taker, a scribbler of *marginalia*, and his notes in the margins of such books as the *Contrat Social*, Condorcet's *Esquisse*, and Priestley's *Doctrines of Heathen Philosophy* form a debate between John Adams and some of the most famous eighteenth-century thinkers, a debate between John Adams and his own conscience, a debate between John Adams and the American people.

Adams's habit of expletive he took over into his note-taking. 'Fool! Fool!' he writes in the margin of Condorcet's *Esquisse*. 'Thou beliest thy species, Satyr. Thou makest him worse than Swift's Yahoo', on a page of Rousseau's *Essay on Inequality*. When the Abbé de Mably assumes that 'we can find happiness only in the common ownership of goods', Adams's conviction, which was apparent in his draft of the Declaration of Rights, that all men are not born free and equal, but free and independent, came out with the simple criticism, 'Stark mad!'

His great reading and his great sense of fairness prevented his violence from getting the better of him, and even in writers that he disliked intensely he could find occasional virtues and frequent morals for his own time. Of all the French thinkers of the eighteenth century, Turgot was the one he disliked most, and his own *Defence of the Constitution of America* was written specifically 'against the attack of M. Turgot'. But when Turgot reproached the American States for including a religious test in their constitutions, Adams leapt to his support and wrote in his neat handwriting in the margin of Turgot's book:

This enmity to test has my most hearty good wishes and prayers. I would try the experiment where a State could exist without the shadow of a test.

Later in his life his countrymen were prepared to go to war a second time against the brutality implied by England's Navigation Acts; Adams, who loved Navigation Acts no more than the rest of them and wished to see them abolished the world over, nevertheless pointed out to himself that England's guilt in this respect was only as the guilt of other nations. He would have rebelled violently against the exclusiveness of American twentieth-century mercantile policies.

Adams was the one American leader who could stand as umpire in the fight going on among Americans, even while they fought against Britain, the fight for the future of America. Even though – and this was to bring him much animosity – all his life he could see some virtue in monarchy, he was violent in his criticism of such aristocratic institutions as the Society of the Cincinnati; but while Hamilton, a real monarchist, called the American Constitution 'a shilly-shally thing of mere milk and water', Adams greeted it as 'the greatest single effort of national deliberation that the world has ever seen'. As he hated the extremes of the French Revolution, so was he sympathetic to Louis the Sixteenth, but such monarchical tendencies as were undoubtedly his came from purely semantic considerations. He thought that monarchy 'may be hereditary, or it may be for life, or it may be for years, or only for one year, or for months, or for one month, or for days, or only for one day'.

He occasionally shouted at his contemporaries that monarchy was not all bad, because he did not want them to get away with the idea that the American Constitution and American Republicanism was all good. He was optimistic about the future of mankind and optimistic about the future of Americans: he was never optimistic about the future of institutions, either American or European.

Some of the enmity that he aroused was justified. His was the character that could easily make enemies, yet could not easily induce discipleship. But, if prudence and the ability to inspire others were not among his qualities, certainly he deserved the credit for having given all his mental energy to the careful consideration of the accumulated wisdom and folly of his age, and for having attempted to translate it into American action.

Though Jefferson was the principal author of the Declaration of Independence it was Adams's obstinacy and Adams's eloquence – 'the man seemed lifted out of himself' – that persuaded Congress to accept and substantiate the Declaration. As commissioner to France and Holland, as member of the peace commission, and as first American Minister at St James's, Adams gave magnificently of his wisdom and his energy to the creation of a sound foreign policy for the new nation. As first Vice-President and second President of the United States, he courted unpopularity and downright hatred for the sake of his mature convictions.

And with John Adams there must be coupled the name of his wife, Abigail. Not only for sentiment's sake, not only because alone among American women she was wife of one President and mother of another, but also because, being a wife and mother to statesmen, she was herself admitted to the secrets of statesmanship and handled them with such competence and judgement as was ordinarily beyond the training and habit of her sex in that age. Abigail Adams was a typical daughter of revolution, ready for hardship, calm in disaster and in triumph, stridently patriotic and determined to do all that she could to strengthen her country's prospects. She was untypical in that she, unlike most of her countrywomen, could express her hopes and fears, and in the eminence which she shared.

Thomas Jefferson epitomized an eighteenth-century development that had little connexion with nationality and that was, despite his great activity in revolution, in many senses independent of political events in revolutionary America. He was the fine flower of dilettantism; himself political philosopher and active politician, amateur scientist, theological controversialist, amateur inventor and amateur architect, he was also a great patron of the arts and the sciences and, both practically and theoretically, an important educator. Although his personality has been used to symbolize America's rejection of Europeanism, he was, of all his American contemporaries, the one most tied to the European tradition in ideals, inspiration, and activity. Where America followed Jefferson, there was America continuing and improving upon Europe; where America ignored his teaching, there, for the most part, America slipped from Europe's standards.

Of all the great leaders in American history only two, Franklin and Jefferson, have reputations that are easily convertible into foreign currency. The rest, Jackson, Lee, Lincoln, and even to a large extent Franklin Roosevelt among them, achieved greatness for peculiarly American reasons; the comprehension of their stature demands understanding of the American background, and the appreciation of their virtues is only possible when they are placed in the intimate setting of American history. Franklin and Jefferson were theorists as well as statesmen, philosophers as much as practical politicians, speculative scientists even while they were men of action. Both contributed much to the foundation of the United States, both contributed something more permanent than revolution. Of the two, Jefferson was undoubtedly the greater thinker and the greater international figure, his interests were wider, his achievements more lasting and, even on the minute political stage of Revolutionary America, he was the more powerful actor. More than any other revolutionary leader, Jefferson created Americanism.

Jefferson synthesized the American ideal for his own times and the synthesis has stood even for those who have marked themselves as opponents of the party he created. The great eighteenth-century tradition of republicanism was epitomized in the writings and activities of Jefferson. His was the hand which more than any other prepared 'a foundation for a government truly republican'. He favoured the separation of Church and State, the establishment of a system of public instruction, the abolition of primogeniture and entails. He saw the future of America safe in the hands of free and educated people unhampered by close governmental control.

The United States never has lived up to its own ambitions. No nation could. But Americanism is not the American achievement but the American ideal, and this ideal was Jefferson's dream:

I have no fear [he wrote to Hartley in 1787,] but that the result of our experiment will be that men may be trusted to govern themselves without a master. Could the contrary of this be proved, I should conclude, either that there is no God, or that he is a malevolent being.

Devotees of the Third International might find cause for envy in the record of Tom Paine, who, with none of the twentieth-century facilities for rapid communication, contrived to act the prophet in three revolutions: the American fight for independence, the French for liberty, fraternity, and equality, and the English for manhood suffrage. The English repaid him with persecution; his more bloodthirsty French colleagues did their best to grant him the privilege of martyrdom, but, as it was in his efforts to turn indignant but loyal American colonists into ardent secessionists that he achieved his most immediate political success, so was his failure to make the American Revolution into an egalitarian movement the saddest of his humiliations. In the first forty years of the nineteenth century it was Englishmen, and not Americans, who, having lighted their tapers at Paine's 'expiring flambeau', went on to make policy out of his propaganda. Paine's greatest book came later when he published *The Rights of Man*, but Paine's greatest contribution to history was the publication, in 1776, of *Common Sense*. It was this, and this alone, which justified his title as the 'Godfather of America'. His simple and emotional pamphlet, which drove through the brick wall of legalistic argument against independence, was perfectly suited to the moment of its appearance. 'I bring reason to your ears, and, in a language as plain as ABC, hold up truth to your eyes.' The pamphlet was first published on 10 January 1776. Two weeks later General Lee wrote to Washington, 'Have you seen the pamphlet *Common Sense*? I never saw such a masterly irresistible performance. It will, if I mistake not, give the coup de grâce to Great Britain.' Washington agreed. 'The sound doctrine,' he wrote, 'and unanswerable reasoning contained in the pamphlet *Common Sense* will not leave members at a loss to decide upon the propriety of separation.' By the end of March 1776 more than one thousand copies had been sold in the colonies. Students of comparative bookselling statistics may well argue that there has never been, in American publishing, a best-seller to equal *Common Sense*. Students of history can add to the claim by stating that no other book has had such immediate and such profound consequence. The Declaration of Independence, it seems likely, would have occurred without *Common Sense*, but it would not have received such widespread support from a people who only a few months earlier had still been havering on the brink of compromise.

Paine would contribute other things to the American cause, but his reward for his services was slight. The Declaration of Independence ran the measure of Paine's American success; the Constitution with its emphasis on presidential prerogative and bicameral legislature established the fullness of his defeat. The leaders of the Revolution turned their backs on Paine's democratic monument. The Pennsylvania Constitution of 1776 demonstrated ideas of manhood suffrage and an executive so limited that it could not hope to usurp the power of the unicameral legislature. But the power of the people was to come to represent to American leaders, as to English Tories, the rule of the 'worst over the best'. For this, Paine's ideal, they substituted presidential prerogative and bicameral legislature. They had their ideals, but they were not the ideals that Tom Paine had tried to inspire in them. Even Jefferson was defeated in his bold effort to include a clause abolishing slavery, and with this excision went the last sop to *Common Sense*. The span of the Revolutionary War, the years between the Declaration of Independence and the ratification of the Constitution, saw the decline of Paine's power over American ideology from its zenith to its nadir.

It was, it is true, his theology and not his politics which finally ruined his reputation with his American contemporaries and their successors. Paine, the revolutionary, was at least respectable, but Paine, the deist, could never hold the respect of puritanical New England, Catholic Maryland, or Episcopalian Virginia. And his case was the worse for his thorny personality and his aggressiveness. Not for Tom Paine the thoughtful, patient deism of Jefferson or Franklin. God, to him was an *aristo*, and *aristos* were best without their heads. Such vigour could but bring upon him the distaste of good Christians and the hate of men who called themselves good Christians.

Yet, for *Common Sense* alone, Tom Paine deserved more than he ever received from the American people.

The structure of ideas within which Americans achieved their independence was provided by two great intellectual movements, the Age of Reason and the Age of Romanticism. The United States itself, almost purely a creation of the eighteenth century, emerged at a time when the western world was shifting from one system of thought to another, each involving quite different views of man, the world, and the Deity beyond them.

The American colonies were children of the Age of Reason, or the 'Enlightenment'. John Locke, the English political philosopher, wrote a charter for the Carolinas; Rousseau and Franklin were friends; Sir Isaac Newton and

Cotton Mather were contemporaries; Voltaire was still living when the Continental Congress signed the Declaration of Independence. The Enlightenment, not the Puritanism of New England, provided the first *nationalized* pattern of American thought. There was an American Enlightenment, but it was late, eclectic, and singularly American. Eighteenth-century America was not merely an extension or a reflection of contemporary Britain or Europe. First of all, there was a culture lag in the transmission of patterns of thinking from one side of the Atlantic to the other. The Founding Fathers worked with ideas fifty to one hundred years old by European standards, in another continent, for different purposes – and mixed with them later borrowings and adaptations. The Romantics – Goethe, Wordsworth, Coleridge, Schiller, and Kant – it should be remembered, were writing at nearly the same time that Americans were still quoting the men of the Age of Reason – Newton, Locke, and Montesquieu.

Second, Americans chose from British and European thought only those ideas they needed, or those in which they had special interest. For example they adopted Locke's justification of a century-old English revolution as vindication of their own, and used French 'radicalism', aimed at Gallic kings, to overthrow a tyranny that really did not exist. The Americans thus bent the Enlightenment to American uses.

CHAPTER 17

THE WAR FOR INDEPENDENCE

THOMAS Paine's *Common Sense* marked the shift in emphasis of American revolution from the conduct of civil war to the quest for independence. *Common Sense* drew together in clear and logical fashion what others – many others – were groping for, and crystallized in the minds of Americans notions of democracy. Through *Common Sense* the issues were made more straightforward even as the events continued to be confused and complicated.

Pennsylvanian James Wilson's *Consideration of the Authority of Parliament*, was published in August 1774, and climaxed a long argument by concluding that Parliament had no authority over the colonies, no more than 'different members of the British Empire, independent of each other, but connected together under the same sovereign'. In 1776 this principle became, at bottom, the principle and *raison d'être* of independence.

Virginia, which had learnt to hate its royal governor as much because he had offered freedom to Negro slaves who would fight for him as because he had bombarded Norfolk, now took the lead in preaching the doctrines of equality in independence. 'All men are by nature equally free and independent, and have certain inherent rights . . . namely the enjoyment of life and liberty, with the means of acquiring and possessing property and the means of obtaining happiness and safety.' Thus the Virginia Bill of Rights, passed on 12 June 1776. In that same week Richard Henry Lee, on behalf of the delegates of Virginia, was moving at the Second Continental Congress:

That these united colonies are, and of right ought to be, free and independent states, that they are absolved from all allegiance to the British Crown, and that all political connection between them and the State of Great Britain is, and ought to be, dissolved.

The Declaration of Independence, drafted by a master of English prose, still perhaps the greatest of American philosophers, is nevertheless in one sense a document of self-justification and propaganda. The colonies needed support in their revolution, and needed local as well as foreign support. Their actions were an implicit threat to every established government in the world, the resort to war anathema even to many who sympathized with their plight. It was necessary to convince kindlier critics and potential allies that the deeds of Congress were the logical and legitimate produce of decent political philosophy. It was the easier to convince because the men who wrote it and voted for it were themselves convinced. This is no cynical document; though the preamble is in many ways false history and exaggerated principle, it synthesizes in a few words a century of thinking, and those few words are words that the people can understand. Jefferson and Congress showed a realistic and short-range view of what the Declaration must achieve in gaining support, but at the same time they were hopeful that its political principles would prove practical and would endure. In its time the Declaration was the cornerstone of American political thinking, and on it was founded the ideology of the first government. Despite the suggestions of its list of grievances and despite the empty deference which has sometimes been its lot, without any Declaration of Independence the subsequent history of the United States would be incomprehensible.

The adoption of the Declaration of Independence immediately changed the character of the conflict. It made the colonies a new and separate nation, with the ability to solicit aid and recognition from the established powers. It made Congress, which until July 1776 was no more than an illegal and rebellious body, the legislative representative of a sovereign state. Internally, it forced a choice upon the hesitant and vacillating; each colonist must of necessity choose to remain loyal, or to secede, for there was no longer a middle ground within which to temporize or manoeuvre. Within the colonies as well it created a set of questions to which at least partial, if not permanent, answers, had to be given. If the authority of Parliament were denied, and connexions with the sovereign severed, who then would take on the authority of governing the states themselves or the new national government represented by Continental Congress? Congress quite naturally assumed the responsibility for prosecution of the war and the business of governing, but the fundamental question remained unsettled, and would inevitably rise again if the war were won.

In the first skirmishes between Washington's troops and the redcoats the idea of 'An American' came to fullness; in the debates of the Second Congress the idea was given legalistic substance, but still the union of the Thirteen Colonies was weak and uncertain. The frontiersmen were, many of them, more interested in the exploits of Daniel Boone than in the exploits of George Washington. In each of the colonies (now states) there were those – and there were a great many – who were prepared to fight for the safety of their own state, but who could not yet understand that each state depended for its safety upon the security of the twelve others. The very hatred of the British regular forces in America was in itself a deterrent to American unity. For it inspired in American minds a fear of a standing army, be it British or American. American though they now were, the very fact that they needed defeat to arouse in them a sense of urgency proved how much they had inherited from their British opponents.

British strategy was correctly centred upon New York, which both emotionally and geographically seemed the weakest link in the thirteen rebellious colonies. In the summer of 1776 the British seized the City without difficulty. At the same time General Burgoyne was sent to Canada with instructions to move South to join up with General Howe from New York, and thus, by seizing the great Hudson waterway, to split New England from the Middle and Southern States.

Nothing could be more perplexing than the activities of

General Howe in the next months. Brilliant and experienced general that he was, he seemed unwilling to press the American commanders. While Burgoyne moved into the territory of the United States, Howe turned away from his task, moved by sea towards the mouth of the Delaware, then out again, perhaps for the Hudson and perhaps for Charleston. Finally, he came to blows with Washington late in the summer of 1777.

On 22 August, little more than a year after Philadelphia had echoed with Jefferson's idealistic optimism, Washington led his eleven thousand troops through the City, bold in his desperation. But his 'ragged, lousy, naked regiments' were incapable of stemming Howe's advance, and on 11 September the citizens of the birthplace of revolution, divided between hope and fear, took front seats for the noisy symphony of battle. Washington was outnumbered, but Howe's cautious refusal to risk his comparatively fresh troops in the easy pursuit of the exhausted Americans denied to the British the opportunity to turn the victory into a conquest. Like bridge-players arguing over a lost trick the military authorities have penned over Howe's decision to wait until the morning of the 12th before accepting his advantage. Lafayette, most censorious in his after-the-event relief, called this lost night the greatest fault of the British, 'during a war in which they committed so many errors'. Clinton, more moderate, as befitted Howe's successor, wrote 'it is a pity Sir W. Howe could not have begun his march at nightfall instead of eight o'clock in the morning', and Napier, sternly classical, commented that 'had Caesar halted because his soldiers were fatigued, Pharsalia would have been but a common battle'.

Whatever the eventual verdict, at the time Howe's victory seemed definite enough. Boston, Philadelphia, and New York were all in the possession of the British. The American Army, close to mutiny, was freezing at Valley Forge, and Congress sheltered ignominiously at York, where general complained against general and politician suspected politician.

Yet Howe's 'victory' was more accurately described by Robert Burns:

> Poor Tammy Gage within a cage
> Was kept at Boston ha', man,
> Till Willie Howe took o'er the knowe,
> For Philadelphia, man.
> Wi' sword and gun he thought a sin
> Guid Christian blood to draw, man:
> But at New-York, wi' knife and fork,
> Sir-loin he hacked sma', man.

And, meanwhile, Burgoyne pressing further and further into New York State, was receiving no support from the South-East. His supply problem became acute. He lost men in each skirmish, and, on 13 October, near Saratoga, surrounded now by a force three times the size of his own, a British regular force was for the first time compelled to surrender to the forces of the Revolution.

(No man was less tempered for defeat than Gentleman Johnny Burgoyne. With some justice, he blamed the disgrace upon the party which he had once bolstered in Parliament, and for the rest of his life, like so many British generals of the American War, he was a staunch Whig. But Burgoyne's gaiety was not easily quelled. He had been a dramatist of sorts before he became a defeated general, defeat gave him the leisure to improve his writing and, in 1786, at the age of sixty-three, he produced *The Heiress*, one of the most successful comedies of the time.)

Even the gloom around Philadelphia could not hide from American eyes the excitement of the outstanding achievement at Saratoga. The ballad-makers (their chronology somewhat suspect!) set to work to describe the Burgoyne campaign, in terms more adulatory, perhaps, than those that would have been used by American generals who were not at Saratoga:

> Come unto me ye heroes, and I the truth will tell
> Concerning many a soldier who for his country fell.
> Burgoyne, the King's commander, and cursed Tory crew,
> With Injuns and Canajuns he up the Champlain flew.

Before Ticonderoga, full well both night and day,
Their motions were observed before the bloody fray;
Burgoyne sent Baum to Bennington, with Hessians there he went,
To plunder and to murder was fully their intent.

But little did they know then with whom they had to deal,
It was not quite so easy our stores and stocks to steal,
Stark would give them only a portion of his lead,
With half his crew e'er sunset, Baum lay among the dead.

The nineteenth of September, the morning cool and clear,
Gates addressed the army each soldier's heart to cheer.
'Burgoyne,' he cried, 'advances, but we will never fly,
But rather than surrender, we'll fight him till we die!'

The seventh of October, they did capitulate,
Burgoyne and his proud army we did our prisoners make;
And vain was their endeavour our men to terrify,
Though death was all around us, not one of us would fly!

Now here's a health to Herkimer and our commander Gates!
To Freedom and to Washington whom every Tory hates;
Likewise unto our Congress – God grant it long to reign –
Our Country, Rights and Justice forever to maintain!

Burgoyne's surrender forced the British Government to think of reconciliation. Paul Wentworth was sent to Paris in an attempt to persuade the American agents there to bring their countrymen back into the fold of empire. But Burgoyne's surrender had also given the Americans heart, and the two agents, Silas Deane and Benjamin Franklin, stood firm for independence.

Perhaps the fact of a British defeat and perhaps the arrival in Paris of a British conciliator forced action upon the French. On 17 December 1777 the French Government informed Deane and Franklin that they had decided to recognize the independence of the United States. On 8 January 1778 Vergennes informed the American commissioners that France was ready to enter into an alliance with the Americans.

Throughout the Revolutionary period there was a strong relationship between the diplomatic and commercial needs of the American people and a fortunate coincidence of interests that made France the natural ally and, potentially, the strongest ally of the Americans. Anything that was to the detriment of Britain was to the benefit of France.

When, after Lexington, the Americans had begun to think of independence, their ambitious thoughts had turned them inevitably to negotiation with foreign powers. There were no brother rebels overseas and when the Continental Congress set up, in November 1775, the Committee of Secret Correspondence to open negotiations abroad, it was to France that they turned first for support.

Again the element of paradox plays its part in the American story. France, the tired aristocrat of Europe, its monarchy hovering on the brink of its own bloody destruction and its empire second only to Britain's, was to be called in to fight the war for democracy.

America needed a source of supply for the munitions with which to fight the war. The cry of the Committee of Safety of New York to the delegates of the Continental Congress of Philadelphia in July 1775 was constantly echoed in the appeals to the American commissioners in Paris: 'We have no arms, we have no powder, we have no blankets. For God's sake send us money, send us arms, send us ammunition.'

'Send us money!' The Americans needed financial assistance for carrying on the war and, above all, for purchasing strategic imports. By the beginning of 1777 the national debt stood at fifteen million dollars and of the total currency in circulation, some thirty million dollars, more than half was in worthless paper. Washington had been forced to pledge his private fortune in order to pay his troops. Gold specie was badly needed if inflation were to be prevented.

The small American navy could not hope to protect American convoys, and unless the United States could negotiate a friendly base in Europe, American merchantmen and naval vessels in European waters sailed without possibility of refuge or refit.

In their new-found diplomatic agility, the Americans approached every European power of any importance; Spain, the Netherlands, Prussia, Austria, and even Russia, but, above all, France.

France was eager; in fact France actually made the first move to establish relations with the rebellious Americans. As early as December 1775 the Confidential Agent of the French Foreign Ministry was conferring with the Committee of Secret Correspondence. By the beginning of 1776 Silas Deane in Paris had obtained an unofficial agreement whereby France supplied the American States with munitions in return for shipments of tobacco. (Deane actually succeeded in getting eight shiploads of military supplies, and it is not without piquancy that the arrangements for their shipment were left to the great comic dramatist, Beaumarchais.) Unfortunately for the French, the tobacco that was to come in exchange for the most part found its way into British pipes, having been captured on the journey across the Atlantic.

In May 1776 the King of France gave a secret subsidy of a million livres to the American cause. By the middle of 1777 French ports were open to American ships for refuge, refittings, and for the sale of prizes, and many officers from the French Army were serving in the American forces with the connivance of the French authorities. The French Government had some justice on its side when it informed Franklin and Deane that 'we enjoy all the advantages already which we proposed to obtain by a treaty, and that we may depend upon continuing to receive every indulgence in our trade that is allowed the most favoured nation'.

But, after Saratoga, France was prepared to come into the open. Two treaties resulted from the negotiations of the first four weeks of 1778. The first proposed 'to maintain effectually the liberty, sovereignty and independence absolute and unlimited of the said United States as well as in matters of government as in commerce'. The second provided for the exchange of consuls, and a few months later Conrad Gerard was named minister plenipotentiary to the United States Congress, and Benjamin Franklin minister to the French Court. Under the treaties, the United States was given a free hand to seize Canada, and France authorized to capture the British West Indies. American ships were given most favoured nation treatment in French ports.

Thus France offered everything short of war to the American cause, and, as so often happens with such alliances, war soon followed. From the British point of view it was inevitable, from the American point of view eminently desirable, and from the French point of view not unwelcome.

Spain followed closely the French pattern. When Silas Deane was first appointed to the French Court he recommended to Congress that it should dispatch American agents to other European capitals, and, accordingly, in 1777, Arthur Lee was commissioned to Spain. Spanish jealousy of British imperial dominion was more bitter even than that of France, but as Spanish power was less so were the Spaniards less willing to risk a formal and open connexion. At first, Lee was not even admitted to Madrid, but through a Spanish Commissioner he succeeded in negotiating secret financial aid from the Spanish Government. Spanish ports were open to American ships, the Spaniards promised that gunpowder and stores would be deposited at New Orleans, Charles the Third followed the example of Louis the Sixteenth in granting a subsidy to the colonial rebels, and finally Spain too declared war on Britain, though her military intervention was more by threat than by force of arms.

But even at the moment of alliance, Spain was eager to keep open the door for withdrawal. In 1778 John Jay, a young New York aristocrat, was made Minister Plenipotentiary at the Spanish Court with orders to secure a formal treaty, if necessary at the expense of forfeiting America's declared right of navigation on the Mississippi. The King of Spain remained stubborn and refused to receive Jay, and although Floridablanca gave Jay a loan of one hundred and seventy thousand dollars the formalities of alliance were never completed.

Spanish aid during the war amounted to some four hundred thousand dollars in subsidies and two hundred and fifty thousand in loans, as compared to the enormous French subsidy of two million dollars and French loans of almost seven million dollars. But Spain wanted Gibraltar and not American independence, and part of the diplomatic suspicion that existed between the Americans and their new-found French allies sprang from the fact that the Americans in general, and Jay in particular, suspected France of being willing to sacrifice the cause of American independence to the European ambitions of Spain.

So too, in the Netherlands, American diplomatic success was as much dictated by the wishes of the French Foreign Ministry as by the strong pro-American feelings of the Dutch or the skill of American agents. After the conclusion of French treaties with the united colonies, Vergennes sent a copy of those treaties to the Netherlands and the citizens of Amsterdam immediately announced their support of the colonies. Yet another of the ubiquitous Virginian Lees, William Lee, stopped in Amsterdam on his way back from Vienna and Berlin, and there drew up a draft treaty with a Dutch businessman, Jean de Neufville. Neither had treaty-making powers, but this treaty was later used as one excuse by the British to declare war on Holland. France, however, wished to keep the Dutch non-belligerent and therefore persuaded Holland against recognizing American independence. Dutch powder was used in American powder-horns and French supplies for America were often routed via Holland and carried in Dutch ships, but it was not until 1782, when the battle of independence was already won, that the Dutch signed a treaty of commerce and friendship with the Americans and became the second nation to give *de jure* recognition to the United States.

In the meanwhile Congress, as always hard pressed for ready money, had sent Henry Laurens to secure a loan of ten million dollars from the Dutch. It was his capture *en route* by the British which precipitated the British declaration of war on Holland, for with him was captured William Lee's draft treaty. His successor was John Adams who eventually negotiated a much smaller loan of some two million dollars to be paid back at the rate of five per cent interest over ten years, the first of several such loans.

In 1777 Berlin found itself invaded by the Lee family. Frederick the Second was eager for American tobacco, but less eager for American tobacco planters, and when Arthur Lee arrived Frederick refused even to see him, and, as if to demonstrate even further his low opinion of Prussia's un-invited guest, he made no protest when the British Ambassador purloined Lee's private papers. William Lee fared little better, though he did manage to secure an audience and was given a vague promise of support on condition that American tobacco would find its way to Prussia and the American colonies be opened as a market for Silesian linen. Franklin, ever jealous of the dignity of the new State, protested to his superiors that America should 'not go about suitoring for alliances, but wait with decent dignity for the application of others'.

William Lee, the only American ever to have been elected a sheriff and an alderman in London, left no impression whatsoever on Vienna, where the French Ambassador was refused permission even to introduce him at Court. Perhaps it was not surprising that Austria, eager enemy of Prussia, looked in horror on an envoy who was trying to secure treaties of amity and commerce with both countries at the same time.

Congress even attempted courtship with Russia and Francis Dana was instructed to negotiate an alliance. But in the ten years from 1770 to 1780 Great Britain doubled her exports to Russia and Russian interests, commercial and emotional, were all with Britain. Catherine the Second refused point-blank to deal with the people who denied absolute authority. It was not until 1784 that an American ship, *The Light Horse*, was seen in a Russian port.

But after Saratoga, America foreign policy could claim successes which were to have vital effect upon the conduct of war. French arms, money, troops, and officers arrived to provide backbone for the struggling Americans. The French fleet was at sea, and Britain was faced with the threat at least, and possibly the reality, of a simultaneous struggle with the three next most formidable navies in the world, the French, the Spanish, and the Dutch.

However, instead of concentrating on the destruction of the European fleets, Britain continued, in a half-hearted manner, land operations in America itself.

Lord George Germain in London – in many ways, and from the British point of view, the villain of the drama – seemed determined to lose the war by bad orders, contradictory orders, conflict of orders, and delayed decisions. He replaced general with general and then prevented each successive commander from achieving victory. Probably the best of his generals, Sir Guy Carlton, he left rotting in Canada, but with Sir Henry Clinton in particular, who succeeded Howe in Philadelphia, Germain's policies appear in retrospect as deliberately malicious. There was a personal antagonism between the General in the field and the Secretary of State for the Colonies which may explain Germain's attitude. When Clinton had failed in an attack on Charleston in 1776, he had written a letter describing the seige which found its way into Germain's hands. Germain, for some reason best known only to himself, had published Clinton's letter in such distorted form that it had made Clinton seem both coward and fool. There followed an undignified fracas: the General threatening the Secretary of State with a duel and hastening to England to implement his threat; the Secretary of State dispatching a secretary to Portsmouth to urge the General back to America as soon as he landed; the General refusing pacification, but accepting eventually the thanks of both Houses of Parliament and the Order of the Bath; the Secretary of State so nervous for his safety that when he found that Order filled he persuaded the King to let in one more Knight, Sir Henry Clinton, rather than fail in his promise and thus offend the General once more. And behind all this lay ancient memories: George Germain had been censured for desertion at the Battle of Minden, and Henry Clinton, who was both brave and by no means stupid, had no intention of being tactful and threw out frequent reminders of the Minister's cowardice.

This dispute between General and Minister may not have caused Germain's failure to support Clinton in his plans as Commander-in-Chief in North America – it is possible that Germain would not have known how to support a general in the field even if he had liked him – but certainly it did not improve the situation.

Clinton had none of Howe's reluctance to destroy America by violence. Though he was ordered from London to send five thousand troops to the West Indies and three thousand to Florida – this from an army which Howe had already and correctly described as inadequate – and although he was told 'to endeavour without delay to bring Mr Washington to a general action', Clinton had other ideas. He realized the impossibility of a major victory. He appreciated that whereas his predecessor had won victories over the rebel army he had won no political victories over the rebel people, while Washington, even in defeat, had strengthened his hold over the affections of his countrymen. Clinton set about to conquer America piecemeal. His small army moved hither and thither and everywhere was victorious and destructive. Washington had nowhere the strength to defend the countryside against Clinton's intelligent dartings.

But neither had Clinton the strength to hold what he had won, and Germain saw to it that the strength was never his.

Meanwhile, French troopships were constantly arriving in American ports, and the Americans themselves were slowly dragging their way through the miseries of disorganization, of lack of supplies and even lack of enthusiasm on the part of the troops for long-term service with the colours.

Most crass of all Germain's many follies was his order for Clinton to evacuate Philadelphia. As the British Army dragged itself wearily into New Jersey it was offered as sacrifice to Washington. But if the British had George Germain, the Americans suffered no less from Charles Lee, and this double traitor, Washington's second-in-command, so bedevilled his commander into indecision as to justify the comment of the eager Alexander Hamilton: that a council of war at that time 'would have done honour to the Most Honourable Society of Midwives and to them only'.

Washington made his decision for a battle, but against the will of many of his officers and, above all, against the will of Charles Lee, who only agreed to accept the responsibility for the preliminary skirmishes because Washington had accepted his first refusal and ordered Lafayette to take his place.

At Monmouth Court House on 28 June 1778 Washington could have destroyed Clinton's army, and it was here, if anywhere, that the weakness of his tactical generalship was evident. He struck at Clinton's rear instead of at the middle of his column, he used infantry instead of fast-moving cavalry. (The Virginian fox-hunter showed a surprising ignorance of the value of the horse in battle.) But the tactical failure was nothing when compared with the conduct of Lee. When the British forces turned in unexpected fury, Lee turned too – in unexpected haste – and with him all his troops. What should have ended in the destruction of Clinton's army, ended in nothing but confusion.

Monmouth Court House was the last open engagement of the war, but by no means the end of fighting. The British Army reached New York and remained there on the defensive. From now on it was the British policy to take the offensive in the South. Lord Cornwallis was sent down to South Carolina where he won victory after victory and set the Americans to dancing a pretty dance. Charleston fell to him on 12 May 1780, and Cornwallis, with an army of some four thousand men, set out to continue the war into Virginia. Almost it seemed as if Clinton's policies of divide and destroy might be successful. There were further defections from the American side; the greatest of them, which might have also proved entirely fatal to the American party, was the offer of Benedict Arnold to hand over by treachery the great fortress of West Point.

On 13 October 1780, the Honourable G. Damer wrote

to Lord George Germain, 'It is painful to think of what accounts and letters of this date might have transmitted to Europe had not a plan finally settled been disconnected by the Adjutant-General falling into the rebels' hands upon the eve of its execution.' The Adjutant-General, Major John André, in the moments of his capture, trial, and execution, made one of those romantic entries into world history which still the logic of greater events. The Americans, who had condemned him as a spy, wept even as they pronounced sentence. Those who were detailed to escort him to his ignominious end admitted publicly their hatred for the task, and the most loyal secretary to the American Commander-in-Chief turned reproachfully upon Washington the irreproachable and could not keep his disgust for Washington's role in this affair, even from his letter – almost the last before their marriage – to his fiancée, Elizabeth Schuyler:

> André suffers today. Everything that is amiable in virtue, in fortitude, in delicate sentiment, and accomplished manners, pleads for him; but hard-hearted policy calles for a sacrifice – some people are only sensible to motives of policy and sometimes, from a narrow disposition, mistake it.

News of André's execution reached New York and the British Army in North America went into mourning for a mere local major, 'a gentleman whose integrity and uncommon ability did honour to their service, to his country, and to human nature, a gentleman incapable of any base action'.

> André was executed
> He looked both meek and mild
> His face was fair and handsome
> And pleasantly he smiled
> It moved each eye with pity
> And every heart there bled
> And every one wished him released
> And Arnold in his stead.

Arnold, much abused by history for his part in the affair, escaped to serve with some distinction but little honour on the other side, his main fault his overweening pride, his main disadvantage the uncertainty of many men who could not make up their minds about the true calls of loyalty in a civil war.

But most important of all, West Point, and with it the control of the Hudson, was still in American hands. The crisis had been averted.

Seldom can the traditional distaste between soldiers and politicians have reached such peaks of animosity as it did in the Revolutionary War.

Even on the American side the good patriots in the field could not always hide their hatred for the good patriots in the council chamber. And, as the war progressed, there seemed to be fewer and fewer politicians who were either good or patriotic. After the ordeal at Valley Forge, the army was reduced to miserable poverty. Continental paper money, with which the troops were paid, when they were paid at all, was useless as currency, and as paper barely useful for the lighting of bivouac-fires. Prices soared and then soared further under the pressure of foreign debts. 'The true point of light,' wrote Washington to Gouverneur Morris, 'is not simply whether Great Britain can carry on the war, but whose Finances (theirs or ours) is most likely to fall.'

Only the profiteers prospered. In the same letter to Morris Washington poured out his misery:

A rat in the shape of a horse, is not to be bought at the time for less than two hundred pounds; A Saddle under Thirty or Forty; Boots twenty, – and shoes and other articles in like proportion – How is it possible, therefore, for officers to stand this without an increase of pay? And how is it possible to advance their Pay, when Flour is selling (at different places) for five or fifteen pounds per cwt., – Hay from ten to thirty per Tunn, and Beef & other essentials in like proportion.

The profiteers were in government. The honest men were either fighting with the army, abroad on foreign missions, or else had returned home to the pursuit of their private thoughts and their private and local interests. Even Washington's Virginian colleagues seemed to have deserted him:

In the present situation [he wrote in 1778] I cannot help asking – Where is Mason – Wythe – Jefferson – Nicholas – Pendleton – Nelson – and another I would name – and why, if you are sufficiently impressed with your danger, do you not send an extra member or two for at least a limited time till the great business of the Nation is put upon a more respectable and happy establishment.

On the American side too there was always the risk of defection; a risk that was increased by the subtlety and efficiency of British agents and the omnipresence of Loyalists both avowed and secret. Sometimes the risk became a reality, as with Charles Lee and Arnold; sometimes it got no further than correspondence of dubious integrity, as in the case of the exchanges between General Gates and General Phillips in December 1778; but the possibility of treachery in high places was always in Washington's mind.

Nor was the emotional comfort of the armies facing the British increased by the arrival of French troops. At the end of the war Washington, in a 'bread-and-butter letter' to his great lieutenant, Rochambeau, slavered the usual exaggerations of international diplomacy:

We have been contemporaries and fellow labourers in the cause of liberty, and we have lived together as brothers should in harmonious friendship.

But France – and many of the Frenchmen in America – was hardly concerned with the ideal of liberty. Rochambeau himself, sturdily professional and loyal to his king's instructions even to the extent of obeying the non-professional American commander, knew well the purpose of his expedition: to strike where the blow would prove most disastrous to Britain. American liberty was a means to an end, and ideologically, a despised means; the 'cause' was France and the defeat of France's ancient enemy.

Rochambeau's juniors could barely hide their unease in the presence of revolution; their sense of superiority over the 'provincials' they guarded as best they could in public, but could not hide from their private diaries:

All the tailors and all the apothecaries must have responded to the call, one recognised them by their round wigs, nearly all miserably mounted, wearing game-bags and shoulder-belts. I judged that these warriors were not coming to see the enemy too close, but to help eat up our victuals.

As for the American view of the French, it is best drawn by a Frenchman, the Abbé Claude Robin, who served with the Soissonnais Regiment:

Before the war the Americans regarded the French as enslaved to despotism, a prey to all manner of superstitions and prejudices; as people quite incapable of solid and consistent effort, only occupied in such matters as curling their hair and painting their faces, and far from being respecters of the most sacred duties. These prejudices had been spread and emphasized by the English; then, at the beginning of the war, not a few things happened to confirm their unfavourable opinions. The great majority of the French who came to America when the rumour of revolution reached them were men who had lost their reputations and were wholly in debt and who generally presented themselves under false names and titles of nobility to which they had no manner of right. Under these false pretences, some of them obtained high rank in the American Army, also considerable advances in money, and then disappeared.

Although Robin goes on to describe the change from suspicion to idyll wrought by the arrival of Rochambeau's regular army, by 'our mild, careful, and moderate' common soldiers, and by the example of 'complete simplicity' of 'our young nobles', it is the suspicion and not the idyll which best portrays the alliance.

But if all this contributed to *malaise* on the American side, it was nothing when compared to the positive disease of British spirit. The hatred of Clinton for Germain was felt and shared by officers and men alike. Not only the commanders, but also many junior officers and other ranks in the British forces were disgusted by the incompetent administration of the war, not only Howe (and Cornwallis, who had voted against the Stamp Act), but also many in subordinate positions, could not be certain that their armed intervention was based upon right as well as might.

As to the matter of right [wrote one of them, a young Scots officer, Sir James Murray] if the Americans are convinced that it is more for the good of that country to be independent of Great Britain and at the same time are able to accomplish it, they are most indisputably in the right to make the attempt.

At home, after 1778, the administration lost favour even with Tories. Among Whigs – and among the merchant classes generally – such was the bitterness of the opposition that a 'patriotic Duke' told of the fate of a British man-of-war, lost at sea in a storm without one survivor, and told his story 'with joy sparkling in his eyes'. Dr Richard Price, the economist and Nonconformist preacher, used his London pulpit for pro-American propaganda, and used it so effectively that on 6 October 1778 a grateful Congress passed a resolution:

That the Hon. Benjamin Franklin, Arthur Lee, and John Adams esq., or any of them, be ordered forthwith to apply to Dr. Price and inform him that it is the desire of Congress to consider him as a citizen of the United States, and to receive his assistance in regulating their finances; [no inconsiderable task at that juncture] that if he shall think it expedient to remove with his family to America and afford such assistance, a generous provision should be made for requiting his services.

David Hume died in 1776, but already he, though a Tory, had declared himself 'an American in my principles' and had urged that he wished to see America 'revolted totally and finally'. Adam Smith, to the very end of the war, hoped for a federal solution but could never support conquest. Burke and Fox battered at the Ministry in abusive speech after abusive speech.

The Government had some vocal supporters, John Wesley, surprisingly, and Dr Johnson, less strangely, being among them, but James Boswell, like so many of his countrymen on both sides of the Border, could not follow his god in this, 'I am growing more and more an American,' he wrote to Temple early in the War, 'I see the unreasonableness of taxing them without the consent of their Assemblies; I think our Ministry are mad in undertaking this desperate war.'

He refused to 'join in imploring Heaven's blessing on the arms of the present administration', and eventually the news of Yorktown made him so 'inspirited, that though for some time I have been quite lazy in the morning, relaxed and unable to rise, I this day sprung up'.

So much anti-war feeling all over Britain might have ended the War in 1778, when there was a strong move towards conciliation, but then the intervention of France gave the ministerial side a new lease of life. It was liberal to preach amity towards the Americans and respect for the justice of the American cause; it was treason to urge objections to war with the ancient and much-hated enemy. And, just as the Americans themselves found it difficult to excuse – even to themselves – an alliance with despotism, so did British Whigs falter in their opposition to the war in that moment when France became the enemy.

There was a sudden increase in recruiting and a few victories might have swung the country to enthusiastic support of the war. But victories were hard to come by. Taxation reached oppressive levels which seemed to the eighteenth century unbearable, and under oppressive taxation the bourgeoisie recovered its pro-American zeal.

The Gordon Riots, which in origins had little to do with the American War, and which sprang in fact from surprisingly liberal activities on the part of the Government, brought to North yet another chance to continue the war with a united country behind him, for it seemed as if the enormities of the rioters might bring about a coalition; on one occasion, North even found himself in the same lobby as Fox! But all that the Gordon Riots contrived was the stillbirth of a secret mission to Spain, which might have detached that country from the Franco-American alliance.

In Britain everything seemed destined to hasten the day when newsboys would shout in the streets 'Good news for England! Lord North in the dumps, and peace with America.'

For all his treachery, the British policy of divide and conquer had gained an efficient exponent in Benedict

Arnold, and his raids into Virginia at the end of 1780 and early in 1781 paved the way for Lord Cornwallis, who seemed almost bound to destroy the American supply and recruiting bases in the South. The comparatively small American forces in Virginia, under the command of Lafayette and Steuben, could not bring Cornwallis to battle with any hope of success, and Cornwallis was as efficient in the use of cavalry as Washington was inefficient. He gave exercise to the genius of Banastre Tarleton while the Americans left Anthony Wayne to command foot-soldiers, and a major success for British cavalry was narrowly avoided when on 4 June 1781 Jefferson, the retired Governor of Virginia, the newly elected Governor, Thomas Nelson, and many members of the Virginia Legislature (including Richard Henry Lee and Patrick Henry) only escaped capture in Charlottesville by the accident of a visit by a wandering officer of the Virginia militia and a violent dash through the night by that same officer, Captain Jack Jouett.

In the heat of the summer, Cornwallis was faced with the problem of deciding whether he should continue to move westwards or else turn back to the coast to seek the covering support of the Royal Navy and a renewal of communications by sea with Clinton in New York. His decision was for the east, and by way of Richmond and Williamsburg Cornwallis moved to Yorktown to set up his base.

Meanwhile Washington too was having his moment of indecision: as to whether to attack Clinton in New York or Cornwallis in Virginia. At a conference at the end of May Washington persuaded Rochambeau to join in an attack against New York supported by the French West Indian Fleet under De Grasse, but the decision was changed when the news reached Washington early in August that the French Fleet had left the West Indies for the Chesapeake Bay, carrying with it three thousand French reinforcements. Immediately, leaving only a small holding force above New York, the American and French armies crossed the Hudson and moved southwards towards Virginia.

Yorktown was a strong defensive position, but it could also turn into a trap. The wide York River lay to the north and the James not far to the south. To the east lay the sea; if Cornwallis ever needed to escape, the land route to the west was his only hope. That hope was soon damned by the armies of Washington and Rochambeau.

And now the sea gods, who had fought so often on the side of the British, turned against them. Admiral Graves strove bitterly to hold off De Grasse's more powerful fleet, succeeded for a while, but then had to return to New York for refit. Cornwallis was surrounded and, had he but known it, hopeless, for the winds in the Atlantic were against his only chance of succour: the squadrons of Britain's West Indies Fleet.

British troops dug defences in the green fields above the York River. Time after time they sallied out in attempts to bring back the enemy or silence his guns. Night after night in the third week of October 1781 they manned their positions waiting for the enemy's attacks.

The Atlantic weather came down even into the York River to destroy the British. Cornwallis's desperate attempt to ferry his troops across the York was foiled by the winds. It was left to Cornwallis to decide whether to surrender the last British force of consequence in North America or to fight to the death. He had still seven thousand men under command, but many of them were sick and many of them wounded. The town of Yorktown was a shambles and relief seemingly impossible. On 17 October Cornwallis made his decision; he decided, as he was forced to decide, for capitulation. On the 18th, while the bands played 'The World Turned Upside Down', his second-in-command, General O'Hara, acting in his place, made the last gesture of a defiant Old World by offering his sword to Rochambeau instead of Washington.

Six days later Clinton arrived off the Chesapeake with seven thousand reinforcements, but turned back for New York on hearing the news of Cornwallis's surrender. A few months later, and in one battle, the Battle of the Saints,

Rodney, the wind this time on his side, had saved the West Indies and captured De Grasse.

But it was too late, the heart had gone out of the British war effort, and in this moment the Americans were as glad to rest upon their independence and to make a unilateral peace with Britain as were the British to seek peace terms with America. The war was virtually over.

New York, Long Island, Charleston, and Georgia were still in British hands, Canada was still a potent threat to American success, but to detach America from her European allies it was necessary to withdraw every British soldier from the territories governed by Congress.

On 27 February 1782 the House of Commons voted against further prosecution of the war in America. On 5 March, a bill was passed authorizing the Crown to make peace, and on the 20th Lord North resigned, to be succeeded by Lord Rockingham, the minister who had secured the repeal of the Stamp Act in 1766. The completeness of the reversal of circumstances could not have been better demonstrated than by two Ministerial appointments: Shelburne to be Secretary to the Colonies, and Charles James Fox to be Secretary of State for Foreign Affairs.

Only at this moment was Sir Guy Carlton brought down from Canada, his task to begin the evacuation of British troops!

In September, October, and November of 1782, a preliminary Treaty of Peace between the British and the Americans was negotiated in Paris. With Benjamin Franklin's original and extravagant demand that Canada should be ceded, dropped, and with the Congressional Commissioners, John Adams, Franklin, Jay, and Laurens virtually ignoring Congress's instructions that they should act only after full consultation with the French, the terms of the Treaty were not without gratification even to the defeated party.

American independence was recognized and boundaries fixed as follows:

The St Croix River divided Maine from Nova Scotia; the

St Lawrence, the Forty-Fifth Parallel, a line through the
Great Lakes and their connecting waterways, and a line
through Lake Superior to the Mississippi, divided Upper
Canada from the United States; a line through the middle of
the Mississippi south to the Thirty-First Parallel was deemed
to be the boundary with Spanish Louisiana, and the Thirty-
First Parallel and the Apalachicola and St Mary's Rivers
as a boundary with Spanish Florida. The United States was
given the right to fish off Newfoundland and Nova Scotia
and to dry and cure fish on any uninhabited shores in
Labrador, the Magdalen Islands, and Nova Scotia. All
debts due to creditors of either country by citizens of others
were validated, the Congress was pledged, a pledge that it
did not fulfil, to 'earnestly recommend' to the Legislatures
of the states a full restoration of the rights and properties of
the Loyalists.

The fate of these American Loyalists deserves at least a
parenthesis. A few – a very few – returned to the new
United States and settled there more or less happily. One,
Josiah Hoffman, became New York's Attorney General;
another, Samuel Seabury, author of many important
Loyalist pamphlets, including *The Letters of a Westchester
Farmer* and *The Congress Canvassed*, secured the apostolic
succession to the Episcopal Church of America by having
himself consecrated in 1784 by three bishops of the pro-
scribed Scottish Apostolic Church. Most Loyalists, however,
were forbidden to return under Acts of Banishment which,
in the case of some states, remained in force for thirty years.
Many remained in England, where often they were hardly
happier than they had been in Revolutionary America –
despite the surprising generosity with which the British
Government compensated Loyalists for their losses in
America. A few thousand – almost all from Southern states
– settled in the West Indies and there was even a plan for a
Loyalist colony in Australia.

The majority of the Loyalists went to Canada, to Nova
Scotia, to Upper Canada and to the area on the St John
River, soon to be the province of New Brunswick. Some

fifty thousand arrived in one year, 1783. When the First Council of New Brunswick met in 1784, it included three ex-American judges, a Regular Army colonel, two colonels of Colonial Corps and at least two close friends of George Washington!

In the new United States, even in this time of rejoicing, the nation was not without internal dissension. Early in 1783 a group of army officers petitioned Congress for a settlement of their financial grievances. All through the year, while the British Army was leaving and the last of the Loyalists sailing for Europe or Canada, Congress faced difficulties with its own disbanding forces. In June, out of fear of demonstrations and mutiny, Congress was even forced to leave Philadelphia.

So, coinciding with the success of the war for secession, there began the first of a series of battles for the control of the new nation, obscurely at first as the actions of a few disgruntled army officers were inevitably obscure, but in mounting excitement and force as the struggle became more obvious between authoritarianism and *laissez-faire* agrarianism.

CHAPTER 18

ORGANIZING A NATION

THE colonies had become States. The war was won. The British had left for Great Britain and those who favoured the British had either left with them or had fled into the fogs along the Saint John River. It remained to construct the United States.

Much had been achieved towards this end. Even the violent years had created in the minds of some a sense of patriotism towards America in the place of loyalty to the individual colony. The bold words of the Declaration of Independence – and the necessities of war – had won a measure of acceptance for egalitarian principles which would have been inconceivable even a quarter of a century earlier. It is true that no state introduced manhood suffrage or the universal right to hold office, but more men voted than ever before and the new constitutions, in this unlike the colonial governments, had their roots in popular consent and the lives of the people.

The American Revolution was a relatively conservative revolution which, from the American point of view, was fought to protect certain rights and practices which the colonists believed they already possessed. Its intent was not to destroy an established order, but rather to be allowed to create another without interference. American radicals, by European standards, were hardly more than cautious liberals; yet their Revolution was a true revolution in that it wrought irrevocable changes in American society, in some cases simply by allowing movements already under way to continue without hindrance and in others by initiating wholly new trends.

The Revolution did not create an egalitarian, level, homogeneous society. The war did not substantially alter the colonial class structure, which by the mid eighteenth century had already become different from that of Britain or Continental Europe. Wealth, lineage, manners, talent, education and such things counted in post-Revolutionary America much as they had before. Enlightened Americans, like Jefferson, believed in leadership by the 'natural aristocracy of worth' and in the social and political guidance of 'gentlemen'. John Adams, though a committed revolutionary, felt that there had to be stability and order in the new society, with 'decency and respect and veneration introduced for persons in authority, and at every rank'.

It included, of course, rich and poor, educated and ignorant, gentleman and boor, but as Lafayette noted, the gap between the classes was much narrower and more easily bridged than in Europe.

Other revolutions, the French, the Russian, even to some extent the British in the seventeenth century, have rushed from liberalism into extremism, from street-corner tub-thumping to street-corner executions. Despite the tar and feathers, despite the avid confiscation of Tory property, the history of the American Revolution is virtually free from tales of vindictive slaughter, and, both during the war and at its successful conclusion, there was a remarkably small shift in the social structure of the country.

The extremist and violent element in most revolutions has been the deprived group, the peasants working land they can never hope to own, the urban wage-earners who see no way of improving their condition without first destroying their employers. America had neither a peasant population nor a real urban proletariat; only the Negro slaves of the South were in any sense equivalent to the *sans-culottes* or the serfs, and the Revolution had, for the most part, passed by the Negro and left him unchanged, his condition no happier under republic than it had been under king.

Property was the idol of the American people, but many could worship at its shrine, for property meant ten acres or ten thousand, a lean-to store or a great trading-business. Poor men could dream of winning riches without suffering miserable and dangerous wakening to harsh impossibility, for, from the beginning of their history Americans had seen poor men turn, in a very few years, into rich men. The American *mythos* needed no fairy godmothers, only land, hard work, and shrewdness. The land was there. Stretching seemingly to infinity the great West was opening its arms to the pioneer, the adventurer – and to the failure.

As westward expansion had been the cause of so much hope, despair, and military effort in the past, so now, but now more than ever before, it both exercised the thoughts of the nation and served as a safety-valve against disaster and political extremism.

But much was yet for resolution before the country could turn happily from the business of defining itself to the more lucrative business of enlarging itself. The states in combination had defeated Britain, but with the reason for combination achieved there was left a void which needed to be filled by constitution, a lack of organization which could only be rectified by nationhood.

Yorktown did not create the United States. For many Americans, and particularly for many who had served in the army, the struggle for victory had been an experience disastrous to their original enthusiasm. Alexander Hamilton, for example, from being a staunch 'freedom' man in 1775 had by the end of the war come to resent the American lack of discipline. He, like many of his military colleagues, had started out to resist strong government and, in resistance, had learnt to be one of its most ardent admirers. Having overthrown British government in America, Hamilton (and many Americans) now looked for a way of rebuilding it in the American image.

There is nothing more common [wrote a contemporary] than to confound the terms of the American Revolution with those of the late American war. The American war is over, but this is far from being the case with the American Revolution. On the contrary, nothing but the first act of the great drama is closed.

The new war for America was fought in the debating chambers and the printing shops. Its generals were, on the one hand, Alexander Hamilton and John Marshall with their belief in a system of government founded upon the sanctity of contracts and well protected against democratic interference, their confidence resting upon the dual privileges of capital and aristocracy, and, on the other, Franklin, Jefferson, and a generation later, John Taylor and Andrew Jackson, whose ideal was to continue those agrarian elements in colonial society which had made the way of America, in their view, utterly different from the old way of Europe.

To the Jeffersonians, Europe had decayed not merely because Europe lacked political democracy but also because it lacked economic democracy; it was, to their thinking, the economic as much as the political advantages of the ruling classes which the American Revolution had overthrown. They did not, they could not as Americans, abhor property, but they were anxious to create a system of equality, of economic opportunity, so that no man could acquire comfort except by his own industry.

Such democracy could not work in Europe:

And if Caesar had been as virtuous as he was daring and sagacious, what could he, even in the plentitude of his usurped power, have done to lead his fellow citizens into good government? I do not say to *restore it*, because they never had it, from the rape of the Sabines to the ravages of the Caesars. If their people indeed had been, like ourselves, enlightened, peaceable, and really free, the answer would be obvious. 'Restore independence to all your foreign conquests, relieve Italy from the government of the rabble of Rome, consult it as a nation entitled to self-government, and do its will.' But steeped in corruption, vice and venality, as the whole nation was (and nobody had done more than Caesar to corrupt it), what could even Cicero, Cato, Brutus have done, had it been referred to them to establish a good government for their country? They had no ideas of government themselves, but of their degenerate Senate, nor the people of liberty, but of the factious opposition of their Tribunes. They had afterwards their Tituses, their Trajans, and Antoninuses, who had the will to make them happy, and the power to mould their government into a good and permanent form. But it would seem as if they could not see their way clearly to do it. No government can continue good, but under the control of the people; and their people were so demoralized and depraved, as to be incapable of exercising a wholesome control.

But in America, where the predominantly agricultural population had enjoyed 'in ease and security the full fruits of their own industry, enlisted by all their interests on the side of law and order, habituated to think for themselves, and to follow their reason as their God', it was not only the right form of government but the most practicable.

Between the Hamiltonians and the Jeffersonians was a gap almost as wide as that which had existed between the colonial governors and their recalcitrant legislatures; Hamilton was for firm government and much government by the informed few, Jefferson for easy government and little government by the will of the majority. In 1787 Jefferson wrote to James Madison:

I own, I am not a friend to a very energetic government. It is always oppressive. It places the governors indeed more at their ease, at the expense of the people. The late rebellion in Massachusetts has given more alarm, than I think it should have done. Calculate that one rebellion in thirteen States in the course of eleven years, is but one for each State in a century and a half. No country should be so long without one. Nor will any degree of power in the hands of government, prevent insurrections. In England, where the hand of power is heavier than with us, there are seldom half a dozen years without an insurrection. In France, where it is still heavier, but less despotic, as Montesquieu supposes, than in some other countries, and where there are always two or three hundred thousand men ready to crush insurrections, there have been three in the course of the three years I have been here, in every one of which greater numbers were engaged than in Massachusetts, and a great deal more blood was spilt. In Turkey, where the sole nod of the despot is death, insurrections are the events of every day. Compare again the ferocious depredations of their insurgents, with the order, the moderation and the almost self-extinguishment of ours. And say, finally, whether peace is best preserved by giving energy to the government, or information to the people. This last is the most certain, and the most legitimate engine of government. Educate and inform the whole mass of the people. Enable them to see that it is their interest to preserve peace and order, and they will preserve them. And it requires no very high degree of education to convince them of this. They are the only sure reliance for the preservation of our liberty. After all, it is my principle that the will of the majority should prevail. If they approve the proposed constitution in all its parts, I shall concur in it cheerfully, in hopes they will amend it, whenever they shall find it works wrong.

The victory in this second phase of the American Revolution was with those who distrusted the wisdom of the majority.

During the Revolution most of the thirteen states had drawn up for themselves new constitutions: only Connecticut and Rhode Island had taken the easy way of continuing to operate under seventeenth-century charters by the simple process of eliminating all references to the Crown.

The Revolutionary leaders agreed that they wanted a government which guaranteed to them all those individual and political and economic privileges which they believed that the British colonial system denied them. They assumed that since they had been unable to govern themselves as they wished under a strong centralized government in London, they could possibly do so under a weaker American government in Philadelphia; furthermore, their whole colonial experience had taught them to distrust any political authority very far beyond their reach. According to the Articles of Confederation, therefore, the United States was 'a firm league of friendship', nothing more, in which 'each state retains its sovereignty, freedom, and independence'.

When the state constitutions were drawn up between 1776 and 1780, they usually placed the essentials of political control – taxes, currency, militia, voting rights, appointments, guarantees of civil and natural rights – with the state legislatures. These new state constitutions were the first step in translating the principles of the Revolution and the Declaration into immediate practical terms, and also established precedents and processes later of great usefulness in political life. The device of the convention, employed by most of the states as a means of evolving their constitutions, became the standard pattern for the actual making of a social compact and long the model for establishing or revising constitutions all over the western world. In addition, these documents introduced into politics the American conviction that government should be based on a written document, which spelled out the principles on which it was founded and which should have the approval of those who were to live under it. The careful, specific construction of written instruments of government on such a large scale was an important contribution to the political tradition.

The fathers of these state constitutions were convinced that the documents they produced should guarantee those 'inalienable rights' of which the Declaration spoke and for which the Revolution was presumably being waged. They were natural rights, ante-dating government and bestowed on men by the Creator, 'rights', wrote Thomas Paine, 'which always appertain to man in right of his existence'. While they were never fully enumerated and defined, there was general agreement that they included the protection of life, the acquisition and security of property, freedom of movement, equal justice before law, and the freedom to speak, write, and think within certain limits. Some of the rights and the privileges deriving from them, so the revolutionaries maintained, had been denied them by British policy; therefore in drafting the new state constitutions it seemed wise to attach to them written 'bills of rights' which listed and defined them. The first of these, the Virginia Bill of Rights (which served as a pattern for the Bill attached later to the Constitution), enumerated the liberties needed by a free society: trial by jury; no taxation without representation; no hereditary offices; prohibition of excessive bail, self-incrimination, and general warrants of search and seizure; the right to bear arms; free press and free speech; the control of military by civil power; and the free exercise of religion. Other state conventions joined similar Bills of Rights to their constitutions, even though in some cases the constitutions themselves were merely re-phrasings of the old colonial charters.

Pennsylvania alone favoured a unicameral legislature,

but all the states put the substance of power in the hands of the lower house. In nine states the lower house originated all money bills, in eight it elected the executive, and in six shared the appointing power.

The old habit of mistrust towards the royal governors continued into the new era and was responsible for the many checks upon the power of the chief executive: a one-year term in nine states, bars against reappointment in seven, no veto power in nine, a council of appointment of which he was but one member in New York, popular election in New York and Massachusetts. But South Carolina, while sharing with its neighbours the desire to limit the power of the governor, was constant in its belief that though a governor should not rule, he should belong without doubt to the ruling class: for the office of Governor of South Carolina a candidate had to own at least ten thousand pounds worth of property.

Most states insisted upon frequent elections. Eight states contrived an appointive judiciary with tenure for good behaviour. New Jersey and Pennsylvania appointed judges for seven-year terms, New Hampshire for five years.

But whatever the virtues or defects of the state constitutions, they were thirteen and unlinked; from them the objects of the Articles of Confederation, drafted in 1777 and brought into operation in 1781 – a common defence, security of liberty and general welfare – were in no whit furthered over America as a whole. There was in fact neither an *American* constitution nor an effective *American* government. The states virtually organized their own foreign affairs, and thus prevented the implementation of some of the terms of the peace treaty with Britain. In the first years of the peace state rivalries for Western trade were intense and led at times, as in the Wyoming Valley dispute between Pennsylvania and Connecticut, to excursions under arms. State set up customs barriers against neighbouring state.

Agreement on a new method of operating the economic affairs of the nation became imperative, and the urgent nature of the need was emphasized by dangers from without.

As Congress had been unable to force upon the states compliance with those clauses of the peace treaty which promised settlement with British debtors and restoration of the property of Loyalists, so the British retaliated by refusing to evacuate North-Western posts. In the South, the Spaniards, with the consent and support of some settlers in Kentucky and Tennessee who preferred affluence under Spain to poverty under the United States, were threatening to close the Mississippi to American trade.

British mercantilism, much hated by the colonials, had nevertheless provided them with protection and encouragement in world markets. With this protection self-abolished, the new nation faced great difficulties in finding for itself an independent position among the trading nations. There was a continuing unfavourable trade-balance, foreign currency was short, and the shortage exacerbated the internal problems caused by the failure to meet obligations towards ex-soldiers of the Revolutionary Army.

Inside Congress a number of attempts were made to strengthen the Articles of Confederation in the direction of greater power for Congress. But as James Monroe of Virginia wrote to Jefferson in 1785, 'Some gentlemen have inveterate prejudices against all attempts to increase the powers of Congress, others see the necessity but fear the consequences.'

Trade had power beyond politics and first Maryland and Virginia, then these two with Pennsylvania and Delaware agreed to meet together to discuss the limited problems of the defence and control of waterways. From this, and at the instigation of Virginia, all the states were invited to confer to consider the condition of the country's commerce and its relation to a strong foreign policy.

A temporary loss of interest by most of the states rendered nugatory the Annapolis Convention of September 1786 – even Maryland itself was not represented. But, at the instigation of Alexander Hamilton, the lonely twelve delegates at Annapolis drafted a report calling upon the states to send representatives to Philadelphia in May 1787, there to consider not merely commercial matters but also to debate the means required 'to render the constitution of the Federal Government adequate to the exigencies of the Union'.

Still the sturdier supporters of the rights of individual states might have avoided decision had not two elements been against them: the aristocratic and propertied minority and the Frontier. Extraordinary cavortings in philosophical argument brought these two elements into surprising if ephemeral agreement.

James Madison, born in the Virginia Piedmont, and therefore a child of the Frontier, but nevertheless a product of the Virginia planter-aristocracy, was well qualified by birth to cement the alliance between hopeful Westerners and the established property-owners of the Atlantic seaboard. His intellect and his response to the minds of others qualified him beyond his social peers. Princeton, America's Scottish university, had reared him; the works of Hume, Smith, James, and Ferguson, as taught by Princeton's vigorous President Witherspoon, had brought to him 'very early and strong impressions in favor of Liberty both Civil and Religious'.

Indubitably a radical, and by 1787 the acknowledged leader of the Virginia radicals in the place of Jefferson (who had been appointed Minister to France), Madison was nevertheless convinced that unless the Federal organization was strengthened the united successes of the Revolution would be squandered in a competitive system of sovereign states, and that the achievement of peace with Britain would be rendered valueless within America by 'an appeal to the sword in every petty squabble, standing armies, and perpetual taxes'.

His letter to James Monroe, written on 5 October 1786, was typical of the arguments he used to bring his fellow-aristocrats and his neighbours to his side:

There is no maxim, in my opinion, which is more liable to be misapplied, and which therefore needs more elucidation, than the current one, that the interest of the majority is the political standard of right and wrong. Taking the word 'interest' as synonymous with ultimate happiness, in which sense it is qualified with every moral 'ingredient', it is no doubt true. But taking it in the popular sense, as referring to the immediate augmentation of property and wealth, nothing can be more false. In the latter sense it would be the interest of the majority, in every community, to despoil and enslave the minority of individuals, and in a Federal community to make a similar sacrifice of the minority of the component parts. In fact, it is only re-establishing, under another name, and a more specious form, force as a measure of right; (and in this light the Western settlements will infallibly view it).

But, if these arguments were close to casuistry, there was deeper and sounder philosophy in Madison's view of the approaching debates on constitutional revision. He it was who, like Hamilton, was to bear the heat of battle for federalism, but, unlike his partner, Madison would neither be blown by the gusts of reaction nor buffeted by gales of desperation. Thought was to him a natural activity for which he was well prepared; emotion he found more difficult, but if emotion was necessary to carry with less philosophical creatures the arguments which Madison founded upon thought, then somehow Madison would contrive emotion for their benefit.

Long before he left for Philadelphia, Madison had begun his preparations for argument. With Jefferson as his book-buyer he collected a library of 'Treatises on the ancient and modern Federal Republics'. He studied the histories of historic confederations, of the Lycian League, the Amphictyonic Council, the Helvetian Republic and the United Netherlands. They gave 'no other light than that of beacons, which give warnings of the course to be shunned, without pointing out that which ought to be pursued'. Political theorists seemed unanimous in the view that sound republican government over a population of varied interests could only be maintained in a compact country. The great empires of the past were all monarchies.

So far Madison's arguments with his own scholarship ran close to the arguments which Hamilton was producing instinctively. But here the ways parted. What had never been achieved was according to Hamilton impossible in America; to Madison it was imperative that America should develop a new theory of federalism. From his own mind and from his research he devised, a month before the Convention met, a practical scheme of governmental organization which accepted the rule of the majority but provided safeguards for the rights of the minority. His scheme became the basis of the Virginia Plan; that Plan, much battered in Philadelphia debates of which he was the undoubted hero – he 'took the lead in the management of every great question' – formed the basis of the American Constitution.

Madison was fearless but he was ready to make allies of the fearful and it was fear, in fact, which brought many political leaders to accept the need for the Philadelphia Convention.

Nagging at the hearts of many Americans of substance was anxiety aroused by the creed 'that the property of the United States had been protected from the confiscation of Britain by the joint exertions of all, and therefore ought to be the common property of all. . . .' The state constitutions, they felt, were none of them strong enough to combat this creed.

Again the lead in argument came from Virginia. 'Our chief danger arises from the democratic parts of our constitutions. It is a maxim which I hold incontrovertible,' said Edmund Randolph, 'that the powers of government exercised by the people swallow up the other branches. None of the constitutions have provided sufficient checks against the democracy.'

But the final demonstration of the need for strengthening central government came accidentally from Massachusetts. There the merchants had continued to enjoy legal support in collecting their debts and when, in July 1786, the State Legislature adjourned without heeding the pleas of the debt-laden farmers for a new issue of paper currency or a law staying foreclosures on mortgages, protest soon led to mob-action, mob-action to active rebellion. Poor Daniel Shays, a destitute farmer who had served with some little distinction in the Revolutionary War, found himself leading more than a thousand discontented farmers against the militia under General Lincoln. Shays was ignominiously routed, but unwittingly he had taught a lesson to men of property in the legislative assemblies of all the states. Madison and Hamilton seized their chance, but they had powers of persuasion even over those who could not be moved by panic.

As Washington had been the one obvious candidate for the leadership of the Continental Army at the outbreak of war with Britain, so now he was necessary to the success of the Convention as the one unchallengeable President. None were better qualified to persuade Washington to attend than Madison, informed and honest, or Hamilton, his ardent ex-secretary. Together they brought Washington to Philadelphia.

The delegates to the Convention who met in Philadelphia in late May 1787 represented a cross-section of the groups that had provided political leadership since the early eighteenth century – landowners, planters, lawyers, businessmen, shippers, bankers. Forty-one of them had served in Congress, seven were former state governors. Jefferson, John Jay and John Adams were absent on diplomatic service, but the powerful state leaders were there, among them Hamilton of New York, James Wilson and Robert Morris from Pennsylvania, Roger Sherman of Connecticut, Luther Martin of Maryland, and the brilliant Virginia delegation of Edmund Randolph, George Mason, George Wythe and James Madison. In attempting one of the most delicate tasks in political history, that of forming a stable union of independent states under a written body of fundamental law, the delegates had few precedents from which to work. They could draw upon the histories of Greek confederacies, the British and classical traditions of political philosophy, their own colonial experience, and little else. The materials which went into the Constitution were not new; the convention, in an act of creative statesmanship, blended them into new combinations, bringing them to bear directly on the specific problems of their place and time.

The delegates did not come to Philadelphia with any concrete concept of exactly what kind of document they should produce, but as debate wore on there seemed to be general consensus on three things. First of all, the national government they envisaged would be republican in form and aim, consistent with the substance of the American revolutionary philosophy. No one had the slightest intention of repealing the Declaration. Second, the central government should be able to act without the mediation of the states to exercise its will directly on the individual citizen; it would have its own administrative agencies, endowed with the authority to make and enforce laws and treaties, collect its own revenues, and to regulate all those affairs which bore directly on the welfare of the nation. Third, the power of the national government would have to be increased (and that of the states correspondingly lessened) while at the same time held in check lest it seriously infringe the rights of states and individuals. The political system would have to be arranged so that the states would be united under some form of federalized, independent central government while allowing them to maintain some degree of power and identity. The problem, and it was a difficult one, was, as Madison put it, of finding that kind of government which would 'support a due supremacy of national authority, and leave in force the local authorities so far as they can be subordinately useful'.

Almost it seems as a reversal of the fine hopes of the Declaration of Independence and the brave struggles for freedom, the men who came together in Philadelphia towards the end of May 1787 were representatives of 'the opulent minority' driven to consult together by threats to their own class, but the reality is less depressing than the appearance. Contemporary circumstances gave urgency to the drafting of a constitution, but the drafters still held in their consciences the principles for which many of them had fought. They suspected the rule of the ignorant but they were determined to make it possible for the 'gentlemen of principle and property' – themselves – to rule well and with enlightened motives. The Constitution which they eventually drafted was less 'republican', less 'egalitarian' than earlier proclamations on American purpose may seem to justify, but the makers of the Constitution hardly realized the nature of their own people. They believed in democracy but their generation was too strong in them. They hoped for freedom – and republicanism – they spoke up even against such institutions as slavery, but they legislated against the licence of the mob, the European mob, which they imagined that they had seen for a moment active on American soil under the leadership of such as Shays.

Madison appreciated the error of judgement, but his first concern was for the immediate implementation of a strong federal system. Thomas Jefferson appreciated it, but he was far away from the scene. Benjamin Franklin alternately patted and scolded to keep opposing groups from each other's throats, saying paternally on one occasion, 'Gentlemen, we were sent here to confer, not to contest with one another.' Only Charles Pinckney of South Carolina seems to have put to the delegates at Philadelphia that 'We have universally considered ourselves as the inhabitants of an old instead of a new country.'

And Charles Pinckney was ignored.

Yet in Pinckney's speech is the germ of all true criticism of the Philadelphia Convention:

The people of this country are not only very different from the inhabitants of any state we are acquainted with in the modern world; but I assert that their situation is distinct from either the people of Greece or Rome, or of any state we are acquainted with among the ancients . . . there is more equality of rank and fortune in America than in any other country under the sun; and this is likely to continue as long as the unappropriated Western lands remain unsettled. . . . Where are the riches and wealth whose representation and protection is the peculiar province of this present body? Are they in the hands of the few who may be called rich; in the possession of less than a hundred citizens? Certainly not. They are in the general body of the people, among whom there are no men of wealth, and very few of real poverty . . . this equality is likely to continue, because in a new country, possessing immense tracts of uncultivated lands, where every temptation is offered to emigration and where industry must be rewarded with competency, there will be few poor, and few dependent. . . .

The colonial had become a republican; this much all accepted. But the completeness of the change from European to American few could yet comprehend.

The actual terms of the American Constitution were fashioned throughout a summer of debate. Even the powers of the Convention were uncertain. The Virginia Plan proposed a new national government comprising a bicameral legislative system representing the States proportionally. The lower house was to be elected by popular vote, the upper by the lower house on the nomination of state legislatures. A chief executive was to be chosen by the national legislature, and a council of revision consisting of the executive and several members of the judiciary was to be given the power of vetoing legislative acts.

To this the delegates from New Jersey replied with their own Plan which retained the loose Articles of Confederation but conferred upon Congress the power to tax and to regulate foreign and interstate commerce.

On 19 June the Convention agreed to adopt as a basis for its work the Virginia rather than the New Jersey Plan. The delegates had accepted the business of creating a new organization for the United States.

And now battle was joined between the small states and the large, the battle over proportional representation by states. Compromise was effected late in July, and the system agreed of representation proportional to population in the lower house and equal representation in the upper. (In reckoning populations one Negro only counted for three-fifths of a white!)

This principle established, it remained to work out the details of function. The two-year term for Representatives, the six-year term for Senators, the four-year term for the President, all were agreed in three weeks at the end of August and the beginning of September.

Finally, on 17 September, each of the state delegations

voted approval and the Constitution was transmitted to Congress.

Still the battle was but half won. A skirmishing-party of anti-Federalists moved to have Congress censure the Philadelphia Convention for going beyond its limit. This attempt having failed, both the advocates and the opponents of the Constitution set about the business of persuasion by propaganda, in an attempt to affect the decisions of state ratifying conventions.

Europeans had become Americans without understanding the meaning of the translation; it was not by any means certain that New Yorkers, for example, or Virginians, would accept conversion into nationals of the United States. All governments, as Hamilton had told the Philadelphia Convention, require an 'habitual attachment of the people. The whole force of the tie is on the side of the State Government. Its sovereignty is immediately before the eyes of the people; its protection is immediately enjoyed by them.' Thus it was that such ardent Federalists as Hamilton and Madison had been forced to accept, against their theoretical inclinations, the continuation of state government.

But such compromise was not necessarily enough to overcome the objections of state patriots. Patrick Henry, fierce and satirical as ever, rose in the Virginia Ratifying Convention and poured out his objections to the Constitution which would take away his right to serve 'his country', Virginia:

What shall the states have to do? Take care of the poor, repair and make highways, erect bridges, and so on, and so on? Abolish the state legislatures at once. What purposes should they be continued for? Our legislature will indeed be a ludicrous spectacle – one hundred and eighty men marching in solumn, farcical procession, exhibiting a mournful proof of the lost liberty of their country, without the proof of restoring it.

Thirteen years earlier, at the First Continental Congress, Henry had claimed with equal dramatic effect, 'I am not a Virginian, but an American', but Henry was an advocate of genius, his logic and his theatricality were fine and ready even for the task of making white what he himself had painted black.

And in the debates over ratification there were many who agreed with his new arguments. In Rhode Island, state patriotism – as well as the natural fears of the representatives of the smallest state that even constitutional guarantees were not enough to protect the interests of small states against the interests of their more powerful neighbours – had held that state from sending representatives to Philadelphia and it was not until 1790 that Rhode Island finally ratified. In North Carolina, state patriotism – as well as a strong agrarian movement, and a longing which was shared with many other states for the inclusion in the Constitution of a Bill of Rights – defeated the first attempts at ratification and held it up for more than a year.

Fortunately, just as there were emotional advantages with the anti-Federalists, so were there advantages with the Federalists, and the greatest of these was the support of Washington. 'I never saw him so keen for anything in my life,' wrote one friend in 1787, 'as he is for the adoption of the new Form of Government.' Monroe, an anti-Federalist, claimed that Washington's enthusiasm was primarily responsible for the victory of the Federalists, Hamilton placed Washington's prestige among the first of the factors which led to acceptance, and a French observer wrote:

The opinion of General Washington was of such weight that it contributed more than any other measure to cause the present constitution to be adopted. The extreme confidence in his patriotism, his integrity, and his intelligence forms today its principal support. It has become popular much more out of respect for the chief of the republic than by any merit of its own. All is hushed in presence of the trust of the people in the saviour of the country.

In the states, too, there were little Washingtons, and in Massachusetts, New Hampshire, Pennsylvania, and Connecticut the Federalist leadership was so much more able and so much more respected than the opposition that ratification was achieved with comparative ease. (Though in some of these states, as in Massachusetts where Governor

Hancock was bribed with the suggestion that the presidency might be his, it was necessary to throw sops to office-holders who preferred to crow over a dung-heap rather than risk their small voices among the choirs of Heaven, who preferred the comfortable certainty of the old order to an uncertain future. In others waverers were won over by the offer of immediate constitutional amendments.)

Delaware was the first state to ratify. On 21 June 1788, after a rough passage, the New Hampshire Federalists won their way; New Hampshire became the ninth state to ratify and, as had been agreed at Philadelphia, the new Constitution came into effect.

But two of the three most powerful states, New York and Virginia, were still debating ratification, and in these two states not only the people but also the share of political genius was divided between Federalist and anti-Federalist. Without New York and Virginia the fact of Union would be reduced to comic fiction. Hamilton and Madison had realized this from the beginning of the ratification debates, and with John Jay they had set about the task of persuasion in the winter of 1787 and the spring of 1788. Then it was that they had begun to produce *The Federalist* – cloaking their activities in decently Latinized anonymity.

Forty years later *Blackwood's Magazine*, surpassing its own habitual pomposity, settled the place of *The Federalist* in the canon of political philosophy above Montesquieu, even above the writings of Aristotle; it was proclaimed 'seriously, reverently' as the 'Bible of Republicanism'. It is unnecessary to accept Blackwood's exaggeration, and to see supranationalism in the voice of *The Federalist* is like seeking squibs for democratic crackers in the plays of Shakespeare. But in *The Federalist*, set out, elaborated and explained, are plain writ the doctrines of American constitutional theory. Here is evidence of the care and logic which gave Madison the victory over Patrick Henry's fire and led Virginia to ratify. Here is evidence of the brilliance which Hamilton used to conquer the New York Anti-Federalists under George Clinton.

With Virginia and New York in, the Constitution moved from the realm of *de jure* to the realm of *de facto*. In 1789 with George Washington (for the third time the obvious choice for important leadership) as President, the Americans began to live under the new Constitution. One of the first acts of Congress was to redeem the pledges made during the campaign for ratification by adding ten amendments to the Constitution, of which the first nine comprised a Bill of Rights. The tenth, which specifically reserved to the states all powers not delegated to the Federal government by the Constitution, served to alleviate the fear of centralized authority still current in several states, and guaranteed to them a measure of autonomy and flexibility in the exercise of their powers in the future.

The Constitution deserves a measure of reverence because, on the whole, it has proved adaptable. The division of sovereignty between Federal and State governments was an effective, and original, compromise which solved the major problem of the new republic, and which for the most part has been successfully implemented ever since, but in that compromise lay the roots of weeds which were to poison the American garden in the next century.

On paper, and for a while in fact, the Constitution limited the power of the majority by the system of indirect election to the Presidency and the upper house. Soon the urge to democracy proved too strong for the provisions; the electoral college became a rubber-stamp cut to the people's wishes.

One of the most important clauses in the Constitution was, so far as explicit statement went, a minor clause: that which forbade the states from impairing the obligation of contracts, for the ultimate defence of the Constitution was placed in the hands of the judiciary and the Supreme Court was independent of popular control or state influence. Here, in the hands of the arch-Federalist, Chief Justice John Marshall, was a weapon for preserving the rights of the few against the bullying of the many. Through this clause was fashioned the link which binds eighteenth-century America to the capitalism of the nineteenth century and which made possible the power of the great trusts of the twentieth century. And here, ultimately, was the weapon which made Federal Government more powerful than State Government.

Theoretically, the American Constitution, as drafted at Philadelphia, is clumsy and inefficient. The system of checks and balances can become too easily a system of delays and divided responsibilities. The inflexibility of election rules makes it impossible to refer disputes immediately to the verdict of the public. There is no clear distinction between legislative and executive powers. From time to time all these disadvantages have paralysed American governmental function. That this has not happened more often stands to the credit not of the American Constitution nor to the genius of its makers but to the wise blindness of the American people. As soon as they had written and accepted a constitution the Americans began to believe that they had written something else, and began to accept the imaginary as the real. By custom, the imaginary became the real: the Constitution which Americans revere is not the Constitution as it was written in 1787.

This process began in the very first Congress, and once more the men who fathered it were Hamilton and Madison, though now their views were in violent opposition. From their struggle grew the American party system; a system foreign to the Constitution and yet ultimately far more powerful than the constitutional provisions.

Hamilton, as Secretary of the Treasury, took his chance to establish by administrative manipulation a strong oligarchical core in government. Suspicious of the 'the disease' of democracy he set about uniting the propertied interests of the Atlantic seaboard and at the same time, by unscrupulous use of the spoils system, he attempted to fatten the power of the executive and to weaken the power of Congress.

Madison, seeing his erstwhile ally undermining their joint work, leapt to the attack. The Hamiltonian programme was 'unconstitutional', this was his constant theme. Hamilton must be prevented from achieving his designs. And the very people who had feared Madison as the arch-exponent of

Federalism now rallied to him as the arch-guardian of the interests and the rights of every class of citizen. The agrarians, headed by Jefferson, stood by Madison, the one-time Federalist.

For twelve years, however, Hamilton was the virtual ruler of the United States, Washington, canonized already in his lifetime, was the subject of occasional reproach and even of occasional calumny, but while Washington accepted office there was no other man who could take it from him. (The very fact that Washington refused a third term became constitutional law by custom, and for no other reason than that it was the gospel according to Saint George of Mount Vernon, so that when, eventually, Franklin Roosevelt shattered history, his opponents growled at his blasphemy and then made certain that it could never happen again by codifying the Washington precedent.) John Adams, with less prestige than Washington, was nevertheless still an all-party President. But behind them both, making policies – and creating dissension – was the erratic and arrogant genius of Alexander Hamilton.

The skein of personal rivalries and philosophical conflicts spun around Hamilton came close to obscuring for all time hope of success for the ideals on which America had been founded, and did in the end bring Hamilton himself to death. The man who had served Washington so faithfully during a war fought to destroy the hold of European institutions over the American people, was himself the least American of all American leaders, and used his vast political influence in attempting to reverse the trend away from Europe which he had started. The man who had joined in the creation of the Federalist movement and who had been one of its leading propagandists, quarrelled first with his collaborator, James Madison, and then with the leader of his party, President John Adams. The man who despised the agrarian way of life, who voiced his hatred of the common, slipshod, unaristocratic habit of the frontier in a hundred bitter phrases, found himself finally, in the election of 1800, in uneasy alliance with the anti-Federalist Party, the Democratic-Republican Party, led by the apostle of agrarianism, Thomas Jefferson. And even this alliance (which took Hamilton back for a while to the side of his old colleague, Madison, now also a Jeffersonian), brought only tragedy – Hamilton's death in a duel with Jefferson's vice-president, Aaron Burr.

'This American world,' wrote Hamilton to Gouverneur Morris in 1802, 'was not made for me.' It is a clear, and in many ways a sound verdict. Yet it is a verdict based only on the failure of his political activities. Young Hamilton had helped to make the American political organization and then in his later years had failed to subvert it to his own liking. But in those years of impotent effort, Hamilton had successes which have lasted beyond the term of his wildest dreams. As Secretary of the Treasury, Hamilton created and made part of the American world the paradox which has since coloured all American economic thinking: a mistrust of government intervention in all areas of economic endeavour save only as a device to protect private enterprise. Protective tariffs, subsidies for manufactures, a chartered national bank controlled by private citizens, the national debt funded at face value, and the encouragement of speculative investment in the West; all these innovations were proposed by Hamilton and adopted by Congress. These precedents, though some have since been denied, some altered out of recognition, and some abandoned, have remained as part of the American principle. The American people have never accepted government by aristocrats but they have maintained to this day the Hamiltonian faith in government for capitalists.

The political eclipse of Hamilton, the growth of a two-party system, and the coincident end of the real power of the electoral college were hastened by events in Europe. The sympathies and interests of the American people became involved in the violent events in France.

Gratitude for favours received and a natural wish that their own newly won liberty should be shared by the nation which had contributed so much to the American cause made it inevitable that, at the outset, most Americans would favour the French Revolutionary cause. For a while the French tricolour became an American patriotic emblem. But then, as the bestiality of Revolutionary rule became apparent, pity and fear combined to bring doubt into the minds of many. The American Revolution had kept itself decently free of massacre, but the winds of hate were blowing from the Place de la Guillotine. The rich merchants of the East and the planter-aristocrats looked uneasily around them. Perhaps the American Revolution would be continued through the French, and they, who had led the way to the overthrow of British aristocratic rule and had then let the British go home unharmed, would be themselves the next victims of mob hatred.

Even Washington was perturbed, for in Washington as in his friend Lafayette there remained an obstinate conviction that although democracy was good, democracy was best guided by aristocrats.

But, while Washington was President, the nation could held to some sort of sanity even when the issues aroused by events in Europe were intensified by the outbreak of war between the old ally, France, and the old enemy, Great Britain. Once Washington's sensible influence was removed anxiety and partisanship became intense.

The Federalist group was for Britain, the anti-Federalist for France. The anti-Federalists were not an absolute majority, and indeed in the early stages of the War of the Coalition against the French it had seemed possible that America might intervene for the Republic against the armies of the kings. But the follies of Citizen Genet, the French representative in Philadelphia, worked to his own disadvantage. Even Jefferson, the Francophile, could not support Genet's infringements of American national sovereignty, and as the years passed, while popular sentiment in America remained on the whole sympathetic to the ideals of the French Revolution, the high-handedness of Revolutionary chiefs, above all of the one-time refugee in America, Talleyrand, awakened America to the knowledge that French ideals were not always equivalent to French actions. By 1798 it seemed probable that if the United States embroiled itself in European affairs at all it would be on the side of the British angels. Indeed, in 1798, Washington was recalled to the command of the army (with Hamilton as his second-in-command!), the treaties with the French were formally repealed, and from 1798 until 1800, though a state of war did not exist, the United States Navy was at sea against the French.

But the efforts of the Anglophiles were as insane as the efforts of the French. Fear drove them to pass through Congress in 1798 an Aliens and Sedition Act which was odious to the spirit of democracy, odious to the spirit of the American Constitution, odious to President Adams, and even odious to Hamilton.

Hamilton fell, the victim of his own party's fright. Adams was discredited. Jefferson and Madison seized their chance. Jefferson spoke up for the Constitution, using the voice of the new State of Kentucky; Madison joined him, speaking through the Virginia Legislature. Behind them stood the full force of the agrarians. The principle was established that the Constitution was above Congress and the judiciary, that the states as true and close representatives of the people had the right to nullify 'all unauthorized acts done under color of that instrument'. The way was clear to the election of Thomas Jefferson as third President of the United States, the first to be chosen by a party, the first to be chosen deliberately by the mass of the people and against the wishes of a powerful few.

On 14 December 1799 Washington died at Mount Vernon. On 4 March 1801, at the new capital city named in honour of the great leader, and in a ceremony from which ceremonial and ceremoniousness were deliberately excluded, Thomas Jefferson was sworn in as President.

CHAPTER 19

ARTS FOR THE NEW NATION

A NEW nation needs political organization. The United States was in this respect well served by the drafters of the Constitution and by the leaders of the first years of its history who in debate and disagreement hammered precept into action.

A new nation needs saints and heroes to strengthen the feeling of patriotism in minds as yet unaccustomed to think of the nation as a reality. America found only one saint, George Washington, but the bitter struggle for independence threw up enough heroes – heroes for the many and heroes for the few – to last the country for several generations.

A new nation, and particularly a nation whose political existence is founded upon a federal organization, needs a national centre. During the Revolutionary War the make-shift nature of the American experiment had been emphasized by the mobility which exigency had forced upon the seat of government. At various times Baltimore, Princeton, Annapolis, Trenton, Lancaster, York, and Philadelphia had all served as capital city for the Americans. Once the war was won, New York and then again Philadelphia became the temporary capital, and no fewer than twenty-four towns put in claims for the honour of providing a permanent home for government.

The first loyalty of most Congressmen, like the first loyalty of most of their constituents, was still to the State; that new and untried entity, the Nation, had not as yet aroused the same fervent patriotism from its citizens. In the year of Washington's inauguration therefore the debate on the location of a Federal centre brought bitterness to Congress; state wrangled with state and the jealousy inspired by regional interests made it seem possible that no decision could be reached either by bold originality or by shifting compromise. Indeed a Federal Town bill, moved by Southern

Congressmen and proposing a new capital city on the 'Easterly bank of the Potomac', was heavily defeated by their Northern rivals, and the defeat so wounded the South that there was for a while a grumbling rumour of secession.

Finally, a decision was reached through the machinations of a pair who were now but seldom in alliance: Jefferson and Hamilton.

Hamilton was anxious that the Federal Government should assume the war debts of the States and his bill had been defeated by the Southern members; Jefferson wanted the capital on the Potomac. The Secretary of State and the Secretary of the Treasury dined together and in the comfortable after-dinner warmth which has settled so many personal, national and international affairs agreed to exchange the votes of their followers on these two controversial issues. The District of Columbia with the capital city of Washington and the foreign credit of the United States may thus be said to have been born at the same dinner table.

The bill creating the District was passed in 1790 and the President himself was asked to select a site on the Potomac near his home Mount Vernon. Washington chose the site and then appointed Jefferson, Daniel Carroll of Maryland, and his family friend, Dr David Stuart of Virginia, as commissioners to start the arduous work of turning a muddy and swampy tract of land into a seat worthy of housing the capital of the nation. The commissioners, in their turn, appointed Andrew Ellicott to survey the land. On 18 March 1791, the *Maryland Gazette* reported from Georgetown:

> Some time last month arrived in this town Mr. Andrew Ellicot, a gentleman of superior, astronomical abilities. He was employed by the President of the United States of America to lay off a tract of land, ten miles square on the Potomac, for the use of Congress – is now engaged in the business.

The overall design of the city was placed in the hands of a French veteran of the American Revolutionary War, Major Pierre L'Enfant, and L'Enfant's European mentality has left such a firm imprint on the American capital that it seems to deny altogether Jefferson's insistence that it should be based on an American model. Almost it is as if the bitter experience of Paris in recent months was uppermost in L'Enfant's mind as he worked, for his long straight avenues and the whole rectangular conception is redolent of the 'whiff of grape-shot' mentality.

President George Washington, for one, was not satisfied and discharged L'Enfant in a scathing letter of reproof, but Ellicott, who took over the work, seems merely to have followed L'Enfant's conception.

Almost every architect then living in America, and many from outside, had some hand in designing the major buildings of state. The competition for a design of the Capitol, for example, was won by a doctor born in the West Indies, William Thornton, who had only recently turned to architecture. The original building was carried out under the direction of Stephen Hallett (who had submitted one of the unsuccessful designs), by James Hoban, an Irishman, and by George Hadfield, an Englishman. In 1803 Benjamin Latrobe, who had spent only six years in the United States but who was already recognized as America's leading exponent of the Greek revival, took over Thornton's plans and modified them to a considerable extent. In 1817 Charles Bullfinch succeeded Latrobe and it was Bullfinch who completed building in 1830.

Hoban was also the architect of the President's house, the first public building to be started in Washington. This, which has become the very symbol of America, was in fact designed on the model of the Duke of Leinster's residence in Dublin. First occupied by President Adams in the last weeks of his Administration, his poor wife, Abigail, was faced with more than the usual problems of a housewife in a new house, for this new house was in a new and almost non-existent town. Abigail could not resist a complaint, though as the loyal wife of the President she warned her correspondent to 'keep all this to yourself, and when asked how I like it say that I wrote to you the situation is beautiful, which is true!'

The misery behind her more public explanation was in the body of the letter:

I arrived about one o'clock at this place known by the name of 'the city', and the Name is all that you can call so! As I expected to find it a new country, with Houses scattered over a space of ten miles, and trees and stumps in plenty, with a castle of a House, so I found it.

The President's House is in a beautiful situation, in front of which is the Potomac, with a view of Alexandria. The country round is romantic, but a wild wilderness at present. . . . But this House is built for ages to come. . . . The capitol is near two miles from us. As to roads, we shall make them by frequent passing before Winter! But I am determined to be satisfied and content, to say nothing of inconvenience, etc. That must be a worse place than even Georgetown that I could not reside in for three months! If they will put me up some bells and let me have wood enough to keep fires, I design to be pleased. We have not the least fence-yard or other convenience without, and the great unfinished audience-room I make a drying-room of, to hang the clothes in. The principal stairs are not up, and will not be this winter.

This situation was typical of the Washington occupied for the first time on 11 June 1800, when all one hundred and twenty-six civil servants moved from Philadelphia to their permanent quarters in the Federal City, but this was at least a centre for the new nation.

A new nation needs economic strength to carry it through the difficulties of newness and the men to organize the national economy to the best advantage. American economic opportunities were from the beginning great; the greatest of all America's advantages was the vast unexploited West, and among the great strokes of good fortune that turned the United States into a potent economic force was the brilliance of her early financial organizers and particularly that confident pair, Alexander Hamilton and Albert Gallatin. As first Secretary of the Treasury, Hamilton can be said to have created United States fiscal policy. It was he who recommended the funding of the national debt at par, who advised that the Federal Government should take over from the States the debts that had accrued in the pursuit of independence. Though the process may seem to have overthrown one of the principal motives of the Revolution, it was essential that the national authority and part of the national burden should be brought home to every citizen, and it was Hamilton who organized the excise tax. In 1791, against all opposition, Hamilton forced through his project for a national bank; in the same year he organized subsidies for industry and agriculture and persuaded Congress to finance internal improvements, Gallatin, who took over as Secretary of the Treasury after the defeat of the Federalists, had already contributed to financial policies when, in opposition, his clear criticism had led to the commissioning of a standing committee on finance. His sound handling of fiscal policy in his fourteen years of office under the presidencies of Jefferson and Madison virtually saved American finances in the difficult times of the Napoleonic Wars and the War of 1812. (It is a curious fact that the two ablest financiers of America's first years were both foreign born; Hamilton in the West Indies and Gallatin in Switzerland.)

But a new nation, if it is to have a cogent existence among the nations, needs strength that comes not merely from political health or economic power, but also from the mind. In this respect the United States was slow to organize. The national 'culture' in the terms that are generally given to the word, that is to say in literature, music, and the fine arts, was for many years a poor creature. This was perhaps inevitable, for the best minds of America were occupied with organization and political theory so that they had little time for more obviously 'creative' activity. The American people were still colonials who had learnt from their political success resentment of their artistic indebtedness.

In one issue of Charles Brockden Brown's short-lived *Monthly Magazine* there is an essay, probably written by the editor, in which for paragraph after paragraph the writer bemoans the lack of authors in the new American nation. Rhetorically, and with strenuous sarcasm, he demands of his readers:

I am desirous of knowing the cause of this want of authorship among us. Four millions of persons, generally taught to read and not overpowered with the barbarism of Algonquin savages or the indigence of Polish serfs, have tailors, carpenters, and even lawyers among them, but not one author can be found. Is this deficiency a proof of refinement or stupidity? Is it a topic of congratulation or condolence?

Hardly a year after this passage was published, America's greatest writer, Thomas Jefferson, became President, and America's finest juristic stylist, John Marshall, became Chief Justice. When it was published almost all of the great Revolutionary polemical writers – Jefferson himself, the Adams, Hamilton, Dickinson, and Jay – were still alive and active, and it is a symptom both of the American desire to emulate the activities of the Old World and of the belletristic bias already being given to the word 'author' that such a statement could be made in America in 1800 – and be accepted by the public.

To produce America's own culture, American critics and artists believed they must first establish cultural independence from Britain. Since no educated American could conceivably wish to reject the great tradition of English letters, his problem became one of what to reject and what to retain which might be made American; no amount of patriotism, Noah Webster said, could make him give up his beloved Addison. At the outset, the critics agreed that they should accept Shakespeare, Milton, Addison, Pope, and the rest, but that they must avoid what Webster called 'servile imitation' of any foreign writing. They must also shun anything untrue, immoral or useless, and things which, in Joel Barlow's phrase, 'might prove false and destructive' to American minds. But simply to avoid European models was not enough. What positive steps might be taken to encourage an American artistic tradition? Though Americans did not have Rob Roy, the Thames, or Cromwell to write about, they decided that they did have a number of things which neither Britain nor Europe could equal – the Indian, the frontier, the Mississippi, the Revolution, their own heroes, these were subjects to challenge and excite the native artistic spirit. The robin, the forest, the whippoorwill, and the whispering brook, Joseph Dennie thought, were as fit materials for poets 'as nightingales, or skylarks, dingles or dells'. Yankees, Dutchmen, frontiersmen, Southerners, and other national types were as promising literary timber as any of Scott's borderers or Germany's young Werthers. The American writer, then, must not merely reject what he could not use from Europe, but must find the right way to use the unique resources of his own country, so that he might create from them his own true and correct American art. He must, as critic John Neal wrote, utilize 'the abundant and hidden sources of fertility in our own brave earth'. The novelist Charles Brockden Brown advised the American writer to observe his own land directly, to 'examine objects with his own eyes, employ European models for the improvement of his own taste', and to build his art about 'all that is genuine and peculiar in the scene before him'. In this way, the *Columbian Orator* hoped in 1807, 'Columbian soil' might

> Rear Men as great as Britain's isle;
> Exceed what Greece and Rome have done,
> Or any land beneath the sun.

This was a time, these first years of American national existence, when national ideals were being crystallized. It is perhaps the most cosmopolitan period in American history even as it is one of the most consciously national, a time when the Americans were attempting to state the fundamentals of Americanism in literature, religion, politics, philosophy, and education. Classicism and neo-classicism, science, rationalism, and deism, the contributory forces of primitivism and the idea of progress, of humanitarianism and Gothicism, the ideas that were current in Europe and the new influence that came from the frontier were all at work upon the American mind.

Federalists and anti-Federalists alike followed the traditions of European classicism and found in Cicero, Seneca, and Virgil reasons for faith in the law of nature; all used the classical tradition of substantiation for ideals that were conveniently American: fortitude in the face of adversity and orderly living. Their literary style Jefferson, Brackenridge, Franklin, and Dwight founded upon the neoclassicists of the late seventeenth and early eighteenth centuries; their ideals went back to early and classical examples.

But America was at once a product of classicism and of the Christian tradition. Much of colonial activity had been prescribed by the needs and intentions of the churches, and in America, as in Europe, at the turn of the nineteenth century the predominant spirit of Christianity showed itself in outward activity. The inwardness of the knowledge of evil and the desire for self-reform had developed into humanitarianism and the Christian justification for democracy.

To these processes science and the scientific spirit added their part. Scientific deism, as well as the growth of man's ability to control nature, increased the complacent faith in reason and turned American thinkers from the spiritual to the utilitarian and secular. It is significant, however, that whereas France in revolution became anti-Christian, America in revolution divorced church and state but remained permanently Christian. 'I do not believe,' wrote Thomas Paine, 'in the creeds professed by the Jewish church, by the Roman church, by the Greek church, by the Turkish church, by the Russian church, by the Protestant church, nor by any church that I know of. My own mind is my own church.' America could not go the whole way with Paine, and even American deists like Thomas Jefferson and Benjamin Rush found themselves turning in their tracks to uphold the value of Christian teaching.

Jefferson had engaged in what he himself described as 'the severest contests in which I have ever been engaged' in order to secure disestablishment. He believed fervently in the validity of Locke's maxim 'The care of every man's soul belongs to himself . . . I enquire after no man's religious opinions and trouble none with mine', but to his eager mind toleration, or disestablishment, could not go to the lengths of rejection. Jefferson, particularly after he had come under the influence of Priestley, regarded the Christian philosophy as at least the equal in importance of the classical philosophies. In 1803 Jefferson wrote to Benjamin Rush from Washington outlining his religious *credo*. His views, he stated:

are the result of a life of inquiry and reflection, and are very different from that anti-Christian system imputed to me by those who know nothing of my opinions. To the corruptions of Christianity I am, indeed, opposed; but not to the genuine precepts of Jesus himself. I am a Christian in the only sense in which he wished anyone to be; sincerely attached to his doctrines, in preference to all others, ascribing to himself every *human* excellence; and believing that he never claimed any other. At the short intervals since these conversations, when I could justifiably abstract my mind from public affairs, this subject has been under my contemplation. But the more I considered it, the more it expanded beyond the measure of either my time or information. In the moment of my late departure from Monticello, I received from Dr. Priestley his little treatise of 'Socrates and Jesus Compared'. This . . . became a subject of reflection while on the road. . . . The result was to arrange in my mind a syllabus, or outline of such an estimate of the comparative merits of Christianity, as I wished to see executed by some one of more leisure and information for the task than myself.

In the *Syllabus* Jefferson gave it as his opinion that the teachings of Jesus

were more pure and perfect than those of the most correct of the philosophers . . . in incalcating universal philanthropy, not only to kindred and friends, to neighbours and countrymen, but to all mankind, gathering all into one family, under the bonds of love, charity, peace, common wants and common aids. . . . He pushed his scrutinies into the hearts of man, he erected his tribunal in the region of his thoughts, and purified the waters at the fountainhead.

These qualities, so eminently humanitarian and parenthetically so much in accord with the American spirit of the time, demonstrated for Jefferson, 'peculiar superiority in the system of Jesus over all others'. Perhaps even more than Jefferson himself, his friend Rush, revolutionary, scientist, philanthropist, and amateur philosopher, is typical of a generation that was groping for an intellectual code. The groping belonged with the times and not with the nation: Coleridge and Goethe were among its greatest exemplars, but the 'newness' of the American nation made the groping of Americans more urgent and more obvious.

Benjamin Rush of Philadelphia slips into the record of American history at many points – as a signatory of the Declaration of Independence, as medical pioneer, as feminist, as educator – yet he has always remained a vague figure, a footnote to other men's biographies, hardly deserving of fame save as the opponent of men greater than he. Sometimes he is remembered for his bold attempt to reform the military hospitals of the Continental Army and sometimes for his energetic and selfless work during the great fever epidemic of 1793, but more often his medical career stands damned by history because his drastic cure of yellow fever – copious bleeding followed by violent purging – helped to hasten the death of George Washington. Sometimes he is remembered as one of Pennsylvania's representatives at the Continental Congress, and sometimes for his part in the overthrow of Pennsylvania's first and radical constitution, but of his own part as a Founding Father he himself could only write that 'he aimed well', and the political activity for which he is best remembered is one which rests entirely on rumour: his association with the 'Conway Cabal' in their attempt to substitute for Washington the double traitor, Charles Lee. If he has achieved any immortality, it is as the principal target of William Cobbett's enmity during his American stay, and it was the crippling libel suit instigated by Rush that drove Cobbett home from America.

And Rush too, from his vast acquaintanceship and vast reading, resolved, to his own satisfaction at least, the conflict between science and Christianity. As early as 1791, he, whom many of his countrymen regarded as second only to Franklin for scientific inventiveness, had stood up to defend the use of the Bible in American education:

In this defence of the use of the Bible as a school book, I beg you would not think that I suppose the Bible to contain the only revelation which God has made to man. I believe in an internal revelation, or a moral principle, which God has implanted in the heart of every man, as the precursor of his final dominion over the whole human race. How much this internal revelation accords with the external, remains yet to be explored by philosophers. I am disposed to believe, that most of the doctrines of Christianity revealed in the Bible might be discovered by a close examination of all the principles of action in man: But who is equal to such an enquiry? It certainly does not suit the natural indolence, or laborious employments of a great majority of mankind. The internal revelation of the gospel may be compared to the straight line which is made through a wilderness by the assistance of a compass, to a distant country, which few are able to discover, while the Bible resembles a public road to the same country, which is wide, plain, and easily found. 'And a highway shall be there, and it shall be called the way of holiness. The wayfaring men, though fools, shall not err therein.'

Neither let me in this place exclude the Revelation which God has made of himself to man in the works of creation. I am far from wishing to lessen the influence of this species of Revelation upon mankind. But the knowledge of God obtained from this source, is obscure and feeble in its operation, compared with that which is derived from the Bible. The visible creation speaks of the Deity in hieroglyphics, while the Bible describes all his attributes and perfections in such plain and familiar language that 'he who runs may read'.

How kindly has our maker dealt with his creatures, in providing three different cords to draw them to himself! But how weakly do some men act, who suspend their faith and hopes upon only one of them! By laying hold of them all, they would approach more speedily and certainly to the centre of all happiness.

Most of the influences on American artistic-intellectual life at the time were derived from European sources. But the frontier was a physical fact which was to America unique. The frontier and its principal inhabitant, the American Indian, represented something which could be intellectually translated into essentially American terms.

For a century and a half the Americans (reflecting the prevailing British and European concepts of what would become in the next century the science of anthropology) looked upon the American Indian with feelings that were a mixture of impatience, contempt, and admiration; impatience, because he stood in the way of white American expansion, moral, geographical, and economic; contempt because he was a savage incapable of the finer civilization of the European, and admiration, perversely perhaps, because of his obstinate opposition to the progress which white Americans imagined as their prerogative. They fought with him, they attempted to re-make him to their own image, and, having destroyed him, in the last years of the nineteenth century the sensitive conscience of America began to work: regret took the place of pride only when regret could have no practical expression.

But, whatever the conflicts and contributions of foreign and American forces to the arts of the new nation, it must be admitted that in sum those arts were hardly distinguished. Philip Freneau, the most 'hellishly keen' satirist of the British during the American War, had fought his nation's enemies more successfully with poem than with sword, and his hopes for the American nation were wide-eyed and wonderful. Yet there is an element of rhetorical despair in his verse:

> Can we never be thought
> To have learning or grace,
> Unless it be brought
> From that damnable place?

Sydney Smith had justice as well as malice on his side when he wrote in the *Edinburgh Review* for December 1818:

Literature the Americans have none – no native literature, we mean. It is all imported. They had a Franklin, indeed; and may afford to live for half a century on his fame. There is, or was, a Mr. Dwight, who wrote some poems; and his baptismal name was Timothy. There is also a small account of Virginia by Jefferson and an epic by Joel Barlow; and some pieces of pleasantry by Mr. Irving. But why should the Americans write books, when a six weeks' passage brings them, in their own tongue, our sense, science, and genius, in bales and hogsheads? Prairies, steam-boats, gristmills, are their natural objects for centuries to come. Then, when they have got to the Pacific Ocean – epic poems, plays, pleasures of memory, and all the elegant gratifications of an ancient people who have tamed the wild earth, and set down to amuse themselves. – This is the natural march of human affairs.

Though there were few American writers of quality, there was a considerable market for books and papers. In the ten years after 1800 the number of newspapers in the United States almost doubled; from two hundred in 1800 to three hundred and seventy-five in 1810. By 1835 there were almost twelve hundred newspapers, a number greater than that of France and England together. Sentimental novels, by sentimental authors – most of them ladies and many of them English – were read as avidly on the frontier as in the withdrawing rooms of Boston or Philadelphia. A visitor to the bookshop of Hoquet Caritat in New York wrote that:

> Its shelves could scarcely sustain the weight of *Female Frailty*, *The Posthumous Daughter* and *The Cavern of Woe;* they required the aid of a carpenter to support the burden of *Cottage on the Moor*, *The House of Tynian* . . . they possessed alluring, melting, irresistible titles such as, *Delicate Embarrassments*, *Venial Trespasses*, *Misplaced Confidence* . . . they were called for by the young and the old; from the tender virgin of thirteen, whose heart went pitter pat at the approach of a beau, to the experienced matron of three-score, who could not read without spectacles.

Sensibility, 'meliorated into something gentler', was the delight of most American readers, Sterne and Goldsmith were its high priests, their less worthy but no less successful acolytes dropped 'lucid emanations' to wring 'pure drops of celestial sensibility' from thousands of American eyes. The most successful novel of the first years of the American nation was a miserably sentimental book by an English ex-actress, Susanna Rowson, called *Charlotte Temple, A Tale of Truth*, which had the advantage over most contemporary saccharine in that it had an American setting.

As in England, sensibility hardened into Gothicism. The American playwright, Royall Tyler, struck at the Gothic novel with lively exaggeration,

Dolly the dairymaid and Jonathan the hired man, threw aside
The Ballad of the Cruel Stepmother, over which they had so often
wept in concert, and now amused themselves into so agreeable a
terror with the haunted house and hobgoblins of Mrs. Radcliffe,
that they were both afraid to sleep alone.

But his blow did nothing to the sales of *Mysteries of Udopho*
or of the books of 'Monk' Lewis and their American imitators, Charles Brockden Brown and Isaac Mitchell.

Gothicism moved on into Romanticism and no place was
more admirably suited to receive with enthusiasm Scott and
Byron than the confident, idealistic, and adventurous
United States. Scott, indeed, was to set the pattern of culture
for part of American society – the upper crust in the South –
for more than half a century, but Byron's greater vigour,
and the interest aroused by his name and reputation, were
even more satisfactory to an adolescent society which was
once more apeing the habits of its sophisticated elders.
When Byron died the *North American Review* wrote, almost
with surprise, that the price of stocks or the election of the
President had not been affected, but there had been,
nevertheless, 'a deep and general feeling of regret throughout the country'.

Much of Romanticism fitted the facts and necessities of
American life; some of it did not. As an intellectual movement, Romanticism in America turned out to be more constructive, individualistic, and democratically based than
Romanticism in Britain or Europe. Romantic individualism
produced rebels (something Americans could understand),
but the American Romantic rebel had a much more open
and fluid society in which to function and far fewer things
he needed to destroy. The Romantic's self-absorption, his
unconventionality, his cultivation of eccentricity, his rejection of certain moral rules and his lack of restraint did not
fit with the legacy of Yankee Calvinism or for that matter
with Virginia Anglicanism. The melancholy, morbid strain
of Romanticism, attractive though it was to American sentimentality, was never really adapted to the temper of a nation
built on optimism and an aggressive patriotism. American

Romanticism produced not Byron but Longfellow, not Napoleon but Jackson. Americans had too much faith in the individual and too much hereditary Calvinistic intensity of moral feeling, so they put their own distinctive stamp on the Romantic movement as they imported it.

The less glamorous and less extravagant exponents of Romanticism were received with no equal enthusiasm in the United States. There was a flutter of patriotic gratification in America at the realization that the great personalities of English literary life were much preoccupied with the American experiment, that Coleridge, Southey, and Lamb, for example, dreamed of peace to come and Heaven on earth 'on the banks of the Susquehanna'. Thomas Campbell was respected in the United States more because *Gertrude of Wyoming* glorified the American scene and the American showing in the Revolutionary War than because he shared Byron's love for liberty but not Byron's lack of respectability. Yet, in their own time, the Americans do not seem to have noticed the claims that they could have made for Americanism in two of the most distinguished English prose writers: William Hazlitt and James Henry Leigh Hunt. A third great prose writer, William Cobbett, seems to have dropped from the American consciousness in the moment when he left the scene of American pamphleteering.

Of the other arts, only painting established itself with any certainty in the new America, and even of painters, the best of them, John Singleton Copley, could write that their work was regarded among Americans as 'no more than any other useful trade . . . like that of a Carpenter or shew-maker'. Copley himself and Benjamin West painted their more sophisticated work for British audiences and British buyers, while Peale, Stuart, Trumbull, Jarvis and Savage contented themselves with producing flattering likenesses of the eager new great and the even more eager new rich of the new country, and with producing great heroic battle-pictures of the glorious Revolutionary War. A hundred other Americans and a hundred more emigré craftsmen from Europe painted portraits when they could get commissions, lived for most of the time like George Rutter as 'an honest sign-painter, who never pretended or aspired to paint the human face divine, except to hang on the outside of a house'. (It is this Rutter who won praise from John Penn in 1788 for his likeness of Benjamin Franklin which hung outside Brooke's Tavern near Reading, Pennsylvania – 'that city and its environs may boast of the best sign-painter, perhaps, in any country'.)

Charles Willson Peale may be credited with other things than the fact that he painted from life eight portraits of George Washington or that he called his seventeen sons and daughters after his heroes, Rembrandt, Rubens, Van Dyck, Kauffman, Titian and so on, for it was Peale who first showed and sold Italian masters to American buyers, and it was Peale who established in Pennsylvania the great and popular exhibition of natural history known as 'Peale's Museum' and who formed in that city, several years before the American Academy was established in New York, the first society for American artists.

The French Revolution, so popular among some Americans, but so much hated by the Federalists, brought to America a host of rivals to native-born artists. *Soi-disant* aristocrats became *soi-disant* musicians; to the exclusion of native-born talent, almost all the theatre orchestras of Boston, Philadelphia, and New York were manned by men fleeing the music of the tumbrils. (The gastronomer, Brillat-Savarin, was for a while a member of the orchestra in a New York theatre.)

Parson Weems was at work collecting anecdotes. 'Washington,' he wrote to his publisher, 'is gone! Millions are gaping to read something about him. I am nearly primed and cocked for 'em.' American hagiology was ready for its first great work. American craftsmen were preparing competent, and sometimes more than competent, imitations of European furniture, buildings, miniatures, glass, and silverware. In creative literature there was an occasional spark of something uniquely American.

But European arts were still to a large extent the inspiration and the measure of American achievement, Europe the Mecca for American men of taste and creative ability. Many who had been active in the Revolutionary cause and in the creation of the United States found little difficulty in regulating their lives according to a dichotomy of loyalties; to the United States went their political patriotism, to Europe, and particularly to Britain, their social and cultural fealty. Once the Revolutionary War was over, Americans of the higher strata of society and Americans with creative ambitions hurried back across the Atlantic to Europe.

Many found it to their liking and stayed, or brought back with them to America a renewed fealty to English culture. Some did not, feeling that English society was corrupt and decadent, and that America would eventually come to maintain the values of the great English tradition. If this were to survive, they believed, it would have to survive across the Atlantic, absorbed into the American context.

It is symbolic of the half-light of nationhood which shone on this period of American history that even the 'Patriot and Artist, Friend and Aid of Washington', John Trumbull, who had served with such distinction in the Revolutionary War, spent most of the early years of the American nation living in London. (Several young Americans, among them Trumbull's illegitimate son, served in the British Army in Napoleonic Wars.)

As yet, the American revolution against British cultural dominion had hardly begun.

CHAPTER 20

THE WAY WEST

JEFFERSON was the most original thinker ever to be elected to America's highest office but he was no great administrator. The brilliant oratory of revolution is seldom suited to the tasks of administration, and genius in theorizing, so useful in the creation of nations and constitutions, is not always capable of controlling the minutiae of routine. Jefferson, out of office or in any office but the Presidency, served as intellectual guardian of the American conscience, but as President expediency was often the master of thought. Nor was Jefferson helped to success by his own complex character. He, the arch-exponent of government for the people, had too much of the aristocrat in his make-up to sit comfortably as the popular hero and his tastes held him aloof from general acclaim. He, the disciple of Americanism, was so close to European culture that he could not easily continue the demonstration of simplicity which he had begun at his Inauguration.

After-knowledge can see in some of the first acts of Jefferson's term of office one of the paradoxes of American history: it was Jefferson who created for America the spoils system later refined by Andrew Jackson. In 1801 he wrote to Dickinson, in terms which would be accepted by all believers in democracy:

My principles, and those always received by the republicans, do not admit the removing of any person from office merely for a difference of political opinion.

But even as he wrote he was at work pulling the shoes off Federalist appointees and thrusting into them men of his own party. Adams, it is true, had forced the issue by his 'midnight appointments': forty-two justices of the peace bustled into office in December 1800, when the second President was already certain of his defeat. Jefferson removed seventeen of them. But within two years of his Inauguration Jefferson had ousted more than one hundred of the three hundred and sixteen office-holders subject to the President's appointment. He did what he did against the advice of some of his friends – among them James Monroe, who wrote from Richmond:

> The principle is sound that no man ought to be turned out for mere difference of political sentiment. . . . By retaining them in office you will give a proof of tolerance, moderation and forbearance, which must command the respect of the benevolent.

He did what he did with protestations of distaste – 'In this horrid drudgery, I always felt myself as a public executioner' – and with a show of disinterest which was probably genuine and worthy in Jefferson but far less worthy in some of his followers: men of the type of George Clinton of New York who practised nepotism as brazenly as any medieval Italian princeling, or Vice-President Aaron Burr whose election had been justly stigmatized by Adams as a 'humiliation' to America, and who had been described by Hamilton, with no less justice, as forming himself 'upon the model of Catiline', and as being 'too cold-blooded and too determined a conspirator ever to change his plan'. During the deadlock which had preceded his election, Adams had warned him in tones of disgust:

> Sir, the event of the election is within your own power. You have only to say you will do justice to the public creditors, maintain the navy, and not disturb those holding office, and the government will instantly be put into your hands.

Jefferson had replied simply, 'I will not come into the government by capitulation,' and still had won office. Whatever the justification, Jefferson did what he did, and the precedent was set.

Among John Adams's latter-day appointments was one which Jefferson could not overturn, the appointment of Adams's Secretary of State, John Marshall, as Chief Justice of the Supreme Court. Marshall was to plague Jefferson and his successors for thirty-five years; the ghosts of the great jurist and the great President still stand up as seconds in every duel between the Judiciary and the Executive.

Jefferson and Marshall were both Virginians, both lawyers, and trained in the same law school, both were men of vast erudition, complete integrity, great charm, and wonderful powers of presentation. Yet the two neither liked each other as men nor much respected each other's office. Jefferson, the unquenchable optimist, believed in the sense of the electorate and therefore stood for the supremacy of the elected representatives. Marshall, who loved the sanctity of contracts more than he loved the people, could but hope that the wisdom of law would support when possible, and control when necessary, the emotionalism of democracy. Jefferson was blind to Marshall's virtues; 'a crafty chief judge', he called him on one occasion, and on another wrote that 'Marshall bears rancorous hatred to the government of his country . . . his twistifications in the case of Marbury, in that of Burr, and the Yazoo case show how dexterously he can reconcile law to his personal biases'. But Jefferson either failed to comprehend or else failed to appreciate the far-reaching and generally worthy objectives for which Marshall worked.

The Constitution had provided for three forces in the state: the Executive, the Legislative, and the Judicial. Until Marshall became Chief Justice the judicial function had never achieved parity with the other two. Indeed, so scant was the respect with which it was regarded that it was difficult to persuade eminent lawyers to serve on the Supreme Court bench – and the architect of the Capitol forgot to include a Supreme Court in his plans, so that it was forced to meet in the basement of the Senate. Marshall was a convinced and partisan Federalist; he believed in the rights of property and was suspicious of popular excesses, and it was his conviction that the Constitution itself was designed to guard property and to prevent the follies of the uninformed. Marshall wrote some five hundred opinions or decisions himself, and participated in five hundred more. In all of them, whenever the opportunity presented itself, he consistently emphasized two principles: that the Supreme Court possessed the power to nullify laws in conflict with the constitution; and that the constitutional authority of the Federal government, in conflict with any other authority, was supreme. 'A Constitution,' he wrote, 'is framed for ages to come, and is designed to approach immortality as nearly as human institutions can approach it.' The Constitution was to him the greatest of contracts; all contracts – and none more than the Constitution – were sacred, and, although his opinions did not always become the final version of constitutional issues, the consistency of his attitudes, carried over a generation of legal interpretations, had much to do with the shaping of American constitutional laws.

In the struggle with Jefferson, Marshall was successful. He carried with him his less principled and less brilliant colleagues and, even if the Court was not always united, it was his power of exposition that usually prevailed. Marshall's service and Marshall's genius made the Supreme Court respectable to the nation.

Other Adams appointees were not protected as was the Chief Justice from losing office at a change of administration, but the full harvest from the seed sown by Jefferson's dismissals was still far in the future, and in other respects Jefferson's first administration began in happy times when the country was prosperous and foreign problems quiescent. America, according to Jefferson's view, was blessed in the fact that it was 'separated by a wide ocean from the nations of Europe'. By reducing the national debt and by keeping America free from European entanglements Jefferson hoped to emphasize the advantages of geography.

Already he was preaching the economic doctrines which became an essential part of the American dream: low taxation and a high standard of living as the equivalent and inspiration of political freedom:

If we run into such debts, as that we must be taxed in our meat and in our drink, in our necessaries and our comforts, in our labours and our amusements, for our callings and our creeds, as the people of England are, our people, like them, must come to labor sixteen hours in the twenty-four, give the earnings of fifteen of these to government for their debts and daily expenses; and the sixteenth being insufficient to afford us bread, we must live, as they now do, on oatmeal and potatoes; have no time to think, no means of calling the mismanagers to account; but be glad to obtain subsistence by hiring ourselves to rivet their chains on the necks of our fellow-sufferers.

And, with the aid of Gallatin, Jefferson's economic and political aspirations seemed likely to succeed, for the uneasy peace in Europe which had followed upon Napoleon's seizure of power in France seemed less uneasy seen from across the Atlantic. Economy could be achieved by reducing the armed services. By cutting contracts with the outside world Jefferson both hoped to bring about financial savings and to reduce the chances of explosion.

But as relations deteriorated between Britain and France, so did Jefferson's chances of bringing his policies to maturity.

Late in 1801 the news reached Jefferson that Napoleon had recovered by secret treaty the Louisiana territories lost to Spain in 1763.

The very name of Louisiana, with its echoes of the great days of French expansion under *Le Roi Soleil*, was bound to excite the ambitions of the new empire builder in Paris. Australia, the target of a French scientific expedition, Egypt, India, and the West Indies were all in Napoleon's mind, and the First Consul could but regret that 'our possessions beyond the sea, which are now in our power, are limited to San Domingo, Guadeloupe, the Isle of France (Mauritius), the Isle of Bourbon, Senegal, and Guiana'. His greatest ambitions were inevitably centred upon Louisiana.

In his efforts to encourage the French people to look beyond home pastures, Napoleon found strong support in the graceful philosophizing of his minister, Talleyrand. The bishop had personal experience of America and, in his wisdom, hoped that some of the maladies of France might be cured by participation in the pioneering activities which, when its own revolution was completed, had helped to

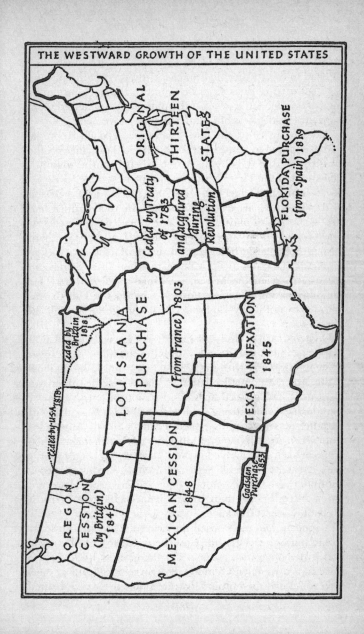

THE WESTWARD GROWTH OF THE UNITED STATES

ORIGINAL THIRTEEN STATES

FLORIDA PURCHASE (from Spain) 1819

Ceded by Treaty of 1783 and acquired during Revolution

LOUISIANA PURCHASE (From France) 1803

Ceded by Britain 1818

Ceded by U.S.A. 1818

TEXAS ANNEXATION 1845

OREGON CESSION (by Britain) 1846

MEXICAN CESSION 1848

Gadsden Purchase 1853

prevent those same maladies from gripping the United States. 'The true Lethe,' said Talleyrand in a paper which he read to the Institut de France in July 1797, 'after passing through a revolution, is to be found in the opening out to men of every avenue of hope. Revolutions leave behind them a general restlessness of mind, a need of movement.'

Already, in 1795, the newly victorious French Republic had attempted to regain from Spain her old province on the Mississippi, but Godoy had stood between the vigorous blackmail of the First Coalition and the miserable weakness of his own King, and had consented merely to the cession of the Spanish part of San Domingo. In 1800 France had stronger cards to play. At that time Napoleon was negotiating a comfortable agreement with the United States, but he was ever one to hide from his left hand the activities of his right; the daughter of Charles the Fourth of Spain had recently married the heir to the Duke of Parma, and, for the glorification of his son-in-law, Charles the Fourth was willing to sign away Louisiana in exchange for the gift of Tuscany.

Godoy was not easily thwarted. He knew full well that Napoleon could not yet risk war with the United States and knew too that war with the United States might soon follow if the Americans realized that a quarter of the American Continent had gone from the possession of a weak power into the hands of a strong. Indeed, when the news leaked out to Jefferson in 1801, that most Francophile of Americans was forced to admit regretfully that in that moment when Napoleon's troops arrived in New Orleans, 'We must marry ourselves to the British fleet and nation'. Godoy played a waiting game in the hopes that waiting would prevent action. Eventually, though Louisiana was lost to Spain it was not gained by France.

Napoleon had now raised the price of Tuscany; not only Louisiana but also Florida must be ceded to him, but even as his demands increased so did his interest in American possessions wane. In October 1802 Spanish officials at New Orleans closed the Lower Mississippi to vessels of the United

States, preparatory to handing over the territory to France. Jefferson now knew that he must either fight for New Orleans or buy it; hurriedly he passed through Congress a secret appropriation of two million dollars for use in the 'intercourse between the United States and foreign nations'. In March 1803 he sent Monroe to Paris with instructions to offer as much as fifty million francs for New Orleans and the Floridas, or more than half that sum for the Island of New Orleans alone. If nothing else was forthcoming, Monroe was to insist upon a guarantee of free passage of the Mississippi for American ships. If even this was not granted, then the course for Monroe was clear:

> Since they find that no arrangement can be made with France, to use all possible procrastination with them, and in the meantime enter into conference with the British Government through their Ambassador at Paris, to fix principles of alliance, and leave us in peace till Congress meets; and prevent war until next Spring.

Even Napoleon could not face lightly the prospect of an Anglo-American alliance; disasters in the French West Indies and the death of his brother-in-law, General Leclerc, in San Domingo in November 1802 seemed to emphasize the unattractiveness of American conquest, while the news from Corfu, Syria, and Egypt promised well for Napoleonic ambitions. A renewal of war between France and Britain seemed inevitable, and Napoleon judged that in the event of war New Orleans would be indefensible. He was, therefore, only too willing to sell to the Americans what was to him an unattractive proposition. Some efforts were made to impress the United States Government with his intentions of actually occupying New Orleans, but they were designed merely to bolster the selling price of Louisiana. Napoleon's activities worked exactly as he intended them to work. He pressed upon the Americans more than they had ever hoped to gain, and the American negotiators accepted the whole of Louisiana and the Floridas for the miserable sum of sixty million francs.

It was an extraordinary event. Almost against their will,

and certainly beyond their wildest dreams, the Americans had achieved Continental power. 'From this day,' said Livingston, the American Ambassador in Paris, as he signed his name to the treaty, 'the United States take their place among the powers of the first rank.' Napoleon, for his part, had sold something which he had never really owned, and Jefferson, for his, had bought something which legally he had no right to buy. To Talleyrand Napoleon said:

Irresolution and deliberation are no longer in season. I renounce Louisiana. It is not only New Orleans that I cede: it is the whole colony, without reserve; I know the price of that which I abandon. I have proved the importance I attach to this province, since my first diplomatic act with Spain had the object of recovering it. I renounce it with the greatest regret: to attempt obstinately to retain it would be folly. I direct you to negotiate the affair.

But Napoleon was able to justify his surrender of France's American ambitions. 'This accession of territory strengthens for ever the power of the United States and I have just given to England a maritime rival that sooner or later will humble her pride.' So far he was right. By the cession of Louisiana, Napoleon had prevented an alliance between Britain and America and revived the rivalries between the English-speaking nations; rivalries that were to be used to France's great advantage, particularly when Nelson's activities made it imperative for Napoleon to seek alliance with a maritime power. But Napoleon went farther, and too far, in his self-justification. 'Perhaps I will also be told in reproach,' he said to Marbois,

that in two or three centuries the Americans may be found too powerful for Europe, but my forethought cannot encompass such distant fears. Besides, in the future, rivalries inside the union are to be expected. These confederations that are called perpetual last only till one of the confederating parties finds that its interest can be served by breaking them.

In fact the Louisiana Purchase made possible, and made logical, the unity of the United States. Jefferson had long realized the impulse westward of the American people and already, before the Purchase was completed, he was preparing an expedition to investigate the routes to American expansion in the West. Indeed, his activities in preparing for the voyages of Lewis and Clark must modify to some extent the conventional view that he was fortunate to get Louisiana from Napoleon. By the Louisiana Purchase, the route Westwards was freed to Americans earlier than even Jefferson had hoped, but he had felt for long that eventually the American people must cross the Mississippi in force and had expected that ultimately American sovereignty would succeed to American passage.

The voyages of Meriwether Lewis and William Clark, prepared through the instigation of Jefferson in 1803 and undertaken between 1804 and 1806, are both symbol and cause of a major change in the American destiny. The period of colonialism was over; American independence had been won; but still the United States clung to its Atlantic coast-line, and the westwards movement which had been part of American history from the very beginning was directed still from its eastern base. A few – speculators, soldiers, Indian traders, adventurers, and failures – groped and stumbled into the lands which are now the Middle West, but with little knowledge of the vastness and incredible opportunity which lay beyond. In 1803 after the Louisiana Purchase was completed, it became apparent to the President, if not to other less acute Americans, that the Mississippi was no longer the frontier of American ambitions, that instead it was now the highway of American ambition, and that beyond it lay the route to the great territory of Oregon, to the fur trade of Canada, to the maritime trade with the Far East, to settlement and the fulfilment of national hopes within obvious geographical boundaries. By the time the Lewis and Clark expedition returned to settled areas it had closed one chapter which was as long as American history; that which told the story of the dream of a North-West Passage. It had opened another chapter: the chapter in which the West was turned from fantasy-land into a reality with which the American mind could deal. In a sense,

Lewis and Clark had discovered the Passage, though its length, appearance and difficulty would have appalled their hopeful predecessors.

It is only by reading once more the admirable journals kept by the two leaders, and the journals kept under instruction by other members of the party, that it is possible to realize the momentous nature of this expedition. Simple things which were to become part of every American's vocabulary first creep into the knowledge of Americans through these accounts. Thus the badger:

Joseph Fields brought in an Anamale called by the French *Brarow* and by the Panies *Cho car tooch* . . . this Anamale Burrows in the Ground and feeds on Flesh, (Prarie Dogs Bugs) & Vigatables.

Magnificent events are recorded with a suitable and inevitable sense of triumph that stands out the more because the language of the journals is for the most part as unemotional as that of a regimental battle-diary:

At the distance of 4 miles further the road took us to the most distant fountain of the waters of the Mighty Missouri in surch of which we have spent so many toilsome days and wrestless nights, thus far I had accomplished one of those great objects on which my mind had been unalterably fixed for many years . . . two miles below McNeal had exultingly stood with a foot on each side of this little revulet and thanked his god that he had lived to bestride the mighty & heretofore deemed endless Missouri.

Many years were to pass before it became a commonplace activity to follow the routes taken by Lewis and Clark, and, while westward travel still retained an element of exploration, it is possible that no other expedition was conducted with such efficiency, with such apparent ease, as this, the first. Planning must be given some of the credit, but planning for the unknown cannot be complete, and to the pioneers of 1804, the Rockies, the Cascades, the high plains and plateaux of Columbia, the North-Western forests with their miserably wet winters, were all as unknown as the cultures of many of the Indian tribes. That such strangeness

was successfully encountered must be placed to the genius
of the two leaders.

The voyages of Lewis and Clark were the first huge steps
in almost a century of westward movement. Within a very
few years the Ohio and the Mississippi had become the highways of America.

> Come all you fine young fellows, who have a mind to range,
> Into some far-off country your fortunes for to change.
> Rise up you fine young women who have a mind to go,
> We'll build you fine log cabins by the blessed Ohio.

The Ohio and the Mississippi – according to legend,
though the rivers meet their waters never mix – carried flat
boats, barges, and soon paddle-steamers. They carried the
pioneers with their fiddles and their bragging. They carried
Bierstadt, Church, and Thomas Moran, painters alive with
the romantic desire to see 'aerial mountain tops with their
mighty growth of forest', men whose Eastern training made
them helpless to portray the vastness of the West. They
carried John James Audubon, a young ornithologist-
painter, who had read Buffon and studied under David, and
it was in the pioneer store which he kept that Audubon first
had the idea for *Birds of America* and *Quadrupeds of America*,
'the most magnificent monument which art has ever raised
to science'. They carried the screamers, the tellers and
hearers of tall stories, Mike Fink and Davy Crockett, 'half
horse, half alligator, a little touched with the snapping
turtle, who could wade the Mississippi, leap the Ohio, ride
upon a streak of lightning, who could whip his weight in
wildcats – and eat any man opposed to Andrew Jackson'.

The West had become not merely an activity for Americans, but in many respects the symbol of Americanism.

CHAPTER 21

THE SECOND WAR

THE growth of the new West strengthened the political power of what could now be termed the old West. Kentucky, Tennessee, and the Western regions of North and South Carolina and Virginia had a congruity of interests each with the other, and all with the Mississippi and Ohio settlements, that seemed to cut them off from the East. Yet territories such as Kentucky were sufficiently established to have developed a class of intellectual and political leaders, men of the type of Henry Clay, born in Hanover County, Virginia, and a member of the Virginia Bar, but essentially a citizen of Lexington, Kentucky, or John Calhoun of South Carolina. There was a division of interest between the slave-owning states and the free states, but it was as nothing when compared to the difference between East and West. As relations between England and the United States were frayed once more by the British decision to employ against Napoleon the weapon which Britain has always wielded most successfully against Continental enemies – the weapon of blockade – it was the West which exacerbated the international situation to the point of war.

Much has been made of the horrors of the press-gang in England; American patriotic fervour was, and still is, aroused to a natural but violent heat at the thought of the British press-gang extending its activities to American ships. But the blockade policies which both Britain and France attempted and the insistence of Britain on its rights of search were but a small part in the general pattern of dilemma which faced Jefferson and his successor, Madison, in international affairs.

Since the Battle of Trafalgar, Britain had maintained undisputed mastery of the seas, but the British were not unique in the lack of respect which they showed towards the insignificant American navy. Napoleon himself referred to the

American flag as 'only a piece of striped bunting'. In 1807 there was a naval incident in the Chesapeake Bay which roused the American nation into unity and was to be remembered with consequence in the next few years. The British frigate *Leopard* stopped the United States navy's *Chesapeake* (a warship, not a merchant vessel), killed or wounded twenty-one men and took four sailors. This was an act of war by any standards, and for a moment the whole of the United States wanted it. When Jefferson forwarded a violent protest to London even the Federalists applauded, so that the President, more used to vilification than praise, could but say, 'Lord, what have I done that the wicked should praise me?'

But Jefferson knew that the country was not ready for war and knew too that trade was vital to the American nation. The British and the French issued a complex and confusing series of orders and decrees intended to control ocean trade, with the result that American ships were likely to be confiscated by either side if they followed the orders of the other. British men-of-war claimed the right to inspect American ships and to search them for British deserters, some of whom (conditions in the British navy being what they were) doubtless did turn up in American crews. British captains, who disregarded the refinements of citizenship, in some cases simply kidnapped American sailors. Jefferson's dilemma was intensified by the disrespect with which Britain treated America's protests, and the consequent activity of Napoleon, who roared the louder the more Britain shouted. Jefferson did not want war though he could very probably have obtained congressional and public support for it. He was able to launch a comforting exercise against Algerian pirates, but he was helpless before the might of the two greatest empires in the world.

In this situation, Jefferson made one of his finest gestures and his worst error of judgement; he tried, probably for the first time in the history of the world, the experiment of waging an economic war without support of arms. To prevent further humiliation and the risk of war, Jefferson passed through Congress in December 1807 an Embargo Act – 'peaceful coercion', as he called it – which forbade commerce with Europe.

Trade was brought to a standstill and in port towns bankruptcies were common. The philosopher-President found himself in a situation in which neither the comforts of philosophy nor the authority of the presidency could protect him from vilification. 'You Infernal Villain,' wrote one angry New Englander. 'How much longer are you going to keep this damned Embargo on to starve us poor people.' And Jefferson's miserable position was worsened by the knowledge that his policies were almost certain to fail, and by the vicious certainty that there were, for him and for the American people, no signposts pointing unequivocally in the direction of right.

Jefferson, and many of his American contemporaries, hated and feared the power of Napoleon. In 1816 he wrote:

I considered him as the very worst of all human beings, and as having inflicted more misery on mankind than any other who had ever lived.

And again, in 1823:

He wanted totally the sense of right and wrong. If he could consider millions of human lives which he had destroyed or caused to be destroyed, the desolations of countries by plunderings, burnings and famine, the destitutions of lawful rulers of the world without the consent of their constituents . . . the cutting up of established societies of men and jumbling them discordantly together again at his caprice, the demolition of the fairest hopes of mankind for the recovery of their rights and amelioration, and all the numberless train of his other enormities; the man, I say, who could consider all these as no crime, must have been a moral monster, against whom every hand should have been lifted to slay him.

But Napoleon was the heir to the French Revolution – 'so beautiful a revolution', Jefferson had called it – and, for the moment, Napoleon was France, for Jefferson the most civilized of the nations. Against Napoleon stood Britain, the traditional enemy of all things American, 'rotted to the core' by 'commerce and a corrupt government', whose object *'is the permanent domination of the ocean and the monopoly of the trade of the world'*.

By his Embargo policies Jefferson had hoped to play Mercutio. When it became apparent that the chance was remote of spurning both the Montagus of Britain and the Capulets of France, and indeed that New England was threatening secession if Jefferson persisted in the attempt, the logical course left to America – a ridiculous and impossible logic – was to declare war on both Empires.

War was virtually inevitable. But war with whom? Presumably with the British who could enforce their maritime policies.

Jefferson was tired and lonely, anxious only to avoid the responsibilities of office and the responsibilities of decision. He used the precedent created by Washington to refuse the chance of a third term, and, at the price of repealing the Embargo Act, managed to secure the succession for his friend and ally, James Madison.

Madison tried to follow Jefferson's lead. He, too, wanted peace with Britain and freedom for trade. But the 'War Hawks' of the new West were in the ascendant and eager for the chance of removing the British from a position threatening to the American control of the Mississippi Valley.

Madison vacillated. There was little else that he could do. First he tried to help New England by negotiating with the British Ambassador an agreement whereby in return for exemption from the denying provisions of Orders in Council the United States would lift all bans on trade with England and would forbid United States ships to enter French waters.

In Britain, George Canning was Foreign Secretary in Portland's Government, and Canning had no use for the United States. Lancashire and Yorkshire were as anxious to cancel the Orders in Council as New England had been to repeal the Embargo Act – and for the same good reason trade starved in the state of blockade. But Canning had held the Government oblivious to the appeals of the merchants. Now he recalled the British Minister for exceeding his instructions, and those in Britain who did not depend on trade applauded, thinking that strong language and strong actions were the best way of keeping peace with the Americans:

> The altered tone of respect and deference, from one of arrogant and haughty superiority, in the Government of America, produced by the policy of Mr. Canning, and the closing of an apprehended breach between the two countries, which the indiscretions of our British minister have widened, are not the least of the many proofs which he has given of his peculiar fitness for presiding over the foreign policy of England.

Next Madison tried the French. Napoleon, ever ready with promises, offered to withdraw his Decrees if Britain would abolish the Orders in Council. The British refused the bait, Madison leapt at the idle concession. In February 1811 trade with Britain was once more halted and trade with France resumed.

The War Hawks, a group of aggressive young congressmen, chiefly from the West, somewhat encouraged by a fine piece of international larceny on the part of Madison – who read more into the Louisiana Purchase than either Jefferson or Napoleon had intended and thus, with the aid of Congress, brought the Florida possessions of Britain's ally, Spain, into the United States – set their eyes once more on Canada, now the greatest prize on the American Continent outside the control of the United States.

Up on the North-Western frontier, two Indian chiefs, Tecumseh and his half-brother the 'Prophet', had started a movement which was to do them little good and which in the hands of the propagandists became yet another stick with which to beat the American nation into war with Britain. Faced with ever-increasing pressure form pioneering Americans, and exhausted out of patience by America's easy way with Indian treaties, these two rare Indian leaders with the support of the Governor of Canada, contrived to unite the four thousand or so Indians in the area between

Pennsylvania, the Mississippi, the Ohio, and the Canadian border. Their aim was defensive, passive if possible, and active only if need be, but the fears of settlers on the frontier were by now tradition-bound; increased Indian activity in the summer of 1811, including some frontier raids, brought nightmares to the people of Indiana Territory, and they demanded action from Governor William Henry Harrison. Harrison took the field against the Indians and destroyed their capital, Tippecanoe. All doubts that conscience might arouse in the majority of the American people could be expunged by spreading the story that the British were behind the Tecumseh 'conspiracy'.

The War Hawks moved from strength to strength and took with them even such moderates as James Monroe and President Madison. 'War is no terrible thing,' cried Clay, 'there is no terror in it but its novelty', and the Committee of Foreign Affairs under the chairmanship of Calhoun worked itself into a frenzy of patriotic indignation against impressment and blockade, reporting finally that 'your committee recommends an appeal to arms'.

The debate on the report demonstrates that it was geographical more than party affiliations which dictated attitudes to the war.

First came Peter Porter from Western New York to urge that the people of the United States 'occupying half a continent, have a right to navigate the seas without being molested by the inhabitants of the little island of Great Britain'.

Felix Grundy of Tennessee charged Britain with inciting the Indians to attack American pioneers. To remove the source of this danger Canada must be annexed to the United States.

Calhoun of South Carolina urged the patriotic necessity to go to war, to expel the British from their North American possessions and to grant letters of marque and reprisal.

Against the War Hawks stood John Randolph of Virginia and the representatives of the New England states. Randolph was no Federalist; indeed, he was a close friend and colleague of Jefferson and Madison, one who only seven years before had been chief advocate for the Republicans in the attempt to impeach the Federalist Judge Samuel Chase. But now Randolph's brilliant and bitter oratory was turned on the Western group of his own party. He objected to standing armies:

No sooner was the report laid on the table, than the vultures were flocking round their prey, the carcass of a great Military Establishment – men of strained reputation, of broken fortunes (if they ever had any) and of battered constitutions, 'choice spirits, tired of the dull pursuits of civil life', were seeking after agencies and commissions, willing to doze in gross stupidity over the public fire; to light the public candle at both ends.

He pointed out that war with Britain meant an alliance with the forces opposed to civilization and 'his imagination shrunk from the miseries of such a connexion'. He denied that Britain had inspired recent Indian troubles; he even had the courage to argue that 'for this signal calamity and disgrace the House was in part at least answerable'.

Advantage has been taken of the spirit of the Indians, broken by the war which ended in the Treaty of Greenville. Under the ascendency then acquired over them, they have been pent up by subsequent treaties into nooks, straitened in their quarters by blind cupidity, seeking to extinguish their title to immense wilderness, for which . . . we shall not have occasion, for half a century to come. It was our own want of moderation, that had driven these sons of nature to desperation.

If war came, declared Randolph, it would be no war for maritime rights but an imperialist and expansionist war in the interests of the Western States.

Go! march to Canada! leave the broad bosom of the Chesapeake and her hundred tributary rivers unprotected! You have taken Quebec – have you conquered England? . . . Will you call upon her to leave your ports and harbours untouched, only just till you can return from Canada, to defend them? The coast is to be left defenceless, whilst men of the interior are revelling in conquest and spoil. . . . As Chatham and Burke, and the whole band of (Britain's) patriots, prayed for her defeat in 1776, so must some of the truest friends to their country deprecate the success of our arms against the only Power that holds in check the arch-enemy of mankind.

Randolph stood by reason and justice. Seldom has Congress been treated to such an accurate analysis of motives, but reason and accuracy could not stand against the blusterings of hurt pride. All that Randolph and the moderate Republicans could secure was a postponement of the inevitable.

Madison stood out against the war party for a few weeks, but he too had decided for warlike measures in face of the 'evidence of hostile inflexibility in trampling on rights which no independent nation can relinquish'. The situation was exacerbated in March 1812, by the publication of the secret correspondence of a political adventurer, John Henry: correspondence which seemed to identify the Federalist opposition with the British cause. A new Embargo Act directed uniquely against Britain came into force on 4 April and on the 10th of that month the President was empowered to call up one hundred thousand militiamen for six months' service. In May Madison was renominated, and on 1 June he sent a confidential message to the House, reviewing the course Britain had taken and insisting that she was already conducting war *de facto* against the United States.

On 18 June, by a small but sufficient majority, Congress voted for war. Next day the President made the declaration of war public.

The origins of war are never simple, and to say that the United States 'blundered' into the war of 1812 is to overgeneralize. There was the lingering resentment of twenty years of friction between Britain and the new country, memories of impressed seamen and haughty captains, the land-hunger of Western expansionists. Paradoxically, the chief opposition to the war came from New England, whose maritime interests had been most clearly endangered; its chief support came from the West, where ocean trade was less important. Much of the war's motivation came perhaps from nothing but vague feelings that national pride and integrity were at stake for, as Andrew Jackson of Tennessee said, 'We are going to fight for the re-establishment of our national character, for the protection of our maritime citizens, to vindicate our right to a free trade, and to open market for the productions of our soil because the *mistress of the ocean* has forbid us to carry them to any foreign nations.'

Three days earlier George Canning's rival, Lord Castle-reagh, had announced to Parliament the suspension of the Orders in Council. The virtual end of American trade, coupled with the increased effectiveness of Napoleon's Continental System, had brought British industry to the verge of ruin and had forced Perceval's Ministry to accept, albeit with reluctance, the abandonment of this vital economic weapon of war. Had it not been for the assassination of the Prime Minister which disrupted temporarily the machinery of government, the decision might have been announced in sufficient time for the news to reach America before Congress could vote for war.

In the same week the true villain of the story, the Emperor Napoleon, had turned his back irrevocably on the puny affairs of the United States. His dreams sped always eastwards, and, in addition, Russia's imperfect participation in the Emperor's Continental System threatened to undermine the economic structure which Napoleon had designed for Europe. The Emperor set out across the Niemen bent upon the destruction of his recent ally, the Tsar Alexander.

As it had started so did the War of 1812 continue, unnecessary and inconclusive. One of the principal reasons for war had vanished before ever the first shot was fired. The mercantile States were bitterly opposed to the war and went almost to the ultimate of treason or secession to prevent its prosecution. The enemy, the British, were for the most part uninterested in distant campaigns and remote grievances, or else regarded them as an unimportant and impertinently inspired diversion from the great struggle with Napoleon. From the War neither side gained anything of practical importance. The most notable battle of the war was fought at New Orleans after a peace treaty had been concluded.

Certain advantages were with the Americans from the outset; above all the fact that Britain was so completely involved with Napoleon that the British Government neither would nor could look with any seriousness upon the distant American War. It seemed that the comparatively small population of Canada would succumb easily to the Americans.

But even in their bellicose eagerness the War Hawks had built up difficulties which were to plague Madison in his conduct of the war.

Early in 1811, for example, their Anglophobia had driven them into alliance with more conservative Republicans to bring about the end of the first United States Bank. When the charter of the Bank was up for renewal the Anglophobes voted against it because two-thirds of its stock was in the hands of British stockholders and because they hoped to divert the new profits of the West into state-chartered banks; moderate Republicans saw in the Bank the last vestiges of Federalist power. A few months later and with the country at war the President would have been grateful for the financial resources of a national bank.

In New York there were anti-war meetings almost from the moment the President declared war. In Massachusetts the Governor declared a public fast in view of the war 'against the nation from which we are descended' and the militia was encouraged to rebel. Financiers not only refused money for the American cause but actually sent specie to Canada. The Governor of Connecticut would not authorize the dispatch of state militia to the Federal forces. From New Hampshire came the Rockingham memorial, drafted by a thirty-year-old lawyer, Daniel Webster, protesting against 'hasty, rash, and ruinous measures'. 'We are from principle and habit attached to the Union,' said Webster in a speech on the outbreak of war, 'but our attachment is to the substance and not to the form. . . . If separation of the States should ever take place, it will be when one portion of the country undertakes to control and regulate and sacrifice the interests of the other.' Timothy Dwight of Yale stepped boldly into his pulpit and preached secession to the text, ' Come ye out from among them.'

Not satisfied with dissension in the United States the war party saddled the country (for the second time in a generation) with the illusion that Canada was ripe for the picking. A three-pronged attack into Canada – General Dearborn along the Lake Champlain route to Montreal, General Van Rensselaer over the Niagara River, and General Hull from Detroit into Upper Canada – would take little time to bring Canada into the United States. Further, according to the armchair strategists, there was every chance that the time would be shortened by a Canadian rebellion. On his first day in Canadian territory, Hull hinted at this hope in a speech which had been drafted for him by the Secretary of War. 'The United States,' de declared, 'offers you peace, liberty, and security. Your choice lies between these and war, slavery, and destruction.'

Yet to all but the few perennial optimists in Washington it was obvious that the Canadians would choose war. The leaders of Upper Canada were the men or sons of the men who had fled the United States out of loyalty to the Crown. The leaders of Lower Canada, Catholic almost to a man, had little reason to ally themselves with the American cause; revolution was to them anathema, the French Revolution had alienated them finally from their Mother Country, the American Revolution was, in their eyes, a Protestant and even an anti-religious revolution. Their faith, interest, and comfort all combined to persuade them into eager opposition to the forces of the heirs to the American Revolution now fighting on the side of the heirs to the French Revolution.

With, at first, few British regulars to support them, but with a new ally, the Shawnee chief Tecumseh, the Canadian militiamen threw back all three invasions.

Hull spent two weeks in Canada, withdrew under pressure to Detroit, and there surrendered to a small pursuing force.

Hull was court-martialled and his name dropped from the army roll.

Van Rensselaer made little progress on the Niagara front; the New York Militia refused to move into action in the very first battle because movement would have taken them beyond the call of duty out of New York State. Van Rensselaer was superseded by General Alexander Smyth. But the change of commander made no difference to the enthusiasm of the troops; a feeble effort to cross the Niagara was repulsed with ease. Smyth was relieved of his command and his name dropped from the army roll.

The largest American force, under the command of General Dearborn, moved boldly from Plattsburg towards Montreal. The border was reached almost without incident and there, as at Niagara, the militia struck, perhaps fortunately because opposite them stood the only substantial force of seasoned British regulars. The army marched back to Plattsburg. Somehow Dearborn kept his name on the army roll.

But for the Americans there was in the first year of the War ample consolation at sea for the humiliations on land. 'The half-a-dozen fir frigates, with bits of bunting flying at their heads', Canning called the American fleet, but these fir frigates, though nominally the same rate as the British frigates opposed to them, were better designed, more heavily gunned, and more strongly timbered. They were, in addition, operating close to their bases, and they were superbly handled.

'The charm of the invincibility of the British Navy' was destroyed in August, when in a battle off Cape Cod, which lasted scarcely an hour, the *Guerriere* was sunk by the *Constitution*. The commander of the American frigate was the nephew of General Hull; an additional compensation for the fiasco at Detroit in the same week. There followed a series of similar duels, and similar victories. The United States Navy had proved itself and in the process kept the war alive for the American Government to put out peace-feelers, but to refuse peace on any terms but its own – and made possible Madison's re-election.

But the defeat, destruction, and capture of British men-of-war aroused the British Admiralty from its nonchalant attitude to the American War, and the changing situation in Europe, where Napoleon was held on all fronts and mastered on many, made it possible for the British Government to release troops, sailors, and ships for North American campaigns.

A vigorous blockade of the American East coast was set up by a naval force under Sir George Cockburn. Raiding parties were landed along the shores of the Chesapeake, and the Bay was for a while a British naval base. The mouth of the Mississippi, the harbours of New York, Charleston, and Savannah were all closed by the vigilance and strength of the British fleet, and although American privateers slipped out to harry British merchantmen in the Irish Sea, the Channel and the Atlantic (by 1814 eight hundred and twenty-five British vessels had been captured by the Americans), the effect on the American economy was well nigh crippling.

Even in the business of duels between frigates, the British began to have successes. On 1 June 1813 the 38-gun American frigate *Chesapeake*, with a green and mutinous crew, engaged the 38-gun British frigate *Shannon* only thirty miles out of Boston and was soundly beaten.

> Brave Broke he waved his sword, crying: Now, my lads, aboard,
> And we'll stop their playing Yankee-doodle-dandy-oh.

John Lawrence, commanding *Chesapeake*, also had something to say for himself, and his dying command, 'Don't give up the ship', was to become the rallying cry of the United States Navy. But the British towed *Chesapeake* into Halifax!

Yet from near-disaster the United States gained new strength. The British Government had hoped to encourage New England's distaste for the war into positive disaffection, and had therefore, in the early days of the blockade, exempted New England ports from naval attrition. New England was never an enthusiastic ally in the War of 1812 – 'We in New England are no patriots,' said Daniel Webster – but, out of the scarcity of foreign goods caused by the blockade, New England learnt the advantages of a new industrial economy which would eventually outstrip her shipbuilding and mercantile interests. New Englanders were not above selling to the British (those were days when mercantile morality was less certain or less regulated than it is today; Napoleon's Grand Army marched to Moscow in British-made boots), but the British had less need than the Americans for New England's goods and so New England sold at home. Eventually, in April 1814, the British were forced to extend the blockade to New England.

And although, when the thirteenth Congress met in May 1813 the War Hawks were noticeably lacking in exuberance, the Federalists' strident disloyalty and their urgent criticism of the Administration and its 'drivelling campaigns' brought only discredit to their party, so that even in New England there was a renewed flutter of patriotic zeal.

In the face of a threatened invasion the nation rallied. A new spirit was infused into the Army and reforms in Washington increased the possibility of military efficiency. The recruiting agents were at work, and their aides, the writers of patriotic songs.

> Enemies beware, keep a proper distance,
> Else we'll make you stare at our firm resistance;
> Let alone the lads who are freedom tasting,
> Don't forget our dads gave you once a basting.
> To protect our rights 'gainst your flints and triggers,
> See on yonder heights our patriotic diggers.
> Men of every age, color, rank, profession.
> Ardently engaged labor in succession.
> Pick-axe, shovel, spade, crow-bar, hoe and barrow,
> Better not invade, Yankees have the marrow!
>
> Scholars leave their schools with patriotic teachers,
> Farmers seize their tools, headed by their preachers,

> How they break the soil – brewers, butchers, bakers,
> Here the Doctors toil, there the undertakers.
> Bright Apollo's sons leave their pipe and tabor,
> Mid the roar of guns, join the martial labor.
> Round the embattled plain in sweet concord rally,
> And in freedom's strain sing the foes finale.
>
> Better not invade, don't forget the spirit
> Which our dads displayed and their sons inherit;
> If you still advance, friendly caution slighting,
> You may get by chance a belly-full of fighting!
> Plumbers, founders, dyers, tinmen, turners, shavers,
> Sweepers, clerks and criers, jewellers, engravers,
> Clothiers, drapers, players, cartmen, hatters, tailors,
> Gaugers, sealers, weighers, carpenters and sailors!

The centre of war now moved once more to the Canadian frontier. In the Detroit region William Henry Harrison was in command – at first with no greater authority than that provided by a group of Kentucky citizens, but ultimately as a general on the establishment. Although he failed in his first drive on Detroit he repulsed the British counter-attacks, and when his supporting naval forces on Lake Erie won a great victory over the British lake squadron, the British were forced to evacuate Detroit and the way into Upper Canada was again open.

Oliver Hazard Perry, the author of the naval victory, became a national hero and the ballad-writers went into legitimate ecstasies over his achievements:

> On the bosom of Lake Erie in fanciful pride
> Did the flat of Old England exaltingly ride,
> Till the flag of Columbia Perry unfurled,
> The pride of the West and the boast of the World.
> And still should the foe dare the fight to sustain,
> Gallant Perry shall lead us to conquer again
> For freedom of trade and our right to the main.

In the course of Harrison's advance into Canada, Tecumseh was killed and the Indians lost heart for the war. The United States military frontier in the North-West was secure. General Dearborn, on the Niagara frontier, hoped to imitate Harrison's action by using Chauncey's naval squadron to seize control of Lake Ontario, but here British and Canadian resistance was stronger, and although his troops captured and set fire to York (Toronto), the capital of Upper Canada, their hold over the region was tenuous.

Again Montreal was the objective of a major American advance, but on this front the British had established their strongest and most experienced force, and the assault was abandoned.

To the American invasion of Canada the British responded with an invasion of United States territory. Bitterness and brutality gripped both sides. As the Americans had burnt York, so the British razed Buffalo. But victory for either side seemed remote, and in November 1813 Lord Castlereagh offered to negotiate a peace.

The news of Allied victories on the Continent of Europe encouraged Madison to accept Castlereagh's offer, and early in 1814 the Senate confirmed the appointment of John Quincy Adams, J. A. Bayard, Clay, Jonathan Russell, and Gallatin as peace commissioners to go to Ghent to conduct negotiations.

Those same European victories had brought about an even greater event. On 6 April 1814 Napoleon signed his instrument of abdication. Britain could now release the veterans of the Peninsular War for service in North America.

The American invaders were driven out of Canada but a spirited American victory at Lake Champlain prevented the British from exploiting their advantage to the full.

In August 1814, as the peace commissioners were meeting for the first time in Belgium, a British force under General Ross sent out directly from France, began harrying selected points on the United States coast. Landing in Maryland the troops advanced against poor opposition towards the capital and camped outside the city. In a display of organized bad temper detachments marched into Washington and wrought damage to the tune of one and a half million dollars.

Admiral Cockburn himself mounted the Speaker's chair in the House of Representatives and asked 'Shall this harbour of Yankee democracy be burned? All for it will say Aye!' All said Aye, here as elsewhere in Washington; wantonly they set fire to public buildings and even private homes, then calmly returned to the British fleet and put to sea.

'The ill-organized association,' fulminated *The Times*, 'is on the eve of dissolution, and the world is speedily to be delivered of the mischievous example of the existence of a government founded on democratic rebellion.'

And so it seemed as Madison and his government crept back into their charred capital city. But three weeks later the British failed to capture Baltimore (and General Ross was mortally wounded).

A young Maryland lawyer who during the bombardment of the key fort to Baltimore was on board the British flagship (for reasons more creditable to the British command than most of the events of this campaign) in elation born of relief wrote a poem to the American flag which, one hundred and seventeen years later, became the American national anthem. (The tune is a British regimental march!)

Oh say can you see by the dawn's early light
What so proudly we hailed at twilight's last gleaming
Whose broad stripes and bright stars, thro' the perilous fight
O'er the ramparts we watched were so gallantly streaming,
And the rockets' red glare, the bombs bursting in air
Gave proof thro' the night that our flag was still there.

In their moments of misery the Americans gained pride – and a measure of national conceit.

And where is the band who so vauntingly swore
That the havoc of war and the battle's confusion
A home and a country would leave us no more?
Their blood has washed out their foul footsteps' pollution.
No refuge could save the hireling and slave
From the terror of flight or the gloom of the grave!

But neither Francis Scott Key, nor for that matter Admiral Cockburn, could alter the fact that both sides were heartily sick of the futile war. The negotiations at Ghent dragged on; news from Washington made the American commissioners truculent, news from Lake Champlain led the British delegates to think that they could dictate terms.

The British wanted a neutral Indian state in the North-West frontier, concessions and navigation rights on the Mississippi; the Americans satisfaction on impressment and blockade, and recognition of American rights to the Newfoundland fisheries. When finally the treaty was signed on Christmas Eve 1814, nothing was said about impressment, navigation, or fishing rights, no changes were made in the boundaries which existed before the war (save that the United States kept West Florida).

It was a strangely inconclusive treaty to a strangely inconclusive war. Yet the Treaty of Ghent was a milestone in the relations between the two signatories, for it recognized the importance of amicable negotiations: each of the matters at dispute was referred for future discussion and four commissions were set up to settle the frontier between the United States and Canada.

'There shall be a firm and universal peace between His Britannic Majesty and the United States,' so ran the preamble to the first article of peace. Unlike most contracts between nations the terms of the Treaty of Ghent have proved enduring.

Two postscripts must be written to the history of the War of 1812.

In November 1814 a British force under Sir Edward Pakenham had left Jamaica for New Orleans. Just as, early in the War, the Americans had thought to take Canada with ease, so now the British imagined that New Orleans would fall to them without a fight. Pakenham, Wellington's brother-in-law, had ready elaborate plans for converting vast captures of sugar and cotton into an investment corporation; his expedition included an official printer with a complete printing press, a full complement of civic officers, and twenty merchant ships.

Fortunately for America, General Andrew Jackson in command of New Orleans and Mobile was well equipped to resist an assault. His efforts were encouraged by the new

Secretary of War, James Monroe. 'Hasten your militia to New Orleans,' wrote Monroe, 'do not wait for the Government here to arm them; put all the arms you can find in their hands; let every man bring his rifle with him; we shall see you paid.'

Martial law was proclaimed in New Orleans, entrenchments dug and strengthened with bales of cotton. The militia was called out and drilled, convicts released, free Negroes and even pirates enlisted into the service. Then Jackson waited for the enemy, and for his own Tennessee and Kentucky militiamen; frontiersmen who had learnt the art of war in fighting under Jackson against the Indians.

The frontier levies arrived, marksmen all armed with the long frontier rifle. Pakenham landed his men on Christmas Eve. (At Ghent the Peace Treaty was being signed.) In a series of fierce minor engagements Jackson held off the enemy while his much smaller force withdrew to a prepared line. On 8 January Pakenham, under orders which he knew to be futile, advanced his troops in fine but stupid order against the breastworks. Pakenham, two other generals, and almost two thousand regulars lost their lives. The American losses were insignificant: eight killed, thirteen wounded.

Fought as it was after hostilities were officially at end the Battle of New Orleans had no military significance. Yet had it not been won and had the British captured New Orleans and Louisiana it is possible that they would have urged the principle of *uti possidetis* and would have insisted on their right to hold the territory.

Beyond the possibility of conjecture, the Battle of New Orleans provided a tremendous fillip to American national pride. The bells which rang out for victory – and for peace – rang the administration back to favour. When the news reached Paris, Henry Clay crowed triumphantly, 'Now I can go to England without mortification.'

The second postscript begins in October 1814, and is in a sense a corollary to the first, for whereas New Orleans is a symbol of the rampant West, the Hartford Convention represents the fears and troubles of the old-established East.

New England's hatred of the war had been occasioned in part by fear that the balance of power in the Union had been upset by the Louisiana Purchase. The destiny of the United States, it was feared, would in future lie in the grasp of the new Western States, and the speed with which this destiny was overriding the wishes of the New England States had been demonstrated by the fact that they were Western politicians who had bustled the country into war.

Therefore the Massachusetts Legislature summoned the New England States to convene in secret sessions at Hartford 'to revise the Constitution'. In three weeks of debate the Convention, composed of moderate Federalist delegates (officially appointed by Massachusetts, Rhode Island, and Connecticut, and appointed by local conventions in New Hampshire and Vermont) agreed upon a series of suggestions, all of them designed to strengthen the State against the Union and to protect New England against the overweening influence of the West.

The resolutions fell far short of secession or treason though in the last of them there was a hint of sterner things to come:

If peace should not be concluded, and the defence of these States should be neglected, as it has since the commencement of the war, it will, in the opinion of the convention, be expedient for the legislatures of the several States to appoint delegates to another convention, to meet at Boston . . . with such powers and instructions as the exigency of a crisis so momentous may require.

The news from Ghent rendered the threat nugatory; the news from New Orleans made in impertinent. The delegates slunk home from Hartford to the tune of much abuse from a rejoicing, proud, and relieved nation.

The Union was safe for a half-century, and when it was threatened again, New England had learnt good reason to spring to its defence.

BIBLIOGRAPHY

IT would be impossible to select from among the many general histories of the United States. Suffice it to say that Samuel Eliot Morison and Henry Steele Commager, *The Growth of the American Republic* (rev. ed. 1962, 2 vols.) and John Richard Alden, *Rise of the American Republic* (1963) are good general surveys. A British historian, Frank Thistlethwaite, has added a useful introduction, *The Great Experiment* (1955). Louis B. Wright *et al.*, *The Democratic Experience: A Short American History* (1963) is a concise yet scholarly book written by ten prominent historians, each writing about the particular period or aspect of American history in which he is a specialist. Another short study, Gilman M. Ostrander, *A Profile History of the United States* (1964) is especially good for social and intellectual developments. One of the most recent additions to the seemingly inexhaustible supply of general histories, John A. Garraty, *The American Nation: A History of the United States* (1966) is well written and well illustrated. *The Statistical History of the United States: from Colonial Times to the Present*, published by the Social Science Research Council in collaboration with the U.S. Census Bureau in 1963, is an indispensable reference work; so too is the Library of Congress bibliography, *A Guide to the Study of the United States of America*, first published in 1960.

Daniel J. Boorstin (ed.), *The Chicago History of American Civilization* (1956–64, 21 vols.) is ideally suited to the needs of the general reader, while the volumes of Henry Steele Commager and Richard B. Morris (eds.), *The New American Nation Series* (1954–65), 40 vols.), are generally longer and more detailed in nature. In addition, Arthur M. Schlesinger and Dixon Ryan Fox (eds.), *The History of American Life* (1927–44, 12 vols.), is still worth consulting.

For materials for the study of Negro life and literature see the continuing series *The American Negro: His History and His Literature* (1968). On the early history of racial attitudes there is a recent book, Winthrop D. Jordan, *White Over*

Black: American Attitudes Toward the Negro 1550–1812 (1968).

Merle Curti, *The Growth of American Thought* (3rd edition 1964) has tended to eclipse Vernon L. Parrington's stimulating *Main Currents in American Thought* (1927–30, 3 vols.) as the standard account of American intellectual development, though Stow Persons, *American Minds* (1958) and Ralph H. Gabriel, *The Course of American Democratic Thought* (2nd edition 1956) are good general studies, while Arthur M. Schlesinger, Jr. and Morton White (eds.), *Paths of American Thought* (1963) is a recent series of stimulating essays on American thought.

Samuel Flagg Bemis, *A Diplomatic History of the United States* (5th edition 1965) and Thomas A. Bailey, *A Diplomatic History of the American People* (7th edition 1964) are two standard works. For a concise recent analysis, see Robert H. Ferrell, *American Diplomacy: A History* (1959).

Wilfred E. Binkley, *American Political Parties: Their Natural History* (rev. ed. 1958) is a lively and well-written account of politics for the general reader, while William B. Hesseltine, *Third-Party Movements in the United States* (1962) is an excellent historical survey of American political protest movements. Richard Hofstadter, *The American Political Tradition and the Men Who Made It* (1956) contains incisive essays on men and events in American politics from Washington to Franklin Roosevelt. Denis W. Brogan, *Politics in America* (1960) is a perceptive analysis of American political development written by a British observer, while Alfred H. Kelly and Winifred A. Harbison, *The American Constitution: Its Origin and Development* (rev. ed. 1963) and Carl B. Swisher, *The Growth of Constitutional Power in the United States* (1963) combine to form an intelligent introduction to American constitutional history.

The standard history of American education is Ellwood P. Cubberley, *Education in the United States* (rev. ed. 1962). A good recent analysis is William M. French, *America's Educational Tradition: An Interpretive History* (1964). Rush Welter, *Popular Education and Democratic Thought in America* (1962) is a systematic and thought-provoking study of the interactions between the American commitment to education and Americal political theory.

Anson P. Stokes, *Church and State in the United States* (rev. ed. 1964) is a solid study, while Clifton E. Olmstead, *History of Religion in the United States* (1960) is a good recent addition. William W. Sweet, *The Story of Religion in America* (2nd rev. ed. 1950) is especially written for the layman, and Willard L. Sperry, *Religion in America* (1946) is especially written for the British layman. Dixon Wecter, *The Saga of American Society: A Record of Social Aspiration* (1957) is an entertaining book on manners, fashions, and social behaviour. Harvey Wish, *Society and Thought in Early America* (2nd ed. 1962) and *Society and Thought in Modern America* (2nd ed. 1962) are penetrating and comprehensive treatments of intellectual history as a phase of social development.

Herbert W. Schneider, *A History of American Philosophy* (2nd ed. 1963) is unique for the way in which philosophical ideas are fitted into the general framework of American historical development. Anton Chroust, *The Rise of the Legal Profession in America* (1965, 2 vols.), and James W. Hurst, *Law and Social Process in United States History* (1960) are two of the better treatments of the history of American law. Perry Miller's *The Legal Mind of America* (1962) is an excellently edited collection of documents illustrating the development of American law and legal philosophy from the Revolution to 1860.

Harold C. Faulkner, *Economic History of the United States* (8th ed., 1960) is probably the best one-volume treatment. Joseph Dorfman, *The Economic Mind in American Civilization* (1946–59, 5 vols.) is more sophisticated but still fascinating, while Seymour E. Harris, *American Economic History* (1961) and John Chamberlain, *The Enterprising Americans: A Business History of the United States* (1963) are valuable and readable. Thomas C. Cochran, *The Age of Enterprise: A Social History of Industrial America* (1961), Robert W. Fogel, *Railroads and American Economic Growth* (1964), Roger

Burlingame, *March of the Iron Men* (1960) and *Scientists Behind the Inventors* (1964), and Foster Rhea Dulles, *Labor in America* (2nd rev. ed. 1960) are studies of particular aspects of economic history. The two books by Burlingame are particularly well suited to the average reader.

Robert E. Spiller, *et al.* (eds.), *The Literary History of the United States* (3rd rev. ed. 1963, 2 vols) is an exhaustive study by a group of scholars, particularly valuable for its excellent biographies. Much shorter but equally important is Spiller's *The Cycle of American Literature: An Essay in Historical Criticism* (1955). Supplementary to these are Carl Van Doren, *The American Novel, 1789–1939* (1940) and Arthur H. Quinn, *A History of American Drama* (2nd edition 1951). Edmund Wilson (ed.), *The Shock of Recognition: The Development of Literature in the United States Recorded by the Men who Made It* (1955) is unique in that it gives the opinions of American writers of their literary colleagues, while James D. Hart, *The Popular Book: A History of America's Literary Tastes* (1950) treats literature from a different angle. Reference should also be made to Frank L. Mott, *American Journalism: A History of Newspapers in the United States Through Two Hundred and Sixty Years, 1690–1950* (3rd edition 1962) and *A History of the American Magazine* (1938–57; 4 vols.). Vernon Loggins, *The Negro Author: His Development in America to 1900* (1964) is a most useful book in a neglected field. A very useful bibliography, T. G. Rosenthal (ed.), *American Fiction*, is published by the National Book League (London).

No entirely adequate history of American music has been written, though Wilfred H. Mellers, *Music in a New Found Land: Themes and Developments in the History of American Music* (1964) is a recent account worth consulting. Oliver W. Larkin, *Art and Life in America* (2nd edition 1960) is a brilliantly illustrated history of painting, sculpture, and architecture; John Walker writes a provocative introduction and some excellent notes to the panorama of two hundred years of American painting in *Paintings from America* (1951). Also see Edgar P. Richardson, *Painting in America: From 1502 to the Present* (1965). For the lighter side of American life, Foster Rhea Dulles, *America Learns to Play: A History of Popular Recreation* (2nd edition 1966) is an entertaining study.

Frederick Jackson Turner, *The Frontier in American History* (1920), is important both to the state of American history and to the state of American historiography. It has had many fruits, among them, Ray A. Billington and James B. Hedges, *Westward Expansion: A History of the American Frontier* (2nd edition 1960). For views hostile to Turner's frontier hypothesis see, for example, Dixon Ryan Fox (ed.), *Sources of Culture in the Middle West* (1934).

Each of the minority groups has had its histories. While recent literature on the Negro in American history is voluminous, John Hope Franklin, *From Slavery to Freedom: A History of American Negroes* (2nd edition 1956) and Roi Vincent Ottley, *Black Odyssey* (1949) remain the most outstanding general studies. Jack D. Forbes, *The Indian in America's Past* (1964), William T. Hagan, *The Indian in American History* (1963), and Irvin M. Peithmann, *Broken Peace Pipes* (1964) are among the more readable recent accounts of the American Indian. Alvin M. Josephy, *The Patriot Chiefs* (1959) is a fascinating study of two centuries of Indian leadership: Alden T. Vaughan, *New England Frontier* (1964) analyses the colonists' attitudes towards and relations with Indians; and Ralph Andrist, *The Long Death* (1963) is a chronicle of the decline of Indian power in the West. Oscar Handlin, *Race and Nationality in American Life* (1957) is more comprehensive and general in scope. Carl Wittke, *We Who Built America: The Saga of the Immigrant* (rev. ed. 1964) and Oscar Handlin, *The Uprooted* (1956) and *Immigration as a Factor in American History* (1959) are the best studies available on immigration and immigrants.

The standard work on pre-Revolutionary America is Charles M. Andrews, *The Colonial Period in American History* (1934–8, 4 vols.). Informative one-volume accounts of the development of the colonies include Louis B. Wright, *The Atlantic Frontier: Colonial American Civilization, 1607–1763*

(1963) and Daniel J. Boorstin, *The Americans: The Colonial Experience* (1958). Clarence L. Ver Steeg, *The Formative Years, 1607–1763* (1964) is a sound recent study well worth reading, and so is A. L. Rowse, *The Elizabethans and America* (1959). James Truslow Adams's venerable three-volume *History of New England* (1923–27) still includes more information general to the colonies than its name would imply and as much pro-Adams bias as the author's name suggests. The definitive account of the colonies within the total framework of empire is Lawrence H. Gipson's recently completed *British Empire before the American Revolution* (1936–65, 12 vols.). For the general reader, Gipson's general thesis is conveniently presented in his one-volume study of *The Coming of the Revolution, 1763–1775* (1962).

There are innumerable histories of the several colonies and states. Among the better ones, and particularly good on the colonial period, are Richard L. Morton, *Colonial Virginia* (1960, 2 vols.), Robert E. Brown, *Middle-Class Democracy and the Revolution in Massachusetts, 1691–1780* (1955), and Robert E. and B. Katherine Brown, *Virginia, 1705–1786: Democracy or Aristocracy* (1964). Matthew P. Andrews, *The Founding of Maryland* (1933) and *History of Maryland: Province and State* (1929) remain the best studies on Maryland, while John E. Pomfret, *The Province of New Jersey, 1607–1702: A History of the Origins of an American Colony* (1965) is a detailed but fascinating study of a very complicated story. There is a voluminous and highly specialized *History of the State of New York*, edited by Alexander C. Flick (1933–37, 10 vols.) which is nevertheless worth attention even by general readers. Edwin B. Bronner, *William Penn's Holy Experiment: The Founding of Pennsylvania, 1681–1701* (1962) and Wayland F. Dunaway, *A History of Pennsylvania* (2nd edition 1948) are both good and readable on the Quaker colony and state, as are Hugh T. Lefler and Albert R. Newsome, *North Carolina: History of a Southern State* (rev. ed. 1963) and E. Merton Coulter, *Georgia: A Short History* (rev. ed. 1960) on those colonies.

The Andrews and Gipson volumes give the best and

clearest notion of the unity and corresponding lack of unity in American colonial history outside the Thirteen Colonies, but reference can also be made to Richard Pares, *Yankees and Creoles: The Trade between North America and the West Indies before the American Revolution* (1956) and *War and Trade in the West Indies, 1739–1763* (1963). In addition, the interested reader might wish to consult Walter A. Roberts, *The French in the West Indies* (1942) as well as Donald G. Creighton, *A History of Canada: Dominion of the North* (1958).

For detailed accounts of early settlement Henry S. Burrage (ed.), *Early English and French Voyages, Chiefly from Hakluyt* (1932) is probably the best general source-book, while those who want even more detail are likely to find it in the publications of the Hakluyt Society. The most recent edition of *Hakluyt's Voyages* (1965) has been edited by Irwin R. Blacker. More popular accounts of early exploration and early settlement are in Roy V. Coleman, *The First Frontier* (1948), a good if occasionally excitable book. George F. Willison, *Saints and Strangers* (1945) is excellent on the European and American story of the Mayflower group, while Philip L. Barbour, *The Three Worlds of Captain John Smith* (1964) gives a picture of the Jamestown colony. On the same subject but in sterner fashion is Bradford Smith, *Captain John Smith: His Life and Legend* (1956), which, in this case, if in no other, should be rounded off with a historian's historical novel, David Garnett, *Pocahontas* (1933).

Thomas J. Wertenbaker, *The First Americans, 1600–1690* (1927), *The Founding of American Civilization: The Middle Colonies* (1938) and *The Puritan Oligarchy* (1965) are all valuable standard accounts, as is Charles M. Andrews, *The Fathers of New England: A Chronicle of the Puritan Commonwealths* (1921), and perhaps best of all, Samuel Eliot Morison, *Builders of the Bay Colony* (rev. ed. 1963).

Most of the recent literature concerning the Puritans and the development of colonial New England has tended to counteract the somewhat hostile account in Parrington's *Main Currents in American Thought.* Aside from the informative and highly readable General Introduction in Perry

Miller and Samuel H. Johnson (eds.), *The Puritans* (1963, 2 vols.), the reader should also consult Miller's *The New England Mind* (1961, 2 vols.) and Samuel Eliot Morison's *Intellectual Life of Colonial New England* (1960). More specialized but equally worth reading is Kenneth B. Murdock, *Literature and Theology in Colonial New England* (1963). Biographical studies of early New England personages are numerous. Among the best are Ola E. Winslow, *Jonathan Edwards, 1703–1758* (1961) and *Master Roger Williams: A Biography* (1956); Perry Miller, *Roger Williams* (1962); Samuel H. Brockunier, *The Irrepressible Democrat: Roger Williams* (1940); and Kenneth B. Murdock, *Increase Mather: The Foremost Puritan* (1926). For additional insight into the New England mind, see Marion L. Starkey, *The Devil in Massachusetts* (1961), which tells the story of the Salem witch trials, and Bernard Bailyn, *The New England Merchants in the Seventeenth Century* (1955).

Wesley R. Craven, *The Southern Colonies in the Seventeenth Century, 1607–1689* (1952) and M. N. Stannard, *The Story of Virginia's First Century* (1928) contain excellent accounts of the South in the seventeenth century. Carl Bridenbaugh, *Myths and Realities: Societies of the Colonial South* (1963) examines three distinct modes of life in the southern colonies and concludes that 'the South' did not emerge as a self-conscious entity before the Revolution, while John Richard Alden, *The First South* (1961) comes to the opposite conclusion. Thomas J. Wertenbaker, *The Shaping of Colonial Virginia* (1958) gives a view of the South more in line with traditional historical thinking, and Louis B. Wright, *The First Gentlemen of Virginia* (1964), like Bridenbaugh's book, discusses the development of the ruling class.

There are many books on Penn and Pennsylvania. In addition to the Bronner volume previously cited, William W. Comfort, *William Penn: A Tercentenary Estimate* (1944) is a remarkably sound study. Among the most recent and readable biographies are Catherine O. Peare, *William Penn* (1957) and Joseph E. Illick, *William Penn the Politician* (1965). In addition, the interested reader might consult

Bibliography

Frederick B. Tolles, *Meeting House and Counting House: The Quaker Merchants of Colonial Philadelphia, 1682–1763* (1948) for a more detailed account of pre-Revolutionary Pennsylvania.

For the eighteenth century in general and for the period immediately preceding the Revolution in particular, there is much good writing and a host of excellent books from which to choose. Charles M. Andrews, *Colonial Folkways: A Chronicle of American Life in the Reign of the Georges* (1921) and James Truslow Adams, *Provincial Society 1690–1763* (1927) remain two of the best studies. Andrews's *The Colonial Background to the American Revolution* (rev. ed. 1958) is highly readable, while Roy V. Coleman, *Liberty and Property* (1951) and Carl Bridenbaugh, *Cities in the Wilderness: The First Century of Urban Life in America, 1625–1742* (1938) provide additional insights into pre-Revolutionary American society. Special aspects are considered in Edmund S. and Helen M. Morgans, *The Stamp Act Crisis: Prologue to Revolution* (1963); C. P. Mullett, *Fundamental Law and the American Revolution* (1933); Arthur M. Schlesinger, *The Colonial Merchants and the American Revolution* (1957); and H. Trevor Colbourne, *The Lamp of Experience: Whig History and the Intellectual Origins of the American Revolution* (1965). Randolph G. Adams's sound but academic *Political Ideas of the American Revolution* (3rd edition 1958) is interesting, but the best and most thorough accounts of events and opinions on both sides of the Atlantic are John C. Miller, *The Origins of the American Revolution* (rev. ed. 1959) and Lawrence H. Gipson, *The Coming of the Revolution, 1763–1775* (1962).

Gerald W. Johnson, *Our English Heritage* (1949) and I. C. C. Graham, *Colonists from Scotland* (1956) are interesting on the two most important sources of colonial immigration, while Wallace Notestein, *The English People on the Eve of Colonization, 1603–1630* (1962) provides an interesting appraisal of the society from which the bulk of early colonists derived.

On the struggle with France for dominion in North

America, the seven volumes of Francis Parkman, *France and England in North America* (1865–92) are still classic; to them should be added *The Conspiracy of Pontiac* (1851), the first of Parkman's works to be written but the last in historical sequence. For a more recent appraisal, see Joseph L. Rutledge, *Century of Conflict: The Struggle between the French and British in Colonial America* (1956).

As Franklin's life and activities are in so many ways the history of America in the eighteenth century, his *Autobiography*, which has been published in what seem innumerable editions, is a most important source-book. Carl Van Doren, *Benjamin Franklin* (1964) and Verner Crane, *Benjamin Franklin and a Rising People* (1954) are by far the best biographical studies, while Carl and Jessica Bridenbaugh, *Rebels and Gentlemen: Philadelphia in the Age of Franklin* (1962) is a fascinating and colourful account of the environment in which 'Poor Richard' lived. Alfred Owen Aldridge, *Benjamin Franklin: Philosopher and Man* (1965) is an instructive recent biography intended primarily for the general reader.

There are a number of good books which describe the retrogression of English sense about American affairs during the eighteenth century, as well as numerous biographical studies which trace the lives of some of those eighteenth-century Englishmen who made and lost the American colonies. See, for example, Sir Lewis B. Namier, *England in the Age of the American Revolution* (2nd edition 1962), Charles R. Ritcheson, *British Politics and the American Revolution* (1954), John W. Shy, *Toward Lexington: The Role of the British Army in the Coming of the American Revolution* (1965); Jack M. Sosin, *Agents and Merchants: British Colonial Policy and the Origins of the American Revolution, 1763–1775* (1965); Gerald S. Brown, *The American Secretary: The Colonial Policy of Lord George Germain, 1775–1778* (1963); John C. Long, *Lord Jeffrey Amherst, a Soldier of the King* (1933); and John Richard Alden, *General Gage in America* (1948).

Richard B. Morris recently has published a revised one-volume edition of Sir George Trevelyan's *The American Revolution* (1964). In addition to this classic study, the reader might consult such recent general accounts as John Richard Alden, *The American Revolution, 1775–1783* (1962); Edmund S. Morgan, *The Birth of the Republic* (1963); Esmond Wright, *Fabric of Freedom: 1763–1800* (1964); Forrest McDonald, *E Pluribus Unum: The Formation of the American Republic, 1776–1790* (1965); and Piers Mackesy, *The War for America, 1775–1783* (1964). Although both are controversial among historians, J. Franklin Jameson, *The American Revolution Considered as a Social Movement* (1925), and Merrill Jensen, *The Articles of Confederation: An Interpretation of the Social-Constitutional History of the American Revolution, 1774–1781* (1963) are two studies which the general reader should not neglect. Carl Becker, *The Declaration of Independence: A Study in the History of Political Ideas* (1922) is dated but in many ways indispensable, while Julian P. Boyd, *A Declaration of Independence: The Evolution of the Text as Shown in Facsimiles of Various Drafts by Its Author* (1945) is especially good for insights into Jeffersonian political theory. The great edition of the Jefferson papers, still being produced under the editorship of Boyd (seventeen volumes in 1965), and the equivalent and even more substantial effort to edit the Adams Papers – under the direction of Lyman Butterfield (six volumes in 1963) which will eventually cover the whole of the remarkable Adams family – are typical of monumental scholarship at its best. Enthusiasts for Jefferson should also read Merrill D. Peterson, *The Jefferson Image in the American Mind* (1962) and Dumas Malone, *Jefferson and His Time* (1948–62, 3 vols.).

The military and naval history of the Revolution are described in Willard M. Wallace, *Appeal to Arms: A Military History of the American Revolution* (1951) and Gardner W. Allen, *A Naval History of the American Revolution* (1962, 2 vols.). More specialized but entirely enjoyable is Lynn Montross, *Rag, Tag and Bobtail: The Story of the Continental Army* (1952). Richard Morris, *The Great Powers and American Independence* (1965) is a study of the European powers and the terms of the Revolutionary war and peace; Forrest McDonald's *E Pluribus Unum: The Formation of the American Republic 1776–1790* (1965) is a definitive account of the internal political development of the new country in Washington's administration. French participation in the war is discussed in Ariane Ruskin, *Spy for Liberty: The Adventurous Life of Beaumarchais, Playwright and Secret Agent for the American Revolution* (1965), Arnold Whitredge, *Rochambeau* (1965), and Stephen Bonsal, *When the French Were Here: A Narrative of the Sojourn of the French Forces in America* (1945). There are many good studies of individual military and naval encounters; among the more recent are Harold A. Larrabee, *Decision at the Chesapeake* (1964), John F. Reed, *Campaign to Valley Forge* (1965), and M. F. Treacy, *Prelude to Yorktown: The Southern Campaign of Nathanael Greene, 1780–1781* (1963).

There are many excellent biographies of the Revolutionary leaders in addition to those which have already been mentioned. The great work on Washington by the late Douglas Southall Freeman, which began to be published in 1948, was continued by Freeman's associates and finished in seven volumes in 1957. Other books on Washington include James T. Flexner, *George Washington: The Forge of Experience, 1732–1775* (1965); Bernard Knollenberg, *George Washington: The Virginia Period, 1732–1775* (1964); Esmond Wright, *Washington and the American Revolution* (1957); and Marcus Cunliffe, *George Washington: Man and Monument* (1958). Stewart Beach, *Samuel Adams: The Fateful Years, 1764–1776* (1965); John C. Miller, *Sam Adams: Pioneer in Propaganda* (1936); Page Smith, *John Adams* (1962); Gilbert Chinard, *Honest John Adams* (1964); and Adrienne Koch, *Adams and Jefferson: Posterity Must Judge* (1963) are all valuable. William E. Woodward's *Tom Paine: America's Godfather* (1945) contains most of the information about the propagandist, but is highly coloured. Alfred O. Aldridge's *Man of Reason: The Life of Thomas Paine* (1961), on the other hand, is sound and scholarly. David L. Jacobson, *John Dickinson and the Revolution in Pennsylvania, 1764–1776* (1965); D. J. Mayers, *Edmund Pendleton, 1721–1803* (1952, 2 vols.); and

George A. Billias (ed.), *George Washington's Generals* (1964), are additional biographical studies well worth reading. Until recently, the story of Loyalism had been but indifferently treated. Since 1960, however, a wealth of new studies has tended to reverse this apparent neglect. See, for example, Paul H. Smith, *Loyalists and Redcoats: A Study in British Revolutionary Policy* (1964); William H. Nelson, *The American Tory* (1961); North Callahan, *Royal Raiders: The Tories of the American Revolution* (1963); and Howard Swiggett, *War Out of Niagara: Walter Butler and the Tory Rangers* (1963). In addition, Thomas J. Wertenbaker, *Father Knickerbocker Rebels* (1948) contains an interesting account of Loyalist activity in New York City.

In addition to the general studies on Loyalism during the Revolution, there has been much attention given to ostensible traitors and near traitors. Carl Van Doren, *Secret History of the American Revolution* (1941) remains the best and most balanced book on the subject. John Richard Alden, *General Charles Lee, Traitor or Patriot* (1951) gives Lee a fair hearing, while James T. Flexner, *The Traitor and the Spy: Benedict Arnold and John André* (1953) – over subjective at times – on Arnold, at least gathers together most of the available information. An interesting account of an awkwardly situated group of Americans is Lewis D. Einstein's *Divided Loyalties: Americans in England during the War of Independence* (1933).

Carl Van Doren, *The Great Rehearsal: The Story of the Making and Ratifying of the Constitution of the United States* (1961); Merrill Jensen, *The Making of the American Constitution* (1964) and *The New Nation: A History of the United States during the Confederation, 1781–1789* (1965); Richard B. Morris, *Alexander Hamilton and the Founding of the Nation* (1957); John C. Miller, *Alexander Hamilton and the Growth of the New Nation* (1964) and *The Federalist Era* (1960); Irving Brant, *James Madison* (1941–61, 6 vols.); Frank R. Donovan, *Mr. Madison's Constitution* (1965); Frank Monaghan, *John Jay: Defender of Liberty* (1935); and Adrienne Koch, *Jefferson and Madison: The Great Collaboration* (1964) together cover the personalities and activities of the period of the Confederation and the making of the Constitution.

The most useful recent biography of Jefferson is Dumas Malone's *Young Jefferson* (1945) and *Jefferson and the Rights of Man* (1951); of Hamilton, Louis Hacker's *Alexander Hamilton* (1957). Those who wish to pursue Constitutional history should consult Samuel Konefsky, *John Marshall and Alexander Hamilton, Architects of the Constitution* (1964). *The Federalist* has been published in many editions since it first appeared in book form in 1788. J. T. Main, *The Antifederalists: Critics of the Constitution* (1964) is a solid study, while William Nisbet Chambers, *Political Parties in a New Nation* (1963) carries the story up to 1809. Clinton Rossiter's account of the Constitutional Convention, *1787: The Grand Convention* (1965), is excellent, while Irving Brant, *The Bill of Rights* (1965) is a history of American civil liberties from their English origins to the sixties. Samuel Eliot Morison (ed.), *Sources and Documents Illustrating the American Revolution and the Formation of the Federal Constitution* (rev. ed. 1964) remains the best source-book available for the general reader.

H. J. Clancy, *The Democratic Party: Jefferson to Jackson* (1962); John Allen Krout and Dixon Ryan Fox, *The Completion of Independence, 1790–1830* (1944); and John C. Miller, *Crisis in Freedom: The Alien and Sedition Acts* (1951) take the political history of the United States through the War of 1812. General studies of this early national period include Marcus Cunliffe, *The Nation Takes Shape* (1963); Charles M. Wiltse, *The New Nation, 1800–1845* (1964); and Edmund S. Morgan, *The Birth of the Republic* (1963). Robert R. Palmer, *The Age of Democratic Revolution* (1959–64, 2 vols.) sets American events against a world background and provides the interested reader with an intelligent and well-written analysis. Henry Adams, *History of the United States of America during the Administrations of Thomas Jefferson and of James Madison* (abridged two-volume edition, 1963) is still very much worthwhile.

On the War of 1812, Bradford Perkins, *Prologue to War: England and the United States, 1805–1812* (1961); Harry L.

Coles, *The War of 1812* (1965); and F. L. Englemann, *The Peace of Christmas Eve* (1962) cover between them the prelude to war, the war itself, and the Treaty of Ghent.

Louis B. Wright, *The Cultural Life of the American Colonies, 1607–1763* (1957) and Russel Blaine Nye, *The Cultural Life of the New Nation, 1776–1830* (1960) provide an intelligent introduction to American social and cultural history during the colonial and early national periods. Some interesting sidelights on social, cultural, and intellectual affairs can be found in Jackson Turner Main. *The Social Structure of Revolutionary America* (1965); J. R. Dolan, *The Yankee Peddlers of Early America* (1934); Mary Earle Gould, *The Early American House* (1949); H. S. Morrison, *Early American Architecture* (1952); S. P. Dorsey, *Early English Churches in America, 1607–1807* (1952); and William W. Sweet, *Religion in Colonial America* (1942). Moses Coit Tyler, *A History of American Literature, 1607–1765* (reprinted 1962) is still among the best books on colonial literature, while the status of women in early American society is most convincingly described in Eugenie A. Leonard, *The Dear-Bought Heritage* (1965) and Carl Holliday, *Woman's Life in Colonial Days* (1960). Additional insights into colonial and early national American society are provided by Seymour C. Thompson, *Evolution of the American Public Library, 1653–1876* (1952); Harold L. Peterson, *Arms and Armor in Colonial America, 1526–1783* (1956); Nina F. Little, *American Decorative Wall Painting, 1700–1850* (1952); and Kenneth Ellis, *The Post Office in the Eighteenth Century* (1958).

Dirk Jan Struik, *Yankee Science in the Making* (rev. ed. 1962) deals with a subject which has been receiving considerable, though belated, attention by American intellectual historians. Additional recent studies include Brooke Hindle. *The Pursuit of Science in Revolutionary America, 1739–1789* (1956); I. Bernard Cohen, *Franklin and Newton* (1956) and *Some Early Tools of American Science* (1950); A. Hunter Dupree, *Science in the Federal Government* (1957), as well as several important essays in Arthur M. Schlesinger, Jr and Morton White (eds.), *Paths of American Thought* (1963).

Brooke Hindle's recent biography of *David Rittenhouse* (1964), moreover, is highly illustrative of the scientific spirit of Revolutionary America.

Apart from the histories of American medicine from the beginning to the present day, there are several good studies which deal primarily with the colonial and early national periods; among the best are Richard H. Shryock, *Medicine and Society in America, 1600–1860* (1960); John Duffy, *Epidemics in Colonial America* (1953); and John B. Blake, *Public Health in the Town of Boston, 1630–1822* (1959). More geographically specialized than the Shryock and Duffy volumes but no less illustrative of colonial medicine are two histories by W. B. Blanton, *Medicine in Virginia in the Seventeenth Century* (1930) and *Medicine in Virginia in the Eighteenth Century* (1931).

Edwin Tunis, *Colonial Craftsmen and the Beginnings of American Industry* (1965); Douglass C. North, *Decisions that Faced the New Nation, 1783–1820* (1964); Curtis P. Nettels, *The Emergence of a National Economy, 1775–1815* (1962); A. P. Middleton, *Tobacco Coast* (1953); and A. E. Smith, *Colonists in Bondage: White Servitude and Convict Labor in America, 1607–1776* (1947) are among the many recent studies which shed light on particular aspects of colonial economic life.

Bernard DeVoto, *The Course of Empire* (1962) is a well-written and provocative study of colonial and early national expansion. Randolph C. Downes, *Council Fires on the Upper Ohio* (1940) is somewhat academic but gives a clear narrative of Indian affairs in that region up to 1795. Bernard DeVoto (ed.), *The Journals of Lewis and Clark* (1963) contains the story of what was perhaps the most important voyage of exploration in American history, while Edwin T. Martin, *Thomas Jefferson: Scientist* (1952) discusses the scientific interests of the President who made the expedition a reality. For additional insights into early westward expansion see the two biographical studies by John Bakeless, *Daniel Boone* (1964) and *Lewis and Clark: Partners in Discovery* (1962).

In addition to those journals, narratives, autobiographies, and collections of letters already mentioned, reference to the following will be in various degrees valuable: Robert Beverly, *The History and Present State of Virginia* (1705; edited by Louis B. Wright and re-issued 1947) and Charles M. Andrews (ed.), *Narratives of the Insurrections, 1675–1690* (1959). The definitive edition of William Byrd, *History of the Dividing Line* was made by William K. Boyd and published in 1929. To it there must be now added Louis B. Wright and Marion Tinling (eds.), *The Great American Gentlemen: William Byrd of Westover in Virginia, His Secret Diary for the Years 1709–1712* (1963) as well as Maude H. Woodfin (ed.), *Another Secret Diary of William Byrd of Westover, 1739–1741: With Letters and Literary Exercises, 1696–1726* (1942). Franklin wrote so much and has had so much written about him that he needs a bibliographical essay to himself, but, from the bibliographical point of view, perhaps the most useful background reading in addition to his *Autobiograph* is Carl Van Doren (ed.), *Benjamin Franklin's Autobiographical Writings* (1948). There are numerous editions of John Woolman's *Journal*, including a recently published paperback edition (1961). The best edition of Washington's writings is the monumental work by John C. Fitzpatrick (ed.), *The Writings of George Washington from the Original Manuscript Sources, 1745–1799* (1940–44, 39 vols.), but for most readers Frank Donovan (ed.), *The George Washington Papers* (1964) will be enough. Dolly Madison has always been a delight to readers, and Lucia B. Cutts (ed.), *Memoirs and Letters of Dolly Madison* (1886) is still worth discovering. Her husband has been well served by Saul K. Padover (ed.), *The Complete Madison: His Basic Writings* (1953).

INDEX

Index

Index

Index

Index

Index

World War I provokes, 660; and anti-'communism', 671; becomes fashionable again, 691

Naturalization laws, 468

Navigation Acts, 212

Navy, American, Continental Congress organizes, 207; seek base in Europe, 225; French ports open to, 226; Spanish ports open to, 227; against the French, 268; and Chesapeake Bay incident, 299; quality of, 309; battle of Cape Cod, 309; defeats for, 310; impresses Japan, 448; and blockade of Confederacy, 480, 494, 511-12; river warfare, 512-13; in Spanish War, 629-30; in World War I, 658-9; fifty destroyers for Britain, 696; in World War II, 701, 702, 703; to protect Formosa, 708

Nebraska, 449, 450, 452, 453, 557

Negroes, immigrants to Virginia, 28-9; and slavery, 76-8; 445; and human rights, 78, 426; young Virginians and Negro women, 144; assessed as part of population, 259; violent feelings against, 388; De Bow on, 427; in race relations, 457-8, 549; Southerners reluctant to arm, 479; march behind Sherman's army, 540; Negro regiment enters Richmond, 544; suffrage, 548, 553, 563, 568, 756; effect of abolition on, 548; and carpetbaggers, 552; Republicans and, 553, 573, 576; cowboys, 558; Fourteenth Amendment, 565, 584; Fifteenth Amendment, 565; and Grant's election, 569, 571; Klu Klux Klan, and, 574-5; in Southern system, 577; Negro Labour, 587; Baptist missionary work among, 593; excluded from Southern Alliance, 616; benefit from war effort, 662; race riots, 671; writers, 692; social and economic progress, 709-10; under-privileged, 737, 748; population, 744; leaders, 744; and civil rights, 744-6, 748-9, 756-7; attack segregation, 746-7

Nelson, Thomas, 239

Netherlands, see Holland

Neufville, Jean de, 228

Nevada, 557, 559

New Amsterdam (New York), 79, 99

New Deal policy, 679, 680, 682-8, 710, 712, 759

New England (see also Northeast), 33, 43, 80; geographical conditions, 40; wealth of, 41; causes of migration to, 42, 44-5, 98; leadership in, 44; Puritans in, 47, 49; culture in, 47, 102-3, 104-10, 403; witchcraft in, 50; trade- 68, 194; provinces under royal Gover-

nor, 89; merchant-ruled, 160; church and state in, 200; British plan to split, 221; attitude to War of 1812, 310, 317; blockaded, 311; Hartford Convention, 316-17; religion in, 344-5, 347, 411; rise of manufacturing in, 354; attitude to tariff policies, 355, 369; Emigrant Aid Society, 451

New England Confederation, 131

New England Council, 42, 43, 54

New England Restraining Act, 195, 196

New Hampshire, 54, 89, 131; obtains a charter, 55; attitude to Crown, 81; ratifies Constitution, 262; Rockingham memorial, 307; textile industry in, 385

New Haven, 54, 104

New Holland, 98

New Jersey (see also Northeast), 79, 80, 131; Quakers find refuge in, 81-2; no newspaper, 155; and Mutiny Act, 167; Restraining Act, 196; and British cause, 198; delegates at Philadelphia Convention, 259

New Mexico, 432; Santa Fe, 116; United States hope to purchase, 436; suggested annexation of, 437; ceded to U.S., 438; admitted to Union, 558

New Netherland, 41, 79, 94-101

New Orleans, 123, 128, 292; settlement at, 117; Napoleon sells, 293, 294; battle of (1815), 307, 315-16; falls to Federal expedition, 499, 512; harbour, 550; Negro music in, 650

New York (see also Northeast), for Prince James, 79; garrison at, 80; harbour, 97, 310; New Amsterdam becomes, 100; music in, 104; immigrants to, 130; police, 141; literary societies in, 146; theatre, 148; King College, 149-50; stage coach to Philadelphia, 152; newspapers, 155; criminal code, 156; patroon-ruled, 160; and Mutiny Act, 167, 168; class struggle and non-importation agreement, 180; Loyalists in, 198; capital, 200; British and, 221, 222, 232, 241; popular election of chief executive in, 251; and Constitution, 262, 263; temporary capital, 269; anti-war meetings in, 307; Militia reluctant to fight, 309; tenements, 589; Negro demonstrations in, 747

New York City, Broadway Tabernacle, 412; transcontinental railway celebrations, 557; Metropolitan Opera Society, 650; Greenwich Village, 676

Newfoundland, 59, 60, 97, 120

Newport, theatre, 148

Newport, Christopher, 23-4

Newspapers and Periodicals, 18th century, 148-9; Franklin's, 150, 151; by time

Index

Index

Index

Toombs, Robert, 444, 449, 475–6, 478, 489

Topeka convention, 451

Toscanini, Arturo, 650

Townshend, Charles, 167–8, 169, 174, 181

Trade, with G.B., 67–8, 132–3, 181, 301, 306; with French West Indies, 131; Board of, 133, 135, 136; free, 151; economic sanctions, 189–90; restrictions, 194; USA and France, 226; Mississippi closure threatened, 252; Annapolis Convention to discuss, 252; effect of Embargo Act on, 300; and blockade of New England, 311; until 1815, 339; and tariffs, 355, 368; Clay's 'American system', 368–9; with Japan, 448, 612–13; with China, 612; and economic development, 631; Wilson's 'open trade' policy, 653; depression, 678; Trade Expansion Act, 742

Trade Unions, 584–6, 684; Mechanics' Union, 399; active during Civil War, 505; A.F.L., 627–8, 684–5; I.W.W., 628; agricultural, 671; U.M.W. and C.I.O., 685; and Taft-Hartley Act, 715, 726; disappointed with Eisenhower administration, 726

Transcendentalism, 410; Emerson and, 405–6; Thoreau and, 406; and Romantic movement, 407–8; Brook Farm community, 409, 413

'Trent affair', 532–3

Truman, Harry S., and atomic bomb, 703; Truman Doctrine, 706, 708, 715; and civil rights, 710, 745; Roosevelt's running-mate, 712; personality and ability, 713; formidable task facing, 713–14; relations with Congress, 713–15, 717, 721, 722; and 1948 election, 715–16; Fair Deal programme, 716–17; and Korean War, 718, 719, 725; assessment of, 722; not to seek re-election, 723; suspected of Communism, 727, 769

Trumbull, John, 283, 285

Turgot, Anne Robert Jacques, 212

Turner, Frederick Jackson, 357, 367

Turner, Nat, 427

Twain, Mark, 559, 595, 600, 601

Tweed, William Marcy, 607

Twiller, Wouter van, 99

Tyler, John, 396, 397, 429, 432, 471

Tyler, Royall, 281–2

Tyndall, John, 592

Ulloa, Antonio de, 128

Union, Lincoln on, 476, 520; Northern belief in, 476–7; Lincoln and, 487, 521, 536; and purpose of Civil War, 519

Unitarianism, 346, 410, 411; Congrega-tionalist controversy, 347; its appeal to cultivated classes, 347; and liberal religious thought, 347–8; unpopular in Northeast, 349; and Calvinism, 405; becomes more liberal, 646

United Nations Organization, American support for, 705; Yalta agreements on, 705; USSR disrupts, 709; and Korean War, 718, 725; and Suez Canal affair, 735; and atomic and nuclear power, 751, 753

Universalism, 347–8, 349

Universities (see also under individual names), 591

Urbanism, 588–90, 644

Usher, John, 64–5

Utah, 441, 557, 558

Utrecht, Treaty of (1713), 120, 122

Vallandigham, Clement, 520

Van Buren, Martin, 392; and Democratic party, 376; Secretary of State, 389; and Peggy Eaton, 389, 390; succeeds Jackson as President, 394–5; national economy in confusion, 395; an aristo-crat, 396; equivocal attitude to Texas, 435; Free Soil Party nominate, 442; retired, 448

Van Dorn, General, 508, 509

Vandenberg, Arthur, 714, 715, 717

Vanderbilt, William Henry, 578

Vanzetti, Bartolomeo, 671

Vaudreuil, Marquis de, 127

Venezuela, 614

Vergennes, Charles Gravier, 224, 228

Vermont, 357

Versailles, Treaty of (1919), 664

Vice, 607

Vicksburg, 508, 519, 535; siege and capture of (1863), 510–11

Victoria, Queen of Great Britain, 531, 532

Vietnam, 733, 759–61

Villa, Francisco, 635

Villeinage, 75, 76

Virgin Islands, 634

Virginia (see also South), 59; Raleigh and, 17; colonization of, 19, 22–38; tobacco, 27; labour, 27–9, 77; women, 29; education, 29–30, 32–4, 387, 389; massacre, 31; House of Burgesses, 35; severe discipline in, 35–6; direct monar-chical government for, 36–7, 58; agriculture, 40; land-tenure in, 42; and Maryland, 62; and Cromwell, 65–6; restricted by trade acts, 68; antagonism to G.B., 69; architecture, 105; and the West, 116; protests against Stamp Act, 137, 138; Gwatkin on social customs of, 142–4; ruled by

XXXV

Index

colonies, 163; and power of Crown, 179; and Radicals, 180; and war with United States, 237, 238

Whigs (American), 181, 468; National Republicans, 395; and presidential elections, 396, 435, 441–2; a party of 'cons', 397; Tyler alienates, 429; oppose annexation of Texas, 432; attitude to Mexican War, 436–7; gloss over slavery problem, 447; divided over Nebraska, 450; a dying party, 453; and Fillimore, 454; Lincoln, 461, 463; and Knownothings, 467

Whistler, James Abbott McNeill, 604

White, Father Andrew, 60

White, John, 19–20

White House, 271, 272, 338, 379

Whitfield, George, 111, 112, 122

Whitman, Walt, 595, 596–9

Whitney, Eli, 271, 580

Wilkes, Captain Charles, 532–3

Wilkes, John, 178, 179

Willard, Frances, 645

William III, King of Great Britain and Prince of Orange, 63, 91, 118

William and Mary, College of, 141, 142; *Cato* produced at, 73; opened, 74; cock-fighting forbidden, 146; clubs at, 146; training for ministry at, 149; loses status, 387, 389

Williams, Roger, 47, 51–2, 53

Williamsburg, 70, 75, 87; theatre, 73, 147; architecture, 74; music in, 104; Duke of Gloucester Street, 141; Gwatkin in, 142; Raleigh Tavern, 145, 153–4; taverns, 153; powder magazine at, 197

Willkie, Wendell, 696–7, 712

Willoughby, Sir Hugh, 12

Wilmot, David, the 'Wilmot Proviso', 438–9, 442

Wilson, James, 256; *Consideration of the Authority of Parliament*, 219

Wilson, Thomas Woodrow, 681; President of Princeton, 111; on Republican party, 452; on government, 604; governor of New Jersey, 625; result of Progressivism under, 627; and Mexican affairs, 634–5; attitude to Monroe Doctrine, 635; proposes international court of justice, 636; becomes President,

640–41; personality and experience, 641; his political philosophy, 641–2; his Inaugural Address, 642; his progressive administration, 643–4; and World War I, 653, 654, 656–7, 659, 661; his personal struggle over War, 655; his 'Fourteen Points' speech, 660; and Labour, 662; on war, 663; and Treaty of Versailles, 664–5; and League of Nations, 664–5, 669; death, 666; on participation, 669

Winthrop, John, 45, 46, 56

Winthrop, John, writer, 106

Winthrop family, 54

Wirt, William, 392

Wisconsin (*see also* Northwest), 356, 414, 434, 439

Witchcraft, 50–51, 53, 156

Wituwamat, 43

Wolfe, James, 115, 125–6, 185

Wolfe, Thomas, 691

Women, price of wives in Virginia, 29; frontier wives, 366; women's rights, 416–17; effect of urbanism on, 590; farm women, 615; changed status in 20th century, 645; and prohibition, 645–6; female suffrage, 646

Wood, Grant, 693

Woolman, John, 82

Wool, General John, 437

World War I, 653–60, 661, 666

World War II, 700–704; outbreak of, 686; America enters, 699; impact on American foreign affairs, 704–9; impact on American internal affairs, 709–12

Wright, Frank Lloyd, 596, 603, 693

Wright, Orville *and* Wilbur, 644

Wright, Richard, 692

Wyatt, Francis, 37

Wyoming, 557

Wythe, George, 157, 158, 256

Yale University, 108, 110, 349, 387

Yalta Conference, 705, 706

Yancey, W. L., 444, 457, 467, 478

Yeardley, Sir George, 35, 36, 37

Y.M.C.A., 594

Yorktown, 207, 238, 239–40

Young, Brigham, 411

Y.M.C.A., 594